THE MIRROR UP TO NATURE

'. . . the purpose of playing, whose end, both
at the first and now, was and is, to hold,
as 'twere, the mirror up to nature; to show
virtue her own feature, scorn her own image,
and the very age and body of the time his
form and pressure.'

Hamlet to the Players : Act III, ii.

THE MIRROR
UP TO NATURE

A Review of the Theatre 1964-1982

by

B. A. YOUNG

WILLIAM KIMBER · LONDON

First published in 1982 by
WILLIAM KIMBER & CO. LIMITED
Godolphin House, 22a Queen Anne's Gate,
London, SW1H 9AE

ISBN 0–7183–0069–6

The extract from a poem by A. E. Housman on page 8 appears by permission of the Society of Authors as the literary representative of the Estate of A. E. Housman, and Jonathan Cape Ltd, publishers of A. E. Housman's *Collected Poems*.

Typeset by Grove Graphics
and printed and bound in Great Britain by
Biddles Limited, Guildford and King's Lynn

FOR MY BROTHER HUGH

Contents

The stars have not dealt me the worst they could do;
My pleasures are plenty, my troubles are two.
But oh, my two troubles they reave me of rest,
The brains in my head and the heart in my breast.

A. E. HOUSMAN

Introduction

THE CRITIC AS JOURNALIST

(*not* by Oscar Wilde)

ADRIAN (*at the piano*) : My poor Bertram, I see you have not been to the theatre this evening.

BERTRAM : On the contrary, I have just returned from the Square Circle. It is as important to be badly dressed there as to be well dressed for the Opera. It reassures the management that they have a satisfactorily democratic house.

ADRIAN : Surely you are more likely to find a democratic audience at the Opera than at the Square Circle.

BERTRAM : Yes, but at the Opera they try to live up to the décor, while at the Square Circle they have to live down to the scripts. I confess I have had an excessively harrowing evening. Where have you put the hash?

ADRIAN : It is hidden in the works of the grandfather clock, as the police advised us. Would you like me to play you something that will soothe your nerves? I have been glancing through this new thing by John Cage. It is quite enchanting, and I play it very well.

BERTRAM : I would prefer to tell you about the play which I have just seen.

ADRIAN : If it contains a scene where a baby is smothered in its own excrement and a scene where some Army deserters hang the mummified body of one of their comrades on a Christmas tree, and a scene where a group of young people improvise that they are being drowned in a flood of digestive juices, I would prefer to wait and read what you have written in the morning paper.

BERTRAM : It contains all that, and it also contains a triangular love-affair between a Negro, a prostitute and a homosexual. From time to time the action is suspended for the rendering of a selection of doggerel ballads of which the words are ill-advisedly displayed on a screen. This hash is quite excellent. Do tell me where you get it.

ADRIAN : You are trying to change the subject.

BERTRAM : I have succeeded in changing the subject. You said you did not wish to hear about the play, and you immediately told me the

9

entire plot. This is typical of the English, who believe that ignorance is a virtue but knowledge something to be excused. If you like, you may play me this mad, scarlet thing by John Cage of which you spoke a moment ago.

ADRIAN: I have been playing it for the last two minutes. It consists only of a single twenty-four bar rest. But I have no intention of allowing you to change the subject. I do not want to know what was in the play, but what you have written about it in the morning paper.

BERTRAM: Then you will be disappointed, for what I have written for my paper consists of an account of what was in the play. I have added my judgment of how well the company performed it, and a note, purely subjective, of what it conveyed to me.

ADRIAN: But have you not explained it?

BERTRAM: Come, my dear Adrian, how could I have explained it when I was unable to understand it? This is a play of infinite complexity directed in the current style, that is to say, every possible step has been taken to apprise the audience of the polymath ingenuity of the director, but comparatively few to adumbrate the ideas of the author.

ADRIAN: But surely it is your responsibility to find out what the play is about before you begin to address your readers.

BERTRAM: It is the responsibility of the author, the director and the players to show me what the play is about before I address my readers. We are often criticised because we hurry away the moment the curtain falls, if we are allowed the luxury of a curtain, and then pronounce judgment without permitting ourselves sufficient time for reflection. We are urged to read the script before coming to the theatre, though it is not often possible to obtain it unless it is available in the bookshops; and we are berated for not allowing our judgment to 'mature' instead of writing while the performance is still fresh and bright in our minds. Had we but world enough and time, we would gladly do all these things, I have no doubt; but this would put us at an advantage relative to the audience, who are unlikely to have read the piece and yet will wish to discuss it on the way home in the omnibus.

ADRIAN: I hope you are not going to tell me that your first responsibility is to the audience.

BERTRAM: My only responsibility is to myself. I do what I can to express what was the effect of the play on me. But I shall be seeing the play from a seat in the stalls and not from the wings, or the box-office, or the manager's house in the suburbs, and the probability is that if it is a new play I shall see it only once before I record my impressions. This is also the situation of the audience.

ADRIAN : In that case, why should the audience pay any attention to what you write, when they may go to the theatre and come to their own conclusions?

BERTRAM : There are a number of reasons.

ADRIAN : Two or three will do.

BERTRAM : Very well, then. In the first place, I go to the theatre far more often than they do, and am therefore more likely than they to penetrate potential obscurities.

ADRIAN : But you said that you would not try to explain a play.

BERTRAM : I would not try to elucidate the playwright's thought, which is something he should have done already. But if, for example, it was clear to me that what we had been watching on the stage had not happened at all, but had been simply the thoughts in somebody's mind, this is something I should mention. Moreover, my wider experience of the theatre, and my constant exercise of writing a thousand words in the time that a novelist would think inadequate to punctuate a sentence, would help me to present an account more coherent than would probably be given over his breakfast by someone who has seldom written anything more ambitious than a bill. I would not regard such an account, however, as a recommendation to see the play or to give it a wide berth. It is the public's duty to make this decision. The best I can do is to give them a clear notion of what they will see if they decide to go.

ADRIAN : You do not consider it necessary, then, to consider the taste of the average audience?

BERTRAM : I do not know what the average audience is. There are only a handful of characteristics that apply to all audiences. For example, they have difficulty in remembering the order of the letters of the alphabet, or of counting from one to thirty, when they are finding their seats. They eat chocolates wrapped in noisy wrappings, and they queue patiently during the interval for quite small drinks. But the only taste with which I am concerned is my own.

ADRIAN : But is it not possible that your taste is so unusual that it will never agree with the public taste as demonstrated at the box-office? I only put this forward as a purely hypothetical case.

BERTRAM : If the people who read my reviews are constant enough to have worked out for themselves what my tastes are, they can match them against their own and decide for themselves whether they are likely to agree or disagree with my opinion.

ADRIAN : Now give me another of your reasons.

BERTRAM : No, on the whole I think I will not. I am in danger of influencing you, and all influence is bad. But I will give you a thought to take to bed with you, though I observe that rosy-fingered dawn is already beginning to stain the sky above Battersea Power Station. A disagreeable director who considered that I had given his play a good notice for the wrong reasons wrote to warn me that if I and my fellow-critics did not show a little more enthusiasm for the theatre, the theatre would die and we should all be out of work. I replied that there had been a notable week when every responsible critic had given a good notice to a new comedy and it had run for ten days; and in the same week only one critic had had a good word to say for a new musical and it had run for six years.

ADRIAN : Then you do not believe that the critic is of any value at all?

BERTRAM : On the contrary, I believe that the critic is of inestimable value to anyone who has any serious interest in the theatre, but that he is neither a ticket-agent nor a public-relations man. Apart from anything else, he will probably write the best prose in the daily newspapers, though I am sorry to see that some notable writing is beginning to fall from the typewriters of even the financial correspondents. But come, the morning editions will already be on the streets. Let us treat them in a civilised manner and retire to bed until lunch-time.

CHAPTER ONE

Starters

'I held it truth,' Tennyson said, 'that men may rise on stepping-stones of their dead selves to higher things.' I rose to be a theatre-critic, something that had not seriously occurred to me to be, on stepping-stones of dead colleagues. Eric Keown of *Punch*, where I was then literary editor, died suddenly, and Bernard Hollowood, the editor, after some discreet hesitation, asked me to take his place. I had been a bare two years in that office when T. C. Worsley of the *Financial Times* became too ill to cope with overnight reviewing any more, and Gordon Newton, the editor, asked me to take his place. As it happened, I was on the point of flying to what was then called Bechuanaland to write a book for the Colonial Office, but as soon as I was back I joined the staff at Bracken House.

That happened in 1964. What a splendid year that was to start being a full-time theatre critic! The great theatrical event of our day was supposed to have been the production of John Osborne's *Look Back in Anger* at the Royal Court in 1956. But 1956 wasn't much of a year in other directions: *Romanov and Juliet, The Chalk Garden, Separate Tables, South Sea Bubble, A View from the Bridge*, there's no indication of a theatrical renaissance there. Indeed the Comedy Theatre had to be turned into a club for *A View from the Bridge*, so that only members might see one man kissing another.

But 1964! There were now two big permanent companies, the National (commuting between Chichester and London) and the Royal Shakespeare (commuting between Stratford-upon-Avon and the Aldwych). There were *Who's Afraid of Virginia Woolf?, Entertaining Mr Sloane, The Royal Hunt of the Sun, Inadmissible Evidence.* (You won't necessarily find all of them here.)

Although Bechuanaland kept me busy until the end of March, I saw a hundred and ninety plays that year. Skilfully edited by John Higgins, the best arts editor I ever knew, including myself, they saw daylight on the pink pages of the *Financial Times* and I cut them out neatly and stuck them in a red-covered book.

This first section contains a selection of the plays that I saw in that first year, the plays that I remember with most pleasure.

*

Hobson's Choice

National Theatre   *7 January 1964*

Harold Brighouse's great Lancashire comedy chooses itself almost as inevitably as *Hamlet* for the repertory of the National Theatre; but the problem of producing it is different today from what it was even ten years ago, and more difficult. As lately as 1958 Brighouse wrote that 'only by exceptional merit . . . can a regional play overcome London's Mayfair prejudice.' Now London's Mayfair prejudice is gone, and Salford, where Henry Hobson's shop stood, is as familiar to us as our own homes, for Salford is the scene of *Coronation Street*. There is a regional play on television almost every night. If there is anything out of character in speech or business or scenery, we shall know it at once.

There is little to complain of in this respect in John Dexter's scrupulous production at the Old Vic, apart from a certain freedom with Lancashire accents which is never serious enough to jar; and he has a cast that serves him, with one exception, almost to perfection. The exception is Sir Michael Redgrave, who is not well chosen to play Hobson. This blustering, ineffectual boozer needs someone who can roar; Sir Michael, effective enough in the quieter moments, and at once comic and moving in his final defeat, does not have a roar in his armoury, and was apt to resort to a squeak when he wanted to express the extremes of emotion.

As Hobson's eldest daughter, Maggie, who marries his gormless benchhand Willie rather than face life as an old maid working in the shop, Joan Plowright has clocked up another triumph. Plain and pasty-faced, her hair dragged back from her forehead, she hectors her way through her several machinations like a North-country Boadicea, never doubting her ultimate success, and never revealing the heart of gold that is reserved to gleam, just once, when – Cordelia wrapped in Goneril's cloak – she waits for her snobbish younger sisters to refuse the chance of moving back into their dying father's home and then at one swoop takes over both her father and his business.

Frank Finlay plays Willie Mossop admirably. You can see the power wielded by Maggie rubbing off on him a little more convincingly the longer he is exposed to it. The happy unambitious shoemaker of the first scene suddenly tries out his newfound ability when Hobson pays his first visit to the cellar where the Mossops live. 'Ay, let 'im come in!' he calls bravely; and immediately his face is contorted with terror at what he has done. But at the end he is able to outface his late employer to such effect that, if we did not see Maggie playing Svengali in the background, we could almost believe he had beaten the old man into conceding him a partnership on his own strength of character. It is a nicely-judged performance.

The two younger sisters, Alice and Vickey, are well done by Mary Miller and Jeanne Hepple, and there are two especially nice performances among the smaller parts – Reginald Green's Tubby Wadlow, the image of what Willie might have become if he had stayed a benchhand at Hobson's all his life, and Anthony Nicholls's fiery Scottish Dr MacFarlane.

Motley's sets continue the vein of pure naturalism that runs throughout the production.

Who's Afraid of Virginia Woolf?

Piccadilly   *7 February 1964*

There are four characters in this pitch-black comedy, and on all of them the author has poured contempt to the dregs and offered them only a thin meed of pity. He has turned their souls inside out before us in the course of a marathon late-night drinking party, and found in them little to admire and nothing to love.

The characters are two married couples, one middle-aged and one young. Both the husbands are on the staff of a small New England college, the older one reconciled to being no more than something in the history department, the younger a new recruit to the biology department who already sees himself forging a swift road to the top.

The play begins when the older couple, George and Martha, have just got back, rather late, from a party given by the college's president, and Martha has invited the younger man and his wife in for drinks. George and Martha have a weakness for private jokes, which they are apt to carry to unmanageable lengths. The difficulty they have is in keeping their jokes from intruding into their lives; 'Truth or illusion, George,' says Martha, pathetically, when the events of the evening have worn her out, 'we don't know the difference.'

So George tells his rather correct young guests how when he was at school he went to a speakeasy with some other boys among whom there was one who had accidentally killed his mother with a shotgun and later killed his father in a motor-accident; and later in the evening when illusion is in the ascendant and both George and Martha are playing their favourite game of humiliating one another in public, Martha takes over these events but places them as the subject-matter of a novel George wrote as a young man which the president of the college couldn't let him publish because of the ill effect it would have on the college's reputation.

But the myth most cherished by George and Martha is the myth of their son, created to fill the position of the son they could never have. This is strictly a private myth, but Martha is careless enough, and drunk enough (there is a prodigious amount of drinking during the three and a half hours of the play), to mention her son to the girl. When George discovers this breach of the rules he brings the son right out into the open, and they drive him at one another like a pair of demented tennis players, each return more wounding than the last, until George plays his ace and tells his wife that their son has been killed in a motor accident.

This is not the *plot* of *Who's Afraid of Virginia Woolf?* There is not so much a plot as the development of a single mood that breaks off after the guests have had enough and George and Martha are left, emotionally exhausted, to end the day in tired companionship until they can raise the steam to start another row. It is what Manet – was it Manet? – called *une composition bien accidentée,* that begins when we happen to begin to see it and ends when we leave.

Edward Albee writes with deep understanding of his unattractive characters; he has created them not only in the round but through and through. No corner of their sad, unhappy personalities has escaped his imagination; everything is brought out into the light for us to see, and everything is completely convincing.

Alan Schneider's direction is faultless. He has brought out the humour, the scarifying criticism, and the tenderness, and the cast are all he could ask for. Uta Hagen is Martha, fighting hard against middle-age with the false weapons of the gin bottle and the easy seduction; Arthur Hill is her husband, sour, intellectual, frustrated, but, as Martha admits, the only person who can make her happy. Richard Easton plays the self-righteous young biologist and Beverlee McKinsey is his silly little wife who is too frightened to have a baby and retreats behind her slim hips. It is a magnificent company, and they play into one another's hands splendidly. They were rightly cheered when the last curtain fell.

And yet . . . And yet . . . For all my admiration of Mr Albee's skill and the splendours of the production, I still find myself asking what the play has to impart to us. Truth or illusion – none of us can tell them apart; but does all this sound and fury ultimately enlarge our understanding? Is there any kind of universal application of what we have been shown? Well, at any rate it is a coruscating display of theatrical talent, and it should be seen for that reason if for no other.

The Master Builder

National Theatre   *10 June 1964*

The protagonist of Ibsen's *The Master Builder* is not the eponymous architect defying heaven like a Scandinavian Prometheus to deny him his just triumph. It is Hilde Wangel, the girl who destroys him out of sheer destructive caprice, who, as we now know, was created out of Ibsen's autumnal affair with the young Viennese Emilie Bardach; and in this fine new production by Peter Wood at the Old Vic it is Maggie Smith's Hilde that rightly towers above the rest like the lofty spire of one of Solness's churches.

What makes Hilde Wangel such a convincingly real character is her total lack of motive for anything she does, unless the gratification of a whim may count as a motive. Hedda Gabler, an equally destructive woman, always had a discernible reason for her vagaries; Hilde Wangel has none. She just wants to see what will happen. This is how girls like that behave.

Miss Smith's conception of her is idiosyncratic; but it happens that Miss Smith's idiosyncrasies fit the part exactly. She strides gawkily on stage at her first appearance, wearing a heavy ginger-coloured costume hooked up for walking, a bright scarf over her hair and this absurd Boy Scout's pole in her hands. She is as confident as Joan of Arc, only more erratic of aim. Miss Smith presents her to us totally, in the round, in the first five minutes; when we have seen her that long we know her completely, there is nothing more to know about her, we can only wonder what the hell she is going to do next. It is a superb perform-ance, every inflection exactly right, every restless move, every nuance of expression on her face.

As her giant-sized puppet Solness, Michael Redgrave matches her well. A self-willed, arrogant bully this master builder may be; but he never raises his voice against those whom he dominates. When he does raise his voice it is to rail against Heaven, and then it comes out like a trumpet. Sir Michael knows exactly the value of the self-doubt that Solness expresses; it is what he employs to whip up his self-esteem.

In the third corner of this singularly scalene triangle Celia Johnson plays poor dotty Aline with exquisite restraint. From the word go there is something about the way she opens her eyes into great round orbs that suggests she is not quite all there, and this mad look takes posses-sion of her completely for a moment, not, as one might imagine, when she reveals the secret about her dolls, but when she complains about the houses built where 'people I've never seen peer at me from behind windows'.

One of the dividends we get from having a permanent company at the Old Vic is that there are first-class players available for small parts; and Max Adrian makes something very complete out of the pathetic old Brovic. Derek Jacobi, an actor I admire more each time I see him, plays young Ragnar Brovik; his long-bottled-up spite, finally released when he convinces himself that Solness won't have the guts to climb his tower, is beautifully suggested.

Restraint is indeed the keynote of the evening. Peter Wood's direc-tion keeps everyone with a sense of power in hand. At the climax of the play, where they all watch from the terrace of the house as Solness makes his foolhardy bid for immortality, a blackbird's song is the only sound to be heard; its innocent note throws into shocking contrast the ensuing shouts of acclaim, so soon to modulate into screams of horror as Solness plunges head-first into the quarry.

There is nothing baffling about the play in this production (in a new adaptation by Emlyn Williams). It all seems as clear as can be, and the credit for this must go largely to Maggie Smith for making Hilde such a plausible character. This said, the rest of the credit must go to the understanding direction and all-round excellence of the company.

Saint Joan of the Stockyards

Queen's   *12 June 1964*

Tony Richardson has made a tremendous theatrical spectacle out of this play of Brecht's, which dates from 1929, although it was not produced until thirty years later. He has done this by giving it a predominantly un-Brechtian production. For all the masks, and the songs, and the ritual gyrations of the big cast, this is something clearly designed to involve the audience in the dramatic events taking place before them. John Addison has written music in a simple diatonic vein which is incorporated in the progress of the play in almost an operatic fashion; instead of interrupting the argument as the songs in Brecht usually do, it heightens the emotions of the moment and involves us deeper than ever.

I at any rate was unprotestingly engulfed. There were moments that were enormously exciting: Joan, who has failed to deliver the letter for the Communists, surrounded by her accusing comrades: Joan desperately crying out her creed against exploitation and disorder, while the packers and stockbreeders sing their own cynical anthem in an attempt to shout her down: Joan, forcibly rehabilitated in the Black Straw Hats, refusing the charitable soup that is held to her mouth. I never expected to weep at Brecht, but I came close to it then.

All this is to the credit of Mr Richardson. But if the production is un-Brechtian, the play is as Brechtian as they come. It is about the manipulation of the market by the Chicago meat-kings in the 'twenties, and it suffers from the usual Brecht trouble – it is written too uncompromisingly in black-and-white. J. Pierpont Mauler, the canned-meat king, is a figure of such comical wickedness that it's quite impossible to feel any resentment against him, especially as he is played by Lionel Stander with the playful panache of J. Worthington Foulfellow in *Pinocchio* (a delightful performance, by the way). It is manifestly absurd to pit a seriously-devised character like this Joan, a poor scion of the Black Straw Hats – a thinly disguised representation of the Salvation Army – against a crowd of caricatures like Mauler and his associates on the meat-market.

But even if this hurdle could be crossed, there is still so little subtlety in the argument that no one can take it seriously. The rich are villains to a man, and so are the religious, who not only believe that distributing free soup and singing hymns are the limits of their responsibility but always side with the rich whenever there is a question of taking sides. On the other hand the workers are honest and heroic, those of them, that is, who support the Communist cause and are willing to cut the Gordian knot in the stock-yards by violence. This is an avowedly Communist-slanted play, more openly so than Brecht's usually are.

However, Brecht has written into it a number of scenes that have a deep emotional content in a purely theatrical way; and it is by taking advantage of these that Mr Richardson has made it such a stirring affair. He is greatly helped by his large cast. I've already mentioned Mr Stander, a welcome import from the United States, whose gritty voice and knobbly face suit Mauler well. Siobhan McKenna is splendid as Joan. She begins as a drab, colourless girl with no personality, and, though she gets drabber in appearance as the evening goes on, her shining spirit shows through more and more clearly until at the end she has the radiant heroism of the other Saint Joan.

There is also a splendidly oily performance by Michael Medwin as Slift, Mauler's broker, in a genre I didn't know he could touch. Most of the twenty-odd other parts are really puppets, and the rich among them wear half-masks to accentuate the effect; but they all fit very neatly into their slots.

The set, based on two removable columns that provide the necessary foregrounds in front of a collage of the Chicago stockyards, is by Jocelyn Herbert, and adds a little touch of menace of its own. I dare say it is no more like Chicago than the Town of Titipu is like the real seat of the Mikado's Court; but I suspect that Brecht chose Chicago, which he had never been within 5,000 miles of at the time, more or less at random to illustrate his theme. As we see it at the Queen's, it serves this purpose well enough.

The good new translation is by Charlotte and A. L. Lloyd.

Entertaining Mr Sloane

Wyndham's   *30 June 1964*

Technically there's nothing *avant-garde* about Joe Orton's black comedy, which has moved on from the Arts to Wyndham's. It is a beautifully constructed play that develops organically from start to finish, has a most elegant shape and is full of cunningly-sprung surprises.

On the other hand the subject-matter is as modern as the morning paper. It couldn't have turned up on the London stage at all until the Lord Chamberlain, that too-much-maligned functionary, began to liberalise his ideas a year or so ago. It involves the simultaneous seduction of a muscular young lout by his landlady and by her brother; it involves the brutal murder of their father; and in every department Evil is allowed to triumph, with a howl of laughter, over Good. In fact, now I come to think of it, Good doesn't even put in an appearance.

Less skilfully handled, the play could have offended. In fact, it is hilariously funny.

'The humorous writer,' Thackeray once wrote, '. . . to the best of his means and ability comments on all the ordinary actions and passions of life almost.' No topic ought to be excluded from the province of the comic writer on the ground of taste alone; there is only one criterion : Is the writing comic ? Mr Orton's writing is almost unceasingly comic, and it is stylish as well. His dialogue has a beautiful formality about it which he derives from the cunning use of demotic clichés : it has the true ring of well-observed common speech, and yet at the same time it has some of the pretty artificiality of Restoration comedy.

Mr Orton is clearly concerned neither to shock us with his theme nor to preach at us, only to make us laugh. *Entertaining Mr Sloane* isn't going to help anyone understand the problems of juvenile delinquents or nymphomaniacs of either sex; it is simply a new, amusing variation of the eternal triangle. If it has a message, it is the salutary one that society comedy need not always deal with the amorous misunderstandings of the upper classes, and is indeed all the saltier for moving out of that somewhat exhausted realm.

Patrick Dromgoole's subtle and inventive production is more or less unchanged from the Arts. My only criticism is that by having both the door and the sofa in the middle of his set some rather awkward moves are forced on him, especially as the set (a gay design by Timothy O'Brien) is rather a small one.

The performances by Dudley Sutton as the boy, Peter Vaughan and Madge Ryan as the brother and sister and Charles Lamb as their father settled down after a rather breathless beginning into something very close to perfection.

The Royal Hunt of the Sun

Chichester Festival Theatre   *8 July 1964*

Peter Shaffer's new play is about honour – the honour of Francisco Pizarro, who had no belief in the established code of chivalry, but who would not break his last promise to the Inca, Atahuallpa of Peru, whose land he had conquered and robbed, because he found that they were fundamentally two of a kind.

His treatment of the subject is monumental, monumental enough to take in, in the first of its two long acts, the astonishing story of how Pizarro with a band of 167 men marched through the trackless jungle of South America and defeated the Inca's 3,000-strong army.

This is possibly too vast a subject to fit on to any stage. In his treatment of it Mr Shaffer has thrown in, with almost insolent boldness, every technique available to him, every dodge ever known to have been dramatically effective in the history of the drama. There are dancing and mime, and a narrator, and a chanting chorus and musique concrète and eerie jungle sounds proceeding from all over the theatre. With John Dexter and Desmond O'Donovan, his two co-directors, he has devised some moments of truly great theatrical genius and diabolically effective invention.

The qualities in which the play is on the whole short are beauty of language and profundity, as opposed to importance, of argument. This is not to say that there are not some very effective passages between Pizarro and the Inca, Pizarro and the priests that accompanied his expedition, Pizarro and his young page, a believer still in the virtues of honour. The page appears in two forms throughout, once as a boy, ably played by Roy Holder, and again as a grown man (played this time by Robert Lang) when he acts as chorus, filling in the gaps of the story for us.

This is one of the most beautiful productions I have seen for a long time. The brilliant, bizarre costumes of the Peruvian Indians (designed, like the scenery, by Michael Annals) are stirred into glorious movement in Claude Chagrin's choreography. The first opening of the golden disc of the sun to reveal the radiant figure of the Inca; the massacre of the Inca's guards; the moment when Pizarro's men fight with gold ingots while the menacing noises of the jungle sound from above and around them – these are moments of great theatre.

Pizarro, lame, old and bent but indestructible, is vividly portrayed by Colin Blakely in a performance that will stay in the memory; and

Robert Stephens, tall, deliberate and dignified as the Inca even in his extreme humiliations, stands at the same level.

This is a play, pageant, call it what you like, that must be seen. We are lucky in having a company with the resources and the courage of the National Theatre to put it on.

Endgame

Aldwych *10 July 1964*

Endgame (or *endgame*, as apparently we must now write it) is the last dynamic work that Samuel Beckett has written for the theatre. There is in it a developing situation; something, as Clov tells us, is taking its course. For Mr Beckett it seems to have marked the end of a journey; from here on he leaves the highway and shuts himself in a closed world where there are no more causes and effects, but where nameless creatures writhe in a state of uneasy equilibrium in the endless search for an identity.

Endgame represents Mr Beckett's arrival at this point. It's interesting, incidentally, that between the French and the English versions he seems to have taken an extra step away from the pleasures of the outside world. '*Le fanal est dans le canal,*' Clov's report on events beyond the room where he and his master Hamm are immured, has a gay, not to say poetic, sound; in English it falls with a dull plonk, 'The light is sunk.' Later Clov is again bidden to see what moves in the world. In the French version there is an excited passage in which Hamm interrogates his servant about the person he claims to see standing a little way off. In the English there are two colourless lines.

CLOV : Looks like a small boy!
HAMM : (*sarcastic*) : A small boy!

A few moments later, Hamm asks Clov for 'a few words from the heart'. In French, Clov sings a little song, *Joli oiseau, quitte ta cage.* In English he goes straight into his soliloquy about love and friendship, which he is instructed to speak 'tonelessly'.

In the current production Donald McWhinnie seems to be chafing a little against the grey monotone Mr Beckett has imposed on him. The bare walls of Hamm's room have been relieved in Ralph Koltai's designs with patches of coarse rough-cast that throw shadows for the eye to rest on, and there is as much light and shade in the way Patrick Magee as Hamm and Jack MacGowran as Clov speak their lines as the lines can bear. Mr McWhinnie is probably right; the text needs all the relief it can get if it is not to relapse into dullness.

Mr Magee's basic nutmeg-grater voice is the right instrument for Hamm's arrogant monologues, but he has overlaid it with a score of variants to cope with the changing personalities that Hamm, like some importunate club bore, assumes for each successive anecdote. At one point (where he represents a rational being come back to earth) he adopts a thick German accent complete with an introductory '*Ach, so!*' that I feel sure is not in the script. Considering that he is confined to a bathchair throughout the action and allowed only a modicum of gesture by the author, he holds the attention wonderfully. I can't help wondering, though, why he wears white glasses instead of the prescribed black; they deprive him of a measure of menace and offer nothing in exchange.

Jack MacGowran is not quite the hopeless hangdog Clov of my imagination; he trots nimbly but onesidedly about the stage like some macabre cross between Ariel and Caliban, and moves with the quick, jerky movements of a frightened blackbird. But it's a viable Clov in its way, though I found it hard to believe he was as helpless as he claims; and Mr MacGowran is an adept at extracting the last squeeze of emotion from what not seldom look like pretty unemotional lines.

There is nothing much to be done with the two legless parents in their sepulchral dustbins, and here the director has allowed Bryan Pringle and Patsy Magee as much grey monotony as they can provide. They speak like people already dead.

One of the Royal Shakespeare Company's nags against the Censor is that he won't allow Hamm to say of God, 'The bastard! He doesn't exist!' At the Aldwych he says 'The swine!' which seems to me a fair translation of *salaud* even if it wasn't Mr Beckett's original choice; and as Mr Beckett has translated '*con*' as '*ape*' at one point I doubt if he can seriously be perturbed by the reduced intensity of the curse.

Endgame is hard work, no doubt about that, but to my way of thinking much better value than *Krapp's Last Tape* or *Happy Days* or *Play*, whose cyclic form is the last word in inconclusiveness. The Aldwych production provides as gentle an initiation as possible into Beckett country for those who are new to it, and a certain pleasure for those already initiated.

Othello

I missed this many-splendoured production when it opened in London; to begin anew on its praises now would be a work of super-rogation, when it has already taken its place as an historic event in the theatre. Its performance on the Chichester open stage, bare of scenery and equipped only with the normal inner stage and balcony of the Elizabethan theatre, is altogether admirable, and the company seems largely to have overcome the tendency to inaudibility that afflicted some of them last week. John Dexter's direction is a jewel of detailed finish; there is never a character on stage who is not clearly where he is, and doing what he is, for a sound reason. The brawl in which Cassio is disgraced is most imaginatively organised, and its happening so closely in our midst gives it an unusual immediacy.

On the subject of Sir Laurence Olivier's Othello there must always be something fresh to say.

Sir Laurence has been criticised for basing his Moor on a pattern that so clearly derives from the Negro of our day. His first appearance on the stage, trailing a flower in his hand, leaning idly against a doorpost and giggling under his breath, certainly owes more to Harlem than Mauretania, and I would rate it as a cardinal mistake, for it gives a quite wrong introduction to the character he is subsequently to portray. The sinuous movement, the pendulous lip, the head lowered in anger like a buffalo about to charge – these are Negro in origin, certainly, but they owe as much to Africa as to the West Indies.

This Othello is in fact an African Chief – not a Westernised political leader like the chaps we saw at the Commonwealth Prime Ministers' conference the other day, but a true fighting chief, a soldier fit to stand by Chaka and Mzilikaze and Lobengula. Everything about him is consistent, whether from Shakespeare's invention or his own.

This explains why he chose Cassio the 'arithmetician', the desiccated calculating machine, as his lieutenant, because he could supply the intellectual qualities he himself lacked while Iago was only a second and smaller edition of himself. (How Othello flinches when Emilia flings at him the deeply wounding epithet, 'as ignorant as dirt!') It explains his obstinate belief in Iago's honesty, for Iago is a man he can understand, while Cassio and the Venetian nobles are something he recognises as his superiors. Sir Laurence emphasises this with a beautifully imaginative touch when he gratuitously stoops to pick up the Duke of Venice's train before the Duke's own man can get to it.

It accounts for his thraldom to witchcraft; when the word is used against him he crosses himself in fear, but later, when his passions have overmastered him, he tears the golden crucifix from about his neck and hurls it away, and prostrates himself on the ground as if in supplication to the gods of the jungle where he came from. For this Othello clearly did come from the jungle, and fought in tribal wars until his delivery from slavery began his service to the Venetians. Sir Laurence makes an occasional miscalculation when the voice of Paul Robeson seems to speak over his shoulder; but whenever this happens it looks out of character: Othello in this production is a Bantu.

It is inevitable that such a part played so prodigiously should dominate the production; and this is possibly unfair, for there are many other fine performances to be seen. Maggie Smith's Desdemona, for example: this is 'our great captain's captain', which Desdemona all too seldom is. Miss Smith's regal carriage and steely voice are well suited to this tough lady who, listening to Othello's tales, sighed first for the pity of them, and sighed then that she could not have taken part in them.

I'm not sure that Miss Smith makes full use of her natural advantages, and it is true that Desdemona's part is a very tearful one for a potential Amazon; but she comes out like a trumpet with 'By Heaven, you do me wrong!' – which renders the subsequent tears all the more effective.

Frank Finlay's Iago, young and ambitious and something of a wit as villains go, is an excellent performance, though I begin to wonder if Mr Finlay, whose voice never lets him down, is beginning to fall into clichés of gesture with his expressive hands. A slight whiff of the drama school accompanied some of his less military elegances; perhaps he learnt them from Roderigo.

There are so many felicities both in the playing and in the direction that one would like to put one's pleasure in all of them on record, but space prevents it. The current season at Chichester is already fully booked, and indeed has been so for some time. I can only hope the production will remain in the National Theatre's repertory for a very long time to come.

The Marat/Sade

The short title used above and authorised in the programme is an abbreviation only; the actual name of the play is *The Persecution and Assassination of Marat as Performed by the Inmates of the Asylum of Charenton under the Direction of the Marquis de Sade*; and if you think that's a devil of a long title I can only say that at times it seemed a devil of a long play.

Short of all the ornamentation, it consists of a debate between Marat on one side, the prophet of the totalitarian state, completely indifferent to the suffering its establishment may bring to the individual; and de Sade on the other, the apostle of individual liberty even it that liberty might be sometimes allowed to stray over the boundaries of recognised morals.

I personally found it a little hard to decide whose side Peter Weiss, the author, was on. He seems to have been scrupulous in putting only their own authentic arguments into the mouths of his principals, and as both of them were persuasive thinkers their cases both come out strong. It happens that today majority opinion is against totalitarianism and increasingly lenient towards sexual deviation, and for that reason de Sade appears the victor; but the dispute is the thing, not the result.

It is presented in the form of a play acted by conventional stage lunatics under the direction of the immortal Marquis, who sits watching them rather aloofly except when from time to time he is roused to a polemic of his own. Patrick Magee plays de Sade; he is not the actor I myself would have chosen, but he exudes the right cold superiority, and his account of the torture and death of the assassin of Louis XV is bloodcurdling. The action alternates mimed scenes from the Revolution with argument, and it is directed with a fantastic richness of kinky invention by Peter Brook.

This is a play that might have been written for Mr Brook. Everything he has been doing and writing about for the last five years is piled in to brilliant effect. No props are employed but Marat's hip-bath and the usual paraphernalia of a bath-house; from these he has constructed the most tremendous scenes of hysteria, tragedy and violence, including a session with the guillotine which ends with a happy lunatic pouring a bucket of blood down the drain. I don't know whether he or Mr Weiss is responsible for the scene where de Sade is whipped with Charlotte Corday's hair, or the sudden breaking off from riot to madrigal, the mouthing of the inmates suddenly giving way to flute-and-guitar strain; they were great moments, anyway.

The translation by Geoffrey Skelton is in decent current English and the verse passages in conscious doggerel, with Byronesque rhymes like 'play the role here' and Richard Peaselee's music, which is plentiful and important, could hardly be bettered.

Costive and repetitious as the play occasionally is, this remarkable production is something that simply cannot be missed.

Inadmissible Evidence

Royal Court   *10 September 1964*

John Osborne has shaken out the accumulated contents of his note-book for the last few years and poured them all into the mould of Bill Maitland, the central and the only fully worked-out character in his new play. Maitland is a shady solicitor of forty, engaged between his fornications in losing such clients as he has. In him, Mr Osborne has devised a marvellous portrait of a man in the last stages of moral disintegration. He is garrulous, self-satisfied and self-pitying. He knows he is only a step ahead of the Law Society, but he blunders on because he has not the backbone to stop. He seduces every girl who comes along as casually as he would pat a dog, and with no more real pleasure in it; his wife and family bore him, and only his mistress remains to give him a real handhold on life.

He is aware that he is slipping too fast for safety, and it gives him a constant delusion that people are avoiding him. At the beginning it is the taxi drivers who will not stop for him although their 'For Hire' lights are on, and the caretaker who ignores him when he arrives at the office. Then the members of his office staff tend to find working with him uncongenial and leave. (Time has been telescoped with some ingenuity during the course of the play.) His sixteen-year-old daughter, whom he loves, slips from his grasp. Finally, even his mistress, though she adores him, decides that she cannot stay with him anymore.

It is an acutely observed portrait and is given an appropriately subtle performance by Nicol Williamson. This splendid actor is at the top of his form in this immensely testing part. The uncontrolled speech, the nervous movement of the limbs, are beautifully managed; the slack face fighting its losing battle with despair is a kaleidoscope of moral degeneracy. None of the other characters is drawn in such detail; they serve only as the stimulant that drives Maitland from one point to the next, as impersonal in their way as the headache pills that he swallows endlessly all day. But there are nice performances by Arthur Lowe as Hudson, the managing clerk who knows when the time has come to make a move, and Lois Daine as the nubile and amenable switchboard operator.

The play runs for $2\frac{3}{4}$ hours and it undoubtedly has its longueurs. I saw little point in the introductory scene showing an incoherent Maitland in a spotlight on trial for having uttered an obscene object (presumably his life); this was just a bit of chi-chi.

There were a number of moments in the second half too, that found me shuffling my feet. The chief of them finds Maitland interviewing a client charged with a homosexual offence. For some reason best known to himself Mr Osborne brings in Maitland's clerk Jones (a very proper performance by John Quentin) to be this client, though they do not appear to have anything in common with anything that has gone before; this young man's confession goes on and on, pointlessly and irrelevantly as far as I could see, until he simply joins the muster of the clients who lose confidence in the firm and walk out. This is simply wilfulness on Mr Osborne's part, unless he felt that he had something new to express about this particular type of offence.

The fact is that Mr Osborne has written what is basically a moving account of a man's failure in life and love, and has had to disguise it as something more ponderous. But on this basic level it is a great success, a moving and exciting portrait of a man in decline, treated with great understanding. It is a pity – though not by any means fatal – to have tried to blow it up into anything more.

Marlene Dietrich

Queen's   *24 November 1964*

It seems almost unfair that the gods should have bestowed so many gifts on one woman as they have on Marlene Dietrich. The tawny beauty alone would see most women happily through life; or the sinuous, imperious dignity; or the mischievous wit. To add the voice and the acting ability as well is sheer extravagance.

Yet to my way of thinking none of those is her dominating quality. What distinguishes everything she does, and makes it so much better than anything of its kind to be seen elsewhere, is her intelligence. In every note she sings, in every movement she makes, you can see how she has studied her material from every side and taken its exact measure. This is why it's never embarrassing to hear her singing foolish American songs like 'My Blue Heaven'. This is why she sings 'Falling in Love Again' just the same now as she sang it in *The Blue Angel.*

Of the eighteen songs she gave at her opening at the Queen's, about half-a-dozen had little but a nostalgic value as songs; yet even these came over with that familiar growling charm. When she did something less familiar, like the little Israeli folksong about the baby that wakes up hungry in the night, she touched such depths as I am constantly forgetting she is capable of.

And there is another instance of her intelligence : the discrimination with which she compiles her programme. When she had finished 'Where have all the flowers gone?' I was in tears. What on earth could follow that? Miss Dietrich knew exactly; she sang 'Honeysuckle Rose' with a dead-pan comedy that brought the sun out again at once.

Her art is above all economical; her gestures are sparing, the range of her voice seldom more than an octave and a half. The songs that gave me most pleasure were a sad, romantic Viennese ballad, *'Frag' nicht warum'* and a French chanson, 'Marie, Marie', a letter from a prisoner to his girlfriend outside; but favourites mean nothing when all is so good.

Burt Bacharach, her arranger, conducts a small orchestra on the stage behind her; his arrangements are tactful and inconspicuous mostly, but occasionally, as in the descant melody to 'Where have all the flowers gone?', ingenious and telling.

When Miss Dietrich had sung 'Falling in love again' and the evening could fairly be considered over, she made countless appearances before the curtain in response to the continuous demonstrations of affection that thundered up at her from the house. One of the remarkable things about the occasion is that the young people who formed a considerable fraction of the audience will not remember that pale golden figure before the flame-coloured drapes in years to come and say, 'I saw Marlene Dietrich when she was over sixty'. They will say, 'I saw Marlene Dietrich'. Perhaps the gods have realised their extravagance, and are determined to compensate for it by adding the additional gift of immortality.

CHAPTER TWO

The Mainstream

And so on to the next decade and a half.

A complete retrospective look at this period would involve about two and a half million words, too much even for the most elaborate coffee-table book. The first task was to make a short list. This would contain notices that still raised a special sense of interest in me when I re-read them. The sources of interest were varied. Sometimes it arose from the obvious importance of a new play; sometimes from the interest of a new production or an outstanding performance; sometimes from a feeling that the play had pushed back the boundaries of what was acceptable in the theatre, as *Saved* did, and *Hair*, and *Oh! Calcutta*. Sometimes I simply recalled the play with a special feeling of affection or excitement, irrespective of its importance in the canon.

My short list worked out at about two hundred thousand words, enough to fill three volumes this size and have a little over. Working on the same principles, but more heartlessly, I prepared a short list of my short list, and this is what you have here.

For convenience, I have subdivided it. I have put the musicals in a section of their own, and the pieces that seemed to enlarge the boundaries. I have extracted the reviews of *Hamlet*, because I particularly want to include my own essay on this play, which I have used as an introduction to this section. I have collected a handful of exotica, not nearly as many as I would have liked. I have separated my own personal favourites, even though they may belong elsewhere.

The rest come under this comprehensive heading 'Mainstream' which applies to this and the following three sections. I can no more explain why these have been my choice than I can explain why I like Schubert better than Elgar. It's a matter of taste.

*

Joyce Grenfell

In Miss Grenfell's world there are no race riots, no Rachmanesque landlords, no doped racehorses, no homosexuals, no Mods and Rockers, no rush-hours, no napalm; when she mentions the Blues, she is referring to the Royal Horse Guards. Ladies write biographies, go to church and to the opera, are elected president of the bridge club; at a lower social level, indicated with the merest hint of condescension, they dance the old-time dances, win pools, see their children off on the train for Australia.

It is the cosy, well-upholstered, air-conditioned world of the upper middle-classes; and if it has as much relevance to the world of 1965 as it has to life on Mars, there is no reason why it should not be a viable source of entertainment, and as a matter of fact Miss Grenfell, with her sensitive eye and ear for behaviour, has extracted from it an evening that is, in its way, as expert as the performance of the American sick-comics, and probably more so. It's a question of being tuned to the right channel.

I suppose you could call Miss Grenfell's art pure humour, as contrasted with the applied humour of the more fashionable entertainers. Applied humour states a point of view, it strives to leave you thinking after the laughter has died down. Pure humour has no other object than to make you laugh. I can't see anything wrong in this; it's the principle that inspires *Three Men in a Boat* and *The Importance of Being Earnest* and *Un Fil à la Patte,* the principle that sustained *Punch* for the seventy years before Malcolm Muggeridge became editor. Miss Grenfell is a clever practitioner of pure humour, and people who are tired of being raked by satirists may well find her one-woman evening a haven of rest and refreshment in a pretty tiresome world.

One thing no one can deny is the sheer talent she brings to bear on her sketches. Every inflection and every movement of her victims is faithfully reproduced, so that even in her long gown by Victor Stiebel she can persuade us that she is the best man at a working-class wedding, or a fat old woman dancing the military two-step. When she sings, she sings *properly.* She has Ruth Draper's ability to people the stage with other characters though they never utter a sound.

She is, to my way of thinking, less successful when she turns serious. The little *scena* about Lally Tullett, the Virginian school-mistress, is written and delivered with consummate skill; so is the sketch about the woman bidding farewell to her emigrant children; but at the end of them I detected a faint aroma of sickly sentiment. But there, we are all so hard nowadays; probably the committed Grenfelliers were as delighted as I was with the fat lady singing the song about the cream cakes; and who am I to deprive them of their pleasure?

Miss Grenfell is accompanied at the piano by William Blezard, who gets one number to himself, a rendering (I'm sure that is the right word) of a piece called Battle March of Delhi, by John Pridham. I take this to be genuine and not pastiche, but the interesting thing is that it produces, with Mr Blezard's terse commentary, exactly the same kind of effect that Miss Grenfell's own sketches do. Miss Grenfell's pastiche is so adroitly done that only a few tiny changes of phrasing and delivery would turn them from comic to serious.

The Homecoming

Aldwych   *4 June 1965*

The story of Harold Pinter's new play is stark and horrible. Teddy, the successful son of a singularly beastly family, comes home from America to pay them a short visit, bringing with him the wife whom none of them has met. Four of the family live in the decaying old North London house : Teddy's father, an aged bully given to sudden spurts of violence; his brother Sam, a taxi-driver of a tidier and more pacific way of life; and Teddy's two younger brothers – Lenny, a successful ponce with the girls working the Greek Street area and Joey, a boxer haunting the gym in the vain pursuit of recognition.

Teddy has somehow become a Doctor of Philosophy in a Mid-Western American university, and his wife Ruth, as we first see her, is the ideal consort for an American professor, cool, attractive, well-dressed, well poised, the mother of three children. At first their impact on the family is what you would expect from the contact of quiet, civilised people with the rough relations they have grown away from. The general level of reserve is dented here and there by bursts of exaggerated affection or familiarity pressed too far, but it maintains an orthodox course on the whole.

And then, in a brilliant Pinterian stroke, an extraordinary change takes place. Ruth gets up to dance with Lenny, and at once they go into an amorous clinch. Teddy watches impassively, neither approving nor disapproving. Lenny is followed by Joey, whose success with Ruth is so immediate that he finally takes her up to his room. The last scene is devoted to a family conference at which they discuss a plan to install her in one of Lenny's Greek Street flats and share her favours when she is off duty. When it is settled, Teddy leaves for America as unperturbed as if his wife were going to her mother's for the week-end.

I've recounted the plot in such detail because Mr Pinter keeps insisting that there's no more in his plays than what you see. It would be easy to read into this story something about original sin, perhaps, or the dangers of rising above one's station. But if I understand Mr Pinter's principles rightly it's simply the story of a woman who found life in an American university intolerable ('it was all sand and rocks, and there were lots of insects') and the prospect of life on the game more attractive.

However you care to take it, it's monstrously effective theatre. Perhaps Mr Pinter keeps us waiting a little too long before he springs the trap, dickering with half-suggested family scandals; but once he does, he raises all the expected *frissons*. Mr Pinter isn't to my way of thinking an *important* playwright, in the sense that he has any message to offer us or any trail-blazing innovations in technique. But he has this enormous capacity for generating a tension among his characters in which the audience becomes irresistibly involved; and to do this is surely the playwright's first responsibility. I defy anyone not to feel concerned with the events presented to them in *The Homecoming*.

The play is splendidly acted by Paul Rogers as Max, Ian Holm as the cunningly-observed wide boy Lenny, John Normington as Sam, Terence Rigby as Joey, Vivien Merchant as Ruth and Michael Bryant as Teddy. The director is Peter Hall, and the set, a cold grey sitting-room as big as a cinema foyer, is by John Bury.

A Patriot for Me

Royal Court   *1 July 1965*

John Osborne's new play tells the story of Colonel Alfred Redl, the subject of a notorious scandal in Austria before the first world war. Redl came of comparatively humble Jewish stock, and he reacted against the snobbish ambience of life in the Austro-Hungarian army by developing an arrogant, selfish character that in his mind set him apart from his colleagues – a character that he conscientiously bolstered by endless hard work that earned him a brilliant reputation and quick promotion culminating in the post of chief of counter-intelligence.

Unluckily he had the misfortune to be a homosexual, and if Mr Osborne's account of his life is to be believed, an almost insatiable one. How his activities escaped notice in that gossipy old army, heaven knows; at any rate they soon attracted attention in the Russian army, whose agents confronted him with an incriminating file and enlisted him on their side. Unfortunately, a letter sent to him at a Poste Restante was intercepted, and Redl was ritually presented with a pistol and invited to commit suicide.

Ironically (though this doesn't come into Osborne's play), no one took the precaution of finding out from him before he shot himself just what information he had sold to the enemy. It turned out to include the plans for the invasion of Serbia the following year . . .

Mr Osborne has treated the story in a more-or-less documentary style in twenty-three short scenes. This is really a very lazy and rather ineffectual way of writing a play, especially when as here, some of the scenes are only of marginal relevance. It is even worse when there has to be a scene change at the end of almost every scene, and we are either kept waiting before a dropped curtain or entertained, rather against our will, by the pleasant music of Tibor Kunstler's *zigeuner* violin. Since the play was written for the Royal Court, one would have thought its author would have taken that theatre's capabilities into account and not expected the resources of Drury Lane. The play as at present performed runs for just on three-and-a-half hours, of which a very significant proportion is spent in manipulating the stage.

A further proportion is occupied with the actual presentation of what could as well be introduced through dialogue or even left to the intelligence of the audience. Structurally, in fact, the play is pretty poor.

However, as we have seen more than once before, Mr Osborne is able to transcend his difficulty in composing a well-shaped play by the sharpness of his characterisation and the agility with which he plays on our emotions. Redl, who is ably portrayed by Maximilian Schell, runs through the centre of the play in exactly the same way as Maitland runs through *Inadmissible Evidence*. All the other parts are feeds for him, but on this occasion there are not half a dozen other parts for forty or so.

The delineation of Redl's character is done with enormous subtlety in the long first act. We see him first acting as second to a brother-office who has challenged another officer to a duel because he charged him with effeminacy. At that time he appears to be a perfectly normal young man. It is occasionally noticed that he takes little interest in women; we even see him in a brothel taking little interest in one; but whenever he is confronted with the other thing he reacts with a burst of disgust. His affair with Countess Sophia Delyanoff (a part that Jill Bennett adorns beyond its real worth) fizzles out – which is lucky, for in the only real *coup de théâtre* of the evening we learn later on that she is a Russian agent.

But by the beginning of the second act he is deeply involved in homosexual society. There is a scene here of a 'drag ball' in Vienna, full of boys dressed as girls, in which he is perfectly at home, though slightly taken aback to find so many of his brother officers there. Mr Osborne has stuffed this scene with all the clichés of camp backchat in the hope, I suppose, that there will be someone in the house to whom they are a novelty. I can only say that to me they were a terrible bore.

But still, even in such compromising surroundings, Redl maintains his arrogant manner – even with his boy-friends, whom he bullies and tortures until, in one case at any rate, they break down altogether. Mr Osborne is remarkably adept at portraying queers. Maples's accounts in *Inadmissible Evidence* of his seduction in the train at Gunnersbury and of his arrest in Piccadilly Underground can only be the result of detailed and authentic research; and here there is an equally remarkable passage where Redl tells the Countess, who has secretly married one of his boy-friends, 'You'll never know his body as I do . . . the backs of his knees, the patterns on the soles of his feet,' and so on. Lines like this show an astonishing intuition into how such people think.

Mr Schell's unerring performance as Redl, all the more impressive because he is so seldom allowed to give rein to his emotions, is at the hub of the play. Among the smaller parts there are good performances by Clive Morton as Colonel von Möhl; George Murcell as Oblensky, the Russian intelligence colonel, and especially by George Devine as Baron von Epp, who presides, disguised as Queen Alexandra, at the curious ball in Vienna.

It's impossible to say that anything so cumbersomely put together is a good play, but Redl's fate, pursuing him as inexorably as Oedipus's, can't be anything but moving; and the play (leaving out of account the impossibilities demanded by its author) is directed as sensitively as possible by Anthony Page.

Ivanov

Phoenix   *1 October 1965*

No Dames, as it happens, and only one Sir, but this is the grand old Tennent formula, a cast glittering with talent from top to bottom and a play with parts in it to display them all. Of the play, more in a moment; but of the acting, the direction, and John Gielgud's adaptation of the play I long to express my complete approval before the glow subsides in the rain-soaked traffic-jams that lie ahead.

The part of Ivanov, in which Sir John has chosen to make his long-overdue reappearance on the London stage, is the kind of thing that shows off his mature talents at their best. He has a positive genius for portraying inward suffering, and this Ivanov, with his shifty eyes, nervous movements and grey, gaunt face, is clearly being consumed by suffering before our very eyes. Even his fleeting moments of happiness fill him with guilt; see him, as he caresses his Sasha's face while his wife Anna lies dying upstairs, his glance flickers involuntarily towards the door in case anyone should come in and see them. This is a terrific performance.

It is flanked by the two women, played excellently by Yvonne Mitchell and Claire Bloom. Miss Mitchell is visibly more wasted in the second act than in the first; she behaves like a dying woman long before Ivanov tells her she is one. Miss Bloom, on the other hand, burgeons with happiness; the happy comrade of the first act swells into the bride of the third act as she sees her influence over Ivanov ripening with his wife's relaxing grip.

For influence, as it happens, is what both of these women are after. It is Ivanov's helplessness that appeals to them, and it is Ivanov's fate to be such a helpless man that the loss of one domination is bound to be followed by the arrival of another.

There are other splendid performances too numerous to recount in detail – Roland Culver's Cheeryble-brother Lebedev, Richard Pasco's priggish young doctor, Ronald Radd's fat well-meaning boor of a Borkin; most impressive of the lot, Edward Atienza's Count Shabelsky, the stiff-kneed Pantoloon whose voice creaks through timeless age while his behaviour lights the least dignified aspects of second childhood. Add to these Angela Baddeley, as the miserly Zyuzyushka, Helen Christie as Babakina, Nora Nicholson as Avdotya Nazarovna – here are riches indeed.

But why *Ivanov*? The fact that Chekhov himself thought it bad and actually produced seven revised versions of it before he relinquished it with the comment, 'No matter how bad the play is, I created a type of literary value' (meaning Ivanov himself), needn't be taken too seriously. After all, plenty of playwrights have admired their own plays when the general consensus has held them to be ghastly; author's opinions are bound to be suspect.

But in this case Chekhov was unquestionably right. The play is very clearly prentice work. The characters are a boring and worthless lot, interesting as it is to see in them the rough workings of the greater characters to emerge later on. The plot is crudely melodramatic, once you remove the veil of nascent Chekhovism that blurs its edges. And a lot of the dialogue is pretty dull stuff; never was small talk quite so small. The horrors of Lebedev's party have been reproduced crudely as if they had been taken down in shorthand and transcribed verbatim into the script; and it's one of the sad facts about playwriting that too-realistic writing about bores simply results in boredom.

There must be more exciting plays to be found for the Sirs and Dames. *Ivanov* is for the library shelf as far as I am concerned. But that doesn't alter the fact that the performances given under John Gielgud's direction in this production hold the attention on their own merits. They don't, alas, blow any extra life into the play, however.

Saved

Royal Court   *4 November 1965*

Edward Bond can handle the current style of curt, laconic speech with considerable skill. It's no light matter to set a mood and advance a narrative in dialogue consisting almost wholly of brief snatches of prefabricated cockney, where it is quite exceptional for any one line to lead on to the next. The opening scene of *Saved*, which shows young Len (John Castle) sporting on the sofa with Pam (Barbara Ferris), picked up ten minutes earlier, is very deftly written and hilariously funny.

Unfortunately, as the evening goes on it becomes clear that the ability to write good dialogue isn't synonymous with the ability to write a good play. The fault is possibly mine that I find Mr Bond's worthless layabouts about as interesting as waste paper blowing about the street. Perhaps I ought to be more concerned with the sinister undercurrents of South London life, that drive girls into casual inter-course without a word of protest from their complaisant parents, and prompt boys to amuse themselves by stoning babies to death.

I can only plead that I have lived a comparatively sheltered life, and if such things are really going on in South London they are properly the concern of the police and the magistrates rather than the audiences of theatres, even the Royal Court.

This holier-than-thou attitude is forced on me because Mr Bond appears to believe that to place these things in front of us with more-or-less photographic realism is all he has to do to make a play. Being a young playwright of the sixties, he is not concerned with anything so old-fashioned as generating dramatic tension. It is true that in the scene where he shows the obscene murder of a baby in a perambulator by five young thugs he certainly generates something, but I found this scene so poisonously objectionable that I can't enter it on the credit side of this ledger.

All the same, there's something to go on the credit side. He has created a bunch of credible characters, scrupulously observed, subtly differentiated, totally consistent in their behaviour, and that isn't a bad score for a young man's first play. The parts, with their taut, elliptical lines, can't be easy to play, but under William Gaskill's direction they are played pretty well on the whole. John Castle and Barbara Ferris are indeed quite outstanding, and there are neat per-formances by Tony Selby as Pam's thug of a boyfriend Fred and by Richard Butler and Gwen Nelson as her father and mother.

The debit side, alas, is overwhelming. When I had done wriggling with embarrassment at the child-murder scene (how much better this situation was handled in that much underrated play *Infanticide in the House of Fred Ginger* a year or two ago!) I gave myself up to wriggling with ennui. So much was shown to us that should have been suggested, so much that it was fair to show us went on too long. For this the blame must presumably be laid on Mr Gaskill, who has chosen this play as one of the three to open his regime with, and has selected this one in particular to direct himself. What we see must be what he wants us to see.

I beseech him to consider whether he may possibly be mistaken. The theatre exists not for the benefit of writers, actors, directors or even shareholders, but for the benefit of audiences. Everything that happens on the stage should happen with the intention of involving the house. If a play comes along that is manifestly too slow, or too weakly founded, or too varying in pace, all this must be ironed out in rehearsal. When Basil Dean, as a young man, was producing a play by Somerset Maugham, then at the peak of his success, he wanted to make some changes in it. Very delicately he put his suggestions to the author. 'Why not?' said Maugham at once. 'The theatre is a workshop.'

The trouble with the Royal Court at the moment is that it seems to be less of a workshop than a showcase. As a founder-member of the English Stage Society, I feel very gloomy about its prospects for the immediate future.

A Song at Twilight

Queen's   *15 April 1966*

It doesn't seem such a long time since we saw Noël Coward in *Present Laughter*, standing on a footstool in order to admire himself better in his new dressing-gown and 'advancing', as he put it, 'with every sign of reluctance into middle-age'. He still wears a dressing-gown for his first appearance in his new play; but this time he is 'growing old gracefully'.

The grace is only an outward and social quality, however; the inward and spiritual graces, if they exist, are kept scrupulously concealed by Sir Hugo Latymer, the hero of *A Song at Twilight*; for Sir Hugo Latymer is, as near as makes no difference, Somerset Maugham.

It would be tedious to set out all the resemblances between the fictional life of Sir Hugo and the real life of Mr Maugham. Sir Hugo, preparing to be the Grand Old Man of English letters, is a novelist and playwright, who, we are told, has spent much time travelling in the East where he tapped the confidence of his acquaintances to bring fresh material to his work. If this were not enough, one need only watch Mr Coward's performance, in which Maugham comes, sometimes quite startlingly, to life – the jutting chin, the mouth turned down at the corners, the brisk but stiff-legged walk. The portrait is authentic; so much so that when Mr Coward permits himself occasionally to relapse into the memorable mannerisms of his earlier style to split the ears of the groundlings, it seems a rather naughty betrayal of his own art.

The play is not much more than an anecdote which a writer less skilful that Mr Coward might have found hard to stretch beyond one act. Sir Hugo is visited in his Swiss hotel by Carlotta Gray, a woman who for two years in the distant past was his mistress. After some fencing she explains that she has come because she has in her possession some of his letters to a young man called Perry Sheldon. She wants to punish him for having been a lifelong homosexual and having been so hypocritical about it, and is going to hand over the letters to a Harvard professor who is keen to embark on a biography of Sir Hugo.

Her motives in this are not very clear to me; I have a feeling they may not have been very clear to Mr Coward, who needed the situation and the character, but found no convincing way of linking the two. So he leaves Carlotta's motives a bit wavery round the edges. It is therefore less of a surprise than it should be when her determination is punctured by the intervention of Sir Hugo's wife, a patient German secretary-cum-companion, who coolly reveals that she has known about Perry Sheldon and the rest of it all her life. I won't disclose exactly how the situation is resolved; if one knew that it would be hard to sit through the second act, which, except for a bravura passage for the wife, is uncommonly straightforward in its development of the story.

The first act contains more of the Old Master's thumbprints – a little fugue about bees and grasshoppers that put me in mind of those immortal judgments on China and Japan, and occasional exchanges like this: 'I met my husband when I was playing Hedda Gabler at Boston.' 'I don't give a damn who you were playing at Boston.' But these, like the Old Master's own ventures into an earlier manner, seem somehow irrelevant.

Carlotta is played shrilly and monotonously by Lilli Palmer; Hilde, the wife, is played sensitively and humorously by Irene Worth. There is also a waiter who performs little beyond a waiter's normal functions and is played by Sean Barrett. The meticulous director is Vivian Matalon, who can't be blamed for the remarkable number of times his principals stumbled over their lines; and the set is designed by Brian Currah.

Suite in Three Keys

Actually the two one-act pieces that make up this double bill, *Shadows of the Evening* and *Come into the Garden, Maud,* are the last two movements of the 'suite'; the first was *A Song at Twilight.* All they have in common is the set (a sitting room in a posh Swiss hotel) and the cast (Noël Coward, Lilli Palmer, Irene Worth and Sean Barrett). Otherwise they are quite independent of each other.

Mr Coward's acting never fails to bring me the highest pleasure. To the selfish, arrogant old man of the first play he now adds a prosperous businessman who has just learnt from his doctor that he has only three months to live, and a rich, rough American tycoon with a vulgar tuft-hunting wife. They are scrupulously observed and faultlessly executed characters. George, the hero of *Shadows of the Evening,* is a cheerful agnostic who has left a solid Anglican wife and gone to live with a frivolous Catholic mistress; now that he is faced with the prospect of death he is beset by doubts he had never allowed to raise their heads before. Every shade in the spectrum that lies between fear and resignation is beautifully conveyed in what seems outwardly an impassive performance.

Verner Conklin, the tycoon, is a rangy, middle-aged man with a crew-cut and a store of good nature for everyone. While his wife is giving a dinner-party for a bunch of hungry titled nobodies (the high-level *mangiare* kids, we used to call them in Florence during the war), Verner dines alone in his room, exiled by the threat of thirteen at table. But there is one high-level *mangiare* kid who was not invited to dinner; and she has a brief encounter with Verner in his suite and ends by taking him off to Rome with her.

I wish I found Mr Coward's writing as dependable as his acting. Alas, it is quite otherwise. *Shadows of the Evening* is a singularly dull piece. The situation is set in an initial duologue for wife and mistress, both of them admirably played, after a rather sticky beginning, by Irene Worth and Lilli Palmer respectively; and thereafter it barely develops at all. I had a feeling that his situation must be one that Mr Coward had encountered somewhere and been very moved by, and consequently couldn't see that he had failed to make it moving when he wrote it down.

To make matters worse the dialogue is flat and commonplace. The only time the audience reacted at all briskly was at the line with which

Miss Palmer replies when Miss Worth says she feels like a governess in her dress, 'I've met comparatively few governesses who are dressed by Molyneux.' I think it was sheer relief.

Still, *Come into the Garden, Maud* ends the evening on an altogether brighter note. Once more the story is pretty thin, but this time a certain amount of dramatic tension is created with it, and the three main parts provide a chance for some really gorgeous comic acting. The honours go to Miss Worth this time for her terrible, ambitious, blue-haired Middle Western matron, happy in the knowledge that if she asks for anything loud enough she is certain to get it; Miss Palmer, as a free-living Anglo-Italian aristocrat, who has come slightly down in the world, has no more to do than look very pretty and very charming, two achievements she can accomplish effortlessly. Mr Coward, whose American accent never quite swamps his well-loved vocal foibles, oscillates happily between them.

Brian Currah's hotel sitting room houses all these events without, as far as I could see, even the bottles on the drink table being changed; and the director is Vivian Matalon.

The Prime of Miss Jean Brodie

Wyndham's   *6 May 1966*

Jean Brodie is a natural leader.

The trouble with natural leaders is that they tend to appoint themselves, to gauge their own capabilities for leadership, and to ascribe all cases where their leadership brings disaster to faults in their followers instead of faults in their own methods. Jean Brodie, a mistress in the Marcia Blane School for Girls in Edinburgh, is blithely unconcerned with curricula. She likes to make teaching interesting, so she declines to teach boring subjects. She crams her pupils' heads with romantic notions about beauty and leadership and never asks what effect such notions will have on their lives.

Conventional virtues are flung to the winds. 'Anna Pavlova is the great *prima ballerina*. The *corps de ballet* have the team spirit,' is one of her object lessons. Naturally she has a following of intelligent girls, 'the Brodie set' as they are somewhat disparagingly called in the school; and inevitably when the Brodie set get old enough to make their own judgments they find that they have been misled.

It is a most interesting character and, even better, a thought-provoking one. Vanessa Redgrave presents it with great intelligence. Her Jean Brodie is fundamentally a gawky provincial, but overlaid with the trappings of home-bred culture – a head of auburn hair like Elizabeth Siddall's, dresses with the faintest trace of bohemianism below their conventional cut, a store of superficial culture remembered in a romantic haze from holidays in Italy and Egypt, and dished out to her little corps of favourites with a garnish of elevated gestures that barely covers the ordinariness of the underlying woman.

The play covers some four years in the lives of one particular Brodie set. (Clearly there was another one before this, and there would have been another one afterwards if circumstances had been different.) At the start the four little girls are all under the spell; but we see as the play progresses how the Brodie influence goes awry. At the climax there is a scene between her and Sandy, one of the set, in which the girl tears away all her pretensions and reveals her to herself as she really is. 'You,' says Sandy, 'really are a ridiculous woman'; and the flat, simple words hold a world of cruelty. Jean Brodie, ridiculous and romantic to the last, rides her bicycle into a lake on the golf-course, from which she is fished, we are told, with her hands still indomitably clutching the handle-bars.

Jay Presson Allen has made an excellent job of adapting the novel. He has used a series of short episodic scenes that flow with perfect smoothness along the narrative course. Although it is basically a one-character play, like *Inadmissible Evidence,* the subsidiary characters are drawn with sympathy and humour – Teddy Lloyd the art master, as first Jean Brodie's lover, later the lover of one of her girls, though not of course the one she had destined for the job; Gordon Lowther the music master, her next elected lover who takes refuge in the arms of the chemistry mistress; Miss Mackay, the unromantically conventional headmistress, who finally has to sack her difficult assistant when she is denounced by her favourite girl for preaching Fascism. And there are all those girls.

The Brodie set themselves are skilfully differentiated from each other, and cleverly played by Vickery Turner, Olivia Hussey, Alison Blair and Jane Carr; they grow up uncannily before our eyes from twelve-year-olds to sixteen-year-olds. Another dozen nymphets are brought on occasionally to dress the scene, and very prettily they do it.

William Squire, Andrew Crawford and Dorothy Reynolds give good performances as Lloyd, Lowther and Miss Mackay respectively. The director is Peter Wood, who has obviously had to work hard to achieve the mastery that conceals art. All those children have been drilled to a hair; and the narrative is kept flowing equably from episode to episode, while Rolf Gerard's effective peripatetic sets glide on and off as needed to set a scene in a moment.

The result is an exceptionally interesting evening. This is a play of ideas and humour quite out of the ordinary; and at the heart of it is a performance by Miss Redgrave that simply mustn't be missed.

US

Aldwych   *14 October 1966*

The equivocation in the title is clearly deliberate. The subject is the war in Vietnam, and the title may be read as 'U.S.' or as 'us' – or as both.

If I believed that *US*, then, would bring the war in Vietnam to an honourable conclusion one minute sooner, it would get the loudest cheer from me that I have ever given. I believe, in fact, that it probably won't, for a variety of reasons, none of which has anything to do with the question of whether or not I agree with the opinions expressed from the stage.

The chief reason is that the appeal made in this remarkable production is directed exclusively at the emotions. The voice of reason is only introduced to be mocked at. Since it was reason and not emotion that began the Vietnam conflict it is easy to see why Peter Brook and his numerous colleagues have taken this attitude; but its weakness is that those who are opposed to the war on purely emotional grounds have already reached their conclusions. *US* will not widen the area of protest, it will only increase the intensity of the protest. Indeed I came away with a serious conviction that emotionally unstable people might well immolate themselves on the steps of the Aldwych in imitation of the desperate Buddhist priests of Saigon whose deaths they may see acted out and discussed on the stage.

The play is not only overtly anti-American and anti-French, it is overtly pro-Vietcong. It is easy enough to amass a formidable case against the Americans and the French from contemporary history, be-

cause the facts are available to us. If we knew as much of what went
on on 'the other side of the hill' the North Vietnamese might possibly
emerge less spotless. This is a small point; the important thing is to
collect all the usable ammunition against the war, without worrying
too much where it comes from as long as it is genuine; but it will not
seem a small point to the French or the Americans, who appear heartless, cruel, obstinate and stupid. If the Vietcong could be made to
appear cruel and stupid as well so much the better; but the data are
not available.

The production takes the form of a chain of scenes representing in
stylised fashion the history of Vietnam and the progress of the war,
interspersed with passages of argument taken from the pronounce-
ments of various public men. It is often violently effective, but
occasionally repetitious and long-winded, especially in the second half,
in which the moral issue is discussed.

This is a bad fault, because if the piece is to have its desired effect
it must take the spectator by the scruff of his neck and hold him down
until the spectacle is done. If his attention is allowed to wander he
may begin to answer the points made seriatim as they come up, and
the spell will be broken. Worse, he may notice the producer's hand
showing behind the performers, and realise that he is only watching a
lot of actors in a play after all.

I do not think anyone would fail to be moved by some of the
scenes, or impressed by Mr Brook's imaginative production, which includes songs, mimes and a dozen other ingenious resources, including
a vast figure with a phallic bomb protruding from its crotch which
descends from the flies like the spirit of Antonin Artaud himself. But
more compressed it would be even more tremendous. That meaningless song 'Tell me lies about Vietnam', to mention only one item, is
enormously overworked. It's not the lies about Vietnam that are so
serious; it's the truths.

I have tried to be absolutely neutral in writing about a strongly
committed piece of theatre. Let no one be discouraged by any existing
opinions they may hold on the subject. Mr Brook and his collaborators
(notably Sally Jacobs, designer, and Dennis Cannan, Michael Kustow
and Michael Scott, compilers) put their case with great brilliance. Dis-
agreement makes it no less remarkable.

Rosencrantz and Guildenstern Are Dead

Old Vic   *12 April 1967*

There is something extraordinarily compulsive about Rosencrantz and Guildenstern, those supreme nullities. Oscar Wilde, in a scathing passage in *De Profundis*, cited them as the contribution of modern life to the antique ideal of friendship; W. S. Gilbert chose them as the heroes of a one-act farce. (Quite an ingenious farce. Claudius in his youth wrote a play so badly received that he has made it a capital offence even to speak of it. When the players come to Elsinore, Rosencrantz, who is in love with Ophelia, eggs on Hamlet to have them produce the play.)

But both Wilde and Gilbert have had to supply the unhappy courtiers with personalities of their own to make their point. Tom Stoppard, whose play *Rosencrantz and Guildenstern Are Dead* is the National Theatre's latest production, has realised that the whole point of them is their lack not only of personality but virtually of existence. 'Why you?' one of them asks the other (it is never quite certain which is which). 'Anyone would have done.'

The play follows the course of *Hamlet* fairly closely, but seen from a new angle, from the angle of the two harmless, foolish courtiers summoned unexpectedly by the King to find out what they can of Hamlet's indispositions, and, having got themselves into this situation, are appointed his escorts on his exile to England, where they meet their undeserved, unnecessary deaths.

Wherever Shakespeare's own plot comes to the fore, the author uses Shakespeare's words. Indeed he uses them more than at first appears, and a sound knowledge of *Hamlet* is advisable. When Hamlet first appears, the stage direction runs :

> Enter Hamlet, with his doublet all unbraced,
> No hat upon his head, his stockings fouled,
> Ungartered and down-gyved to his ankles

All the way to –

> He seemed to find his way without his eyes,
> For out of doors he went without their helps
> And to the last bended their light on me.

This has to be done without words. Discussing the possibility of rendering the soliloquies through the medium of facial expression,

A. A. Milne once wrote 'The insolence of office and the spurns would tax the most elastic face'; but John McEnery, who plays Hamlet with romantic panache (and who would have ever expected John McEnery to play Hamlet at the Old Vic before Peter?), takes this in his stride, making it at once touching and very funny.

When Rosencrantz and Guildenstern are alone, however, they speak in modern idiomatic English, and this is consistent with Mr Stoppard's point that they only take on their familiar significance when they are in contact with the other characters of the play.

There are other characters in the play whose situation is much like Rosencrantz and Guildenstern's – the players. They too are devoid of personalities, and they too play a decisive part in shaping the destiny of the main participants. Mr Stoppard treats them much as he treats his two heroes, and indeed gives them lines that might have suited them. 'The single assumption that makes our existence viable,' says the players' leader, who is admirably played by Graham Crowden with a mixture of the dramatic and the sardonic, 'is that there is someone watching us.'

Mr Stoppard prolongs the dumb-show (*Hamlet* III ii) to the point where Hamlet has gone to England with Rosencrantz and Guildenstern. Later he assumes that the players, flying from the King's disapproval of their play, have stowed away on the very ship that takes the exiled Prince, so that at the end they may very effectively take up the dumb-show once more to the culminating pile of corpses, leaving Rosencrantz and Guildenstern to a final baffled musing on the nature of death.

I must have made the play sound enormously solemn and portentous. In fact it's nothing of the kind; it's extremely funny almost all the way through. Like *Gulliver's Travels*, it can be enjoyed on two levels, there is enough in it to keep an audience laughing constantly for nearly three hours, but behind the laughter there is the deeper question that dignifies the laughter with a serious purpose.

The performances of John Stride as Rosencrantz and Edward Petherbridge as Guildenstern (or vice versa) are masterly. They have given body to perfect vacuity. Rosencrantz is a rather pathetic simpleton whom an insurance company would class as 'accident-prone'; Guildenstern is sharper, more likely to start ideas, though no more likely to carry them through. As they argue about the laws of chance, or test the reality of reality by discussing life, or death, in a box, they are no more than the two ends of a see-saw which, without an outside stimulus, would stay perpetually at rest. But Mr Stride and Mr Petherbridge do more than make them pointless; they reveal that to be pointless can be very sad. There are some dry patches in their duologues, but they are ably gilded over.

Derek Goldby has directed with just the right balance of feeling and irony, never allowing the Shakespearean scenes to fall too far into travesty, since their actuality is the king-pin in the situation besetting the heroes, nor on the other hand allowing them to usurp too much attention. Desmond Heeley's sets are lighted with rare sensitivity by Richard Pilbrow.

The Happy Apple

Hampstead Theatre Club   *27 July 1967*

The Happy Apple introduces me for the first time to Pauline Collins, a diminutive girl with a face like Paul McCartney, a voice like a bandsaw, and a way with cockney speech that could hardly be better. She plays, very amusingly, the part of Nancy Gray, a secretary in an advertising agency who is one of nature's median types. A median type, in advertising jargon, is someone who can be relied on to give the standard reaction to any given proposal, and Nancy's reactions are so unerringly predictable that the three partners in the agency use her as a one-woman depth survey and so raise themselves from imminent bankruptcy to those prosperous heights that only advertising men can envisage.

The three partners, Charles, Freddie and Arthur, are played with a nice regard for the fooleries of the advertising world by Lance Percival, Julian Orchard and Jeffry Wickham. When wealth showers upon them from the cornucopia of Nancy's predictability, Freddie buys a clinic to practise psychiatry in and Arthur buys a farm in East Anglia and a Ferrari. But Charles, who is blissfully ignorant of anything at all outside his business, stays at his desk, though he makes a concession to the world in the shape of a Cultural Adviser, an ambitious educationalist who played Beethoven to the head-hunters in North Borneo for the British Council until the Council sacked him for playing them backwards.

The Cultural Adviser soon sees that his educational gifts can be better used than in teaching Charles to distinguish *Eine Kleine Nacht-musik* from the Albanian national anthem, and he coaches Nancy until she is in a position to twist her employers' arms to the tune of fifty per cent of the profits. The dénouement is kept cunningly hidden by a series of false casts – not that it matters much how it ends, though its conclusion in a fully choral version of the first movement of *Eine Kleine Nachtmusik* by the entire office staff is certainly not a logical development of what has gone before.

Jack Pulman, the author, calls this 'a summer play', but I think that's unduly modest. It's an extremely funny and intelligent comedy about a world where comedy proliferates. This world has been very well caught by the author, and he kept me laughing pretty continuously. His lines are amusing and his characters well drawn, and the cast give them a lively rendering that I can only fault by suggesting that they are all too loud for this little theatre.

Besides those I have mentioned, there is an excellent portrayal of Kenilworth, the culture-vulture, by John Malcolm, a suave bit by Jeremy Hawk as a lecherous client (who seemed, though, to have very little to do with the play except as a bit of trimming), and another well-observed secretary by Kate Brown, to my mind as median as anyone else on the stage. James Roose-Evans directs with wit and vigour, and there are admirable sets by Harry Waistnage.

Long Day's Journey into Night

Nottingham Playhouse   *30 September 1967*

Robert Ryan's performance as James Tyrone is worthy of O'Neill's fine play and I can't say fairer than that. It is beautifully relaxed, pitched very low with the quieter lines slipped into the auditorium at the bare threshold of audibility, and yet charged with all the suppressed passion that O'Neill wrote into this bitter yet affectionate portrait of his father.

All four members of the Tyrone household are faithfully remembered from the O'Neill family, and this company has caught all four of them with a set of above-average renderings. Gillian Martell plays the morphine-addicted wife, tender and decent enough until she has made one of her visits upstairs for a fix. Then at once she becomes hard and febrile, chattering away in a half-absent voice, throwing wild accusations of meanness and drunkenness and infidelity at her loyal husband, slipping away from every reference to her weakness with a counter-charge or a blank profession of ignorance. Miss Martell does it all admirably, even the difficult soliloquies.

Jamie, the elder son, is excellently played by Anthony Langdon, who flaunts his elegant failure carelessly in the faces of his family, caring only for the younger brother, Edmund. In his final scene, where he blurts drunken contempt for his father's theatrical success, he is quite outstanding, the half-mocked quotations rolling out like thunder.

Edmund is Eugene O'Neill's self-portrait. (What I wonder, did he mean by slipping in a brother called Eugene, who dies in infancy?) Alfred Bell gives a touching picture of the sad, poetic young man, his hopes set firmly on literature, his prospects reduced to nothing by the tuberculosis that racks him with helpless coughing. Hollow-chested and hollow-cheeked, he alternates challenge and despair with a pathetic fire that gives out all too soon.

I don't know whether Mr Ryan has acted as a catalyst on the company, but all of them manage their American speech with unusual success. As a rule I find an English cast playing Americans faintly embarrassing : this time it is so convincing that after a while I simply stopped noticing the accent at all. Apart from the comics and the singers, we see too little of American actors over here. The exchange is all the other way, and this is a pity.

Michael Rudman is responsible for the impeccable direction. The play has a long slow patch in the last act that can be very tedious; propelled by the able performances of Mr Ryan and Mr Bell it holds the attention from start to finish, and even last night's ceaselessly coughing audience heard it in silence. The living-room of the Tyrone 'summer residence' in Connecticut is an excellent design by Patrick Robertson, and it is most sympathetically lit, though no one is given a credit on the programme for this.

'I did just stammer,' says the young Edmund of his writing, 'it's the best I'll ever do.' This is the authentic voice of Eugene, who knew that he would never achieve the higher flights of poetry that he aspired to as a young man. But stammering or not, *Long Day's Journey into Night* is a great, great play, so full of sadness, so clear of self-pity. It ought to be seen much more often. Meanwhile, it is worth any kind of journey to see it here.

Jim Haynes's Arts Laboratory

Arts Laboratory   *11 January 1968*

At 182 Drury Lane you can eat a snack, watch a movie, see a play and a dance performance, buy a book, look at (or buy) a picture and argue your head off about the contemporary arts scene all under one roof. If you are over twenty-five, you will feel a bit elderly. If you are a sybarite, you will feel a bit uncomfortable. If you are concerned about people's involvement with the arts, you will be excited.

The Arts Laboratory is the latest, and most ambitious, venture of Jim Haynes. Mr Haynes is a young American who fell in love with the city of Edinburgh during his service with the US Air Force and stayed there to open first a bookshop, then the Traverse Theatre. Two years ago he came to London to open a London Traverse at the Jeannetta Cochrane Theatre; but that rather antiseptic hall, with its minimal facilities for hospitality, could never acquire the same character as the Edinburgh Traverse, and Mr Haynes moved on to something more in line with his concept of a theatre that was not only a place of entertainment but a social centre as well.

He was lucky to find an empty warehouse at 182 Drury Lane; it gives him exactly the right kind of accommodation, and he has a seven year lease on it, renewable for a further fourteen, which should offer reasonable stability.

The modest street door opens into an enormously lofty hall, the bareness of whose whitewashed walls is at present relieved by an exhibition of paintings by P. Zoline, an American painter who has lived in London for the past five years having 'a long and somewhat unhappy relationship with the Slade'. At the foot of a staircase is a desk populated by two girls dispensing tickets and information. Up the stairs is the restaurant, a long table down the middle of the room, small individual tables on each side, a general atmosphere of scrubbed wood and peasant pottery. No licence: the possession of a licence involves endless additional complications, and in any case, as anyone knows who frequents jazz clubs, alcohol is now no great draw among the young.

Beyond the desk is a kind of inner hall. Another picture exhibition (Ilene Astrahan, some amusing *trompe l'oeil* and colourful science-fiction); a bookshop, barely more than a cubicle and the shelves curiously empty; and the curtained entrances to the theatre and the cinema.

The theatre is small (120 seats or so) but protean. It has a raised platform at one end, which can serve as a stage but may also be used to lift the back seats when the theatre is turned back to front and the acting area is transferred to what was the space behind the seats. On the occasion of my visit the raised stage was being used for the dance programme of Graciela Martinez and the Sensual Laboratory.

This is not the place for an assessment of the work of the Sensual Laboratory, nor am I really qualified to make one. I can only say that the projections of light-patterns on the backcloth behind the dancers was startlingly lovely and original and quite uninfluenced by current psychedelic lighting. Unfortunately, I found it so fascinating that I barely had any attention left for the dancers. The Sensual Laboratory is the brain-child of Mark Boyle, who was an award winner at last year's Venice Biennale.

The theatre is small and has no real facilities backstage. But I suppose its drawbacks aren't more considerable than those of the Traverse, and its Spartan ambience will no doubt be softened as resources become available.

The cinema is down a flight of steps into a roomy cellar. The first thing you notice about it is that there are no seats. The floor is covered with a thick layer of sponge rubber, on top of which is spread an assortment of Wilton carpets that Mr Haynes got at bargain prices. This is where you sit; if you are wise you get there early to have a place against the wall, but the mid-floor spaces are not as uncomfortable as they sound. On the nights when the Arts Laboratory is open until 6 a.m. the cinema is the favourite place to go. For hygiene's sake you are asked to take your shoes off before entering.

Not unnaturally, all-night sessions like these attract some undesirable patrons, but Mr Haynes and his staff are firm with them. The Arts Laboratory is a club, and only club members may go in. At the first sign of unacceptable behaviour, out they go again. While I was getting a private run-through of the evening's film programme (two cartoon films by Rubington, *Frabjous Day* and *The Birth of Venus*, and a piece of elegant though not provocative erotica *Kronhausen Psychomontage No 1*) my guide suddenly called out: 'Danny, is the cinema officially open?' 'No, I don't think so.' 'You'll have to ask those people to leave then.' They left at once without argument. Opening hours vary. Sometimes it's 11 a.m. to midnight, sometimes it's 4 p.m. to 6 a.m., and it can almost be anything between these extremes, according to what's going on in the club, except on Mondays, when it is closed.

Ten minutes after the end of Graciela Martinez's dance programme, the theatre was turned around for a performance of a monologue by Kafka (written in 1917) called *Lecture to an Academy*. The lecture is given by an ape dressed in a frock-coat, and explains how, and more importantly why, it, or he, graduated from a cage in Hagenback's circus to his, or its, current intellectual status. Klaus Kammer had a great success with the piece on West German TV before his untimely death. At Drury Lane, Tutte Lemkov impersonated the ape; an hour later, as we squatted on the floor of the cinema, he was impersonating a Yugoslavian peasant in Dimic's *The Very Long Life of Tola Manoylevitch*, a performance enlivened by some of the most skilful audience involvement I have ever encountered. (It includes the offer of Slivovitz all round.)

Besides theatre, dance, films, books, pictures and food, the Arts Laboratory has announced a four-day festival of new music. This leads off today with Erik Satie's *Vexations* – all twenty-four hours of them. There are then programmes of new American music, new English music, and music by John Cage. Concerts of recorded music are given every Sunday at 4 p.m.

As administrator, Jim Haynes is a firm believer in decentralisation. He has a director in charge of theatre policy, one for music, one for the cinema and the art gallery, one for the restaurant. They are responsible to him, but they have a free hand in the running of their own departments.

The Arts Laboratory is the only example we have of what may be called off-off-Shaftesbury Avenue theatre. But it is more than merely a fringe house of entertainment. It is what it calls itself, a laboratory. It will provide opportunities for experimental playwrights, film-makers and musicians to have their work produced before critical audiences. It should also provide, if the responsibility is recognised, opportunities for established workers in the arts to come and see what the experimentalists are up to.

Best of all, it will function as a club where the young can come and talk to each other about all their interests. One of the outstanding qualities of the Traverse in Edinburgh was, and indeed is, the atmosphere of welcome that greeted even strangers, even in Festival time. There's no reason why that same quality shouldn't germinate in Drury Lane.

Jim Haynes's own enthusiasm is boundless. He has such confidence in the support of his public that he is now thinking of establishing a modest hotel near the Arts Laboratory to accommodate the visitors from outlying areas who wish to make prolonged contact with the centre and find themselves debarred from camping out on the foam-rubber floor of the cinema. I bet he will, too.

Oedipus

Old Vic   *20 March 1968*

Seneca's *Oedipus* turns out to be a fine play, more dramatic if less tremendous than the Sophocles version we're used to, and very well done into English verse for the National Theatre by David Anthony Turner and Ted Hughes. No doubt because of my unfamiliarity with the text, I found the dramatic tension actually greater than in the Greek play; certainly there are scenes that make one's hair stand on end in a way that the other one doesn't.

The sequence of events covered is much the same, but is presented in more detail, because less of the action is relegated to reported speech. We hear of the Sphinx's riddle and Oedipus's success in answering it; of the plague that descends on Thebes; of Oedipus's curse on the murderer of Laius. Tiresias presides over the sacrifice of a bull and a heifer in his search for the truth, and Creon, after a visit to hell, reluctantly names Oedipus as the guilty man.

But can this be a plot on Creon's part to succeed his father on the throne of Thebes? Bit by bit the real truth comes out: Oedipus's supposed father died peaceably in bed: an old shepherd is persuaded to remember having received a child from Oedipus's wife Jocasta with the iron wires in its heel that tell Oedipus the facts of his true parentage, and so of the subsequent enormities. In agony of remorse he thinks of suicide, but then, reckoning mere death an unsatisfactory atonement for the endless suffering he has caused, he pulls his eyes out with his bare hands.

This scene is recounted by a narrator, and it is as sickeningly bloody a piece of writing as the theatre can know.

There is much very fine speaking of the text, notably by John Gielgud as Oedipus, Irene Worth as Jocasta his mother-wife and Colin Blakely as Creon. But the production as a whole is disfigured by a wretched lot of tomfoolery.

For twenty minutes before the play begins, the cast is assembled on the stage, sitting on the little boxes that form part of the decor and quietly preparing themselves. We soon perceive that against every pillar in the auditorium there is a further member of the chorus standing; if we don't see it at once we hear it when they begin to imitate the humming of innumerable bees.

In the middle of the stage is a big square box, some ten feet by ten, revolving slowly on a pedestal. The chorus get off their boxes and crouch before them in a position from which they can drum on them with their hands. The drumming rises to a fortissimo, the house lights dim and the stage lights come on, to reveal that the boxes and indeed all the stage are dull-gold-coloured, whilst the actors are in 'rehearsal clothes', dark roll-neck sweaters and flannel trousers.

Accompanying their words with cutting strokes of their forearms, the chorus begins to whisper. 'Show us!' they whisper, and we come to the propounding of the riddle. The chorus is used in an orchestral role frequently during the evening, humming or muttering or crying 'Hah!' to create atmosphere – which they often do, though as often they tend to sound rather silly.

The big central box can be opened by lowering one, two or three of its sides, when it reveals the principals waiting to take their part in the play. Occasionally they are immured in it again at the end of a scene, otherwise they will retire upstage.

As the tension mounts, the style of the speaking is changed, until at the end it is chopped into staccato sections of two or three words that are jerked out in irregular rhythms. This is often effective for the choral passages, but less so for the characters who are speaking in their own persons. Sir John, for example, who has begun by delivering his lines with superb magic, has to speak his last tragic words in this way, and it creates an effect of artificial pathos much inferior to the genuine pathos we know he could instil into them if he were given his head.

None the less, there are many thrillingly impressive moments in the production, and I am glad to have seen it. The conclusion which the director has tacked on to it is unutterably silly. After Oedipus has gone and Jocasta's body has been carried from the stage, a litter is brought on bearing a tall shape covered in red silk and draped with ivy-leaves. The silk is slowly pulled away; it reveals an immense golden phallus.

Do I have to say that the director is Peter Brook? And the designer too? Mr Brook belongs to the Royal Shakespeare Company; let him play the fool nowhere but in his own house.

Hadrian the Seventh

Mermaid   *19 April 1968*

I am absolutely delighted that this adaptation of Baron Corvo's novel has come to London. I saw it at Birmingham this time last year and was very much impressed; on a second seeing I find it even more impressive. It may not be the best, but it is to my mind the most interesting play to be seen in London at the moment; and Alec McCowen's performance as Fr William Rolfe, later Pope Hadrian VII, is certainly the best piece of acting.

Peter Luke, the adaptor, has taken liberties with the novel that give the play additional interest. Baron Corvo's Hadrian VII was called George Arthur Rose when he was a penniless genius with a manic determination to become a priest in the Roman Catholic Church. Mr Luke's is called Frederick William Rolfe, to emphasise the degree of autobiographical wish-fulfilment there is in the character, and the story of the extraordinary call to the Papacy, the singular reforms at the Vatican and the death at the hands of a Belfast Protestant agitator is presented as a dream.

Naturally a good deal of the book has to be left out, and the emphasis is considerably shifted. The novel is chiefly concerned with what Pope Hadrian did at the Vatican, which was considerable and involved the whole range of European politics. This is all of interest to students of church affairs, but it is hardly dramatic; so the play concerns itself mostly with the simple – well, far from simple – story of how an unknown and apparently unsuitable man who has already been chucked out of two ecclesiastical colleges comes to be elected Pope, and how his lay enemies contrive his downfall just as he has won over his antagonists in the Sacred College.

It is crammed with good conversation, and Corvo's orotund dialogue, as virulent and as ornamental as anything in John Osborne, proves to have an intrinsic dramatic life that is comical and cogent. The best of the talk is reserved for Rolfe, and in this part Alec McCowen gives a performance such as doesn't often come our way. He speaks the complex lines as if they fell naturally off his tongue and he has caught exactly the bumptious conceit that wars with the scarifying devotion in his soul. There are the passionate self-loathing and the passionate self-satisfaction, perfectly conveyed in the nervous, rapid speech and the fatuous smile that suggests a cat stuffed to bursting point with canaries. The descent into agony as he defends himself from the accusations thrown at him by members of the Sacred College is memorable indeed.

The remainder of the company are good, too. They are all, I think, new since Birmingham except for Peggy Aitchison as Agnes, the faithful char who comforts His Holiness with a jar of pickled onions. Patrick McAlinney is excellent as Sant, the militant Protestant with a chip on his shoulder who, in this version, shoots down the Pope on his throne, and Margaret Courtney has her tongue just far enough in her cheek as Mrs Crowe, Rolfe's landlady who becomes Sant's confederate. There are admirable performances by Alan MacNaughton as the Bishop of Caerlon and Donald Eccles as the elderly Archbishop of Pimlico (doubling, tellingly, as a couple of bailiffs), by Brian Coburn as the vast Italian Cardinal Ragna and Otto Diamant as Cardinal Berstein. And George Arthur Rose is ingeniously introduced as the unhappy student whom the Pope makes his private chaplain; he is well done by Vivian Meckerrell.

With the Vatican as background, there is endless spectacle available, and Peter Dews, the director, makes splendid use of the vivid robes of the clergy, the Swiss Guards, and so on. When the moment arrives at which the Consistory invites Rolfe to accept the Papacy, a procession comes down the auditorium from top to bottom. There is no scenery, apart from two movable inset stages at the side which provide room for domestic scenes. The director's skilful arrangement of the brightly dressed characters and David Adams' lighting are enough.

Soldiers

New Theatre   *13 December 1968*

When you see the name of Kenneth Tynan among the sponsors of a new play you can be sure that it is not being put on for its entertainment value alone. It is therefore doubly important to know that Rolf Hochhuth's *Soldiers* as presented now is not only a very truncated version of the play, but a version in which what seems to me to be the principal theme is played down at the expense of another, more dramatic but less cosmically important.

But first, what happens in this version, as translated by Robert David Macdonald and directed by Clifford Williams?

In the first act we see Churchill on the deck of HMS *Duke of York*. He is making his plans for Exercise Gomorrah, the conjuring of a 'fire-storm' in Hamburg, here presented as the brain-child of Lord Cherwell. General Sikorski, Minister President of the Polish Government in exile, is also present; he is appalled by the discovery of the assassinations at Katyn, and announces his intention to get the International Red Cross to investigate them, in spite of Churchill's plea that this will so antagonise Russia as to be a real threat to the conduct of the war.

Act two shows Churchill in bed. Gomorrah is over, and the results are satisfactory; because there is no hope of launching a second front in France, Churchill is persuaded that he can tell Stalin that 'our bombers are the second front'. But as the result of Sikorski's complaint to the Red Cross, the Russians have broken off relations with the exiled Polish Government. Lord Cherwell, Churchill's *eminence grise*, puts forward with infinite tact, a proposal for getting Sikorski out of the way.

The third act takes place in the garden at Chequers. It is mainly concerned with a dispute between Churchill and Dr Bell, the Bishop of Chichester, who has come up to plead that civilians are not a legitimate target for bombers. There is some parenthetic material about the sinking of the *Scharnhorst*: and there is also the announcement of General Sikorski's death in an aircraft that failed to take off from Gibraltar, killing all on board except the Czech pilot.

As here presented, the main theme of the play is clearly the conspiracy to kill Sikorski. But as published, the play begins with a long, very dull prologue, quite rightly cut completely from this production; and this makes it absolutely plain that the chief concern of the play is the question of the bombing. Hochhuth is asking for an extension of the Geneva Convention to cover aerial warfare, which so far is not dealt with in any international agreement.

It seems to me quite possible that Hochhuth doesn't really expect us to believe that he thinks Churchill connived at Sikorski's death. No one who has done his prep so thoroughly as Hochhuth so obviously has could seriously put forward such a preposterous theory. And Hochhuth is a dramatist, not an historian.

If indeed Sikorski was murdered (and this is certainly not unlikely; in four successive flights his aircraft, each provided by the RAF, all had mishaps of one kind or another), Churchill's involvement can hardly have been greater than was Bolingbroke's in the death of Richard II. 'They love not poison that do poison need'; no one doubts that Sikorski was a great trouble to Churchill at the time (and so was de Gaulle, for that matter), and it is, I suppose, not impossible that there might have been some character willing to play Sir Pierce of Exton and get rid of him out of mistaken loyalty.

But I believe that Hochhuth has deliberately laid this monstrous charge at Churchill's door as a standard against which the less unarguably monstrous charge of bombing civilians can be measured in truly dramatic terms. Considered out of the context of a world war, either action would be unspeakable. Within the ambit of the war, the one seems defensible and the other not; and yet the absolute measure of guilt involved may well be about the same.

The matter of bombing civilians is relegated to the third act, in the confrontation between Churchill and Bishop Bell, which is in fact the best part of the play. Yet because of the theme of Sikorski's death is so much more horrifying, especially to a British audience, this looms up with an equal, or even a greater, importance. In fact, as I see it, it is only a dramatic allegory; and very effective too, as the reaction to it, even before the play opened, has shown.

As now carved into useful dramatic form, the play is undeniably fascinating. Whether it would be so fascinating if the characters concerned were renamed Smith, Brown, Jones and Robinson instead of Churchill, Cherwell, Brooke and Sikorski is another matter; this is 'theatre of fact' and makes no pretence to any higher step on the artistic level. Its fascination depends on its involvement of ourselves in matters where we may have participated, or which may have had consequences that directly affect us. It does not matter now whether General Sikorski met his death by accident or by design; but it would make a significant difference tomorrow if indiscriminate 'terror-bombing' were to be outlawed by international agreement.

Whereas the historical reality of the characters is an advantage from this point of view, it is a snag from another. Churchill at any rate is so familiar to all of us from his photographs and his records that we could not bear to see him represented other than accurately.

In this at any rate we are fortunate, for John Colicos gives a masterly impersonation of him. His make-up, said to take him three hours to put on, gives him a startling resemblance to the Churchill we remember from the war years, and the voice, painstakingly learned from recordings, is remarkably true. Hochhuth must be allowed his share of the credit in this lifelike representation; Randolph Churchill, when he read the script, expressed wonder at the way in which the author had accurately caught his father's mannerisms in his stage directions.

Whether such a performance can be accounted great acting is another matter. If it can, then Bransby Williams was as great an actor as Henry Ainley. The imitation of the model is exact, but no room is left at all for any creative impulse. At any rate it is very remarkable to see.

For genuinely creative acting, Alec Clunes' performance as Bishop Bell is better, for it is not a photographic reproduction of a well-studied original but an imaginative creation of a dramatic character. This is a very fine performance, and it is no wonder that when Bell and Churchill are on the stage together it is always Bell that seems to be the superior character.

As Lord Cherwell, Raymond Huntley has not gone out for an especially vivid physical likeness, but he produces that rarefied science-fiction personality admirably, muttering his most outrageous suggestions with the dry monotone of a professor.

There is a moving representation of the old, weary, heroic Sikorski by George Coulouris, and Joanna Dunham is good as Churchill's WRNS orderly, a composite portrait of several of the Prime Minister's minions. The minor characters, a Polish lieutenant and two senior RAF officers who seem to have been left in by mistake when the text was being cut to manageable proportions, are adequately taken by John Carlisle, Russell Hunter and William Russell, but one found oneself wondering why they were there at all.

The impressive set, dominated by a great radar dish, is by Ralph Koltai.

Judy Garland

Talk of the Town   *1 January 1969*

Two elements make up Judy Garland – the woman and the myth. The myth is what we encounter first; as soon as the orchestra has embarked on its overture, with strains of 'The Trolley Song' and 'Over the Rainbow', the audience is clapping, even cheering. The magic has been turned on. By the prickling of my thumbs, something remarkable this way comes.

What comes is Judy Garland, the woman. In an old-gold trouser suit that reflects a thousand sparks from the embracing spotlight, she looks tiny and timelessly young, and her little-boy hair-cut gives her now and then a quick flicker of pathos. A smudge of dirt on her face, and she might be telling us how she would sail up the avenue, but she hasn't got a yacht. However, there is nothing really pathetic about her. She prowls around the big thrust-stage of the Talk of the Town like a tigress, tugging at the microphone cord as if her rations were at the end of it, as in a sense I suppose they are. She is the Maria Callas of popular music.

She is hardly ever still. She is constantly making new, delectable patterns with her limbs as she moves. Though her personality is tigerish, her restless mobility has about it something of the sinuous grace as the gibbons in the Zoo. It would hardly have surprised me to see her leap into the air and sing a number hanging head downwards from a chandelier.

Her voice still holds its tremendous charge of suppressed excitement, the product I suppose (though cold analysis is the last process it ought to be subjected to) of that wild vibrato that can skid up and down over a third or a fourth.

But Miss Garland is a much better artist than she gives herself credit for. It is her good fortune – it happens to few people in their lifetimes – that the public sees no need to separate the myth from the person. I daresay if she didn't sing at all, but just loped around the stage waving to her friends and chatting up her conductor a good many of us would feel that we had attended a joyous spectacle enough.

Miss Garland, though, must know that to be a legend in your lifetime is not enough. She did sing one new song in her forty-minute programme, an attractive bit of diablerie called 'I like to hate myself', but most of the time she confined herself to well-tried favourites that had only to be begun to be cheered to the echo. Yet now and then she gave us a glimpse of the talent she hardly needs to draw on. The sustained *piano* of the verse of 'Just in Time', which she sang sitting on a stool far upstage, was moving; so was 'Over the Rainbow', which she did squatting in the lotus position, the spot that held her the only lighting on the stage.

Myth and woman are inextricably entangled. For us at the receiving end this is a misfortune that we can hardly avoid unless we are prepared to throw romance out of our lives altogether. Nor indeed is it so much of a misfortune as long as Miss Garland, coasting along with her engine ticking over, can engulf us to completely in her magic.

But oh, suppose one day the woman cut free from the myth, threw overboard all the prefabricated success, gave once again a performance that had been woven afresh on the limitless tapestry of her talents! Will this, *can* this ever happen now?

Judy Garland began and ended her act with 'I belong in London'. 'A Londoner I'll always be,' she carolled, and we loved her for it. Of course she is no more a Londoner than Maurice Chevalier, but she is as right to say it as President Kennedy was when he said *'Ich bin ein Berliner.'* It makes us both feel good.

Early Morning

Royal Court *14 March 1969*

So 'Bond at the Court' completes its schedule with the first public performance of the last play to be banned by the Lord Chamberlain. *Early Morning* wasn't easy to judge in the makeshift production it had last year, where everyone was looking over his shoulder to see if there was a policeman at the door. William Gaskill has put some decent flesh on its somewhat angular bones this time, and for the first one-third of the evening it seems as if the play will turn out workable after all.

But alas it docsn't. After reading the text and seeing it performed in what I take to be an authorised production, I'm as far as ever from understanding what it is about. The first act is an exercise in what Maurice Baring called 'alternative history'. Queen Victoria's eldest children are Siamese twins George and Arthur. There is a rebellion, engineered by Disraeli, which goes awry when Florence Nightingale, the Queen's lesbian lover, puts poison in the shoe from which Prince Albert is drinking her health. And so on. It is all very funny, but it has less to say than *Don't, Mr Disraeli*, and says it less economically.

It has moreover little to do with what comes after. In the second act we see a plot organised by Prince Arthur, whose Siamese incubus has died and dwindled to a litter of bones. It results in the death of everyone we have seen up to that point. However we meet them again in the last act; this is set in Heaven, where, though we are constantly told that there is no death and no pain, the blessed are always starving unless they are able to eat one another – a process that does no lasting harm, since their missing limbs grow whole again.

These two acts are not even very funny; but this might be forgiven them if they carried either a coherent story line or a coherent theme. They have neither. Dimly, one perceives that Mr Bond's trend is towards anarchy. 'Civilization is just bigger heaps of dead,' he says in a rather impressive bit where Prince Arthur is apostrophising Hitler for his expertise at killing. And 'Wherever you go, someone will always want to kill someone.'

But there is no argument. Mr Bond is like these students who think they are fit to take over the world when they haven't even the patience to finish their education. Like them, he has an enviable liveliness; but like them, he has not the ability to let us know clearly what the hell it is he wants.

Moira Redmond repeats her gay performance as the Queen; her new paramour is Shirley Anne Field, who seems to me not to have put enough magnetism into her rendering. There are entertaining performances by Henry Woolf as Disraeli, John Barrett as Gladstone, Queenie Watts as a cockney virago; best of all there is Jack Shepherd's moving work as Arthur. Nothing is beyond Mr Shepherd's range; whenever he was on stage I felt that behind all the foolery there must be a grain of sense. But the feeling never survived long.

Having now seen all his three plays, I can't believe that the Court are doing Edward Bond a favour by giving him a season to himself. Here, one feels, is someone learning his trade in public. *Saved* points in one direction to a kind of neo-Ibsenism, marred by the obsession with violence and cruelty that seems to be the Royal Court's hallmark. *Early Morning* is an exercise in a totally different (and much harder) style; anything Mr Bond learnt from *Saved* has been jettisoned in *Early Morning*. In *The Narrow Road to the Deep North*, said to have been written in three days, we're on another tack again. I admire Mr Bond for his determination, but what I'd like to see is progress.

CHAPTER THREE

Small Change

In the summer of 1969 my Arts Editor, John Higgins, who had been endlessly helpful to me, left to join *The Times*. It was his idea that I should take over his desk when he went. 'But I don't think,' he said, 'you'd be able to go on doing the theatres as well.' 'Oh, I'm sure I could,' I said confidently as we sat over our after-luncheon drinks in the Morning Room at the Garrick.

In July of that year, the Editor, Sir Gordon Newton, called me up to his office. He would have liked me to take over John Higgins's job, he said, but he thought he should appoint someone younger. 'I want someone who can stay a long time,' he said. I was fifty-seven.

'The chap I have in mind is Anthony Curtis from the *Sunday Telegraph*,' said the Editor. 'Do you think you could work with him?'

I knew Anthony Curtis and liked him very much. 'Of course I could,' I assured him. Tony Curtis moved in on 1 July. Life went on for me apparently unchanged. American students preparing their theses on the variations in the Arts Page of the *Financial Times* won't find much alteration to note in my columns. But at least we can start with the first verses ever to be published in that newspaper. They celebrate the seventieth birthday of Sir Noël Coward.

*

17 December 1969

THE NOELIAD

A Fragment

Now see where gay Thalia, the comic Muse,
Ascends the stage and for attention sues,
Her smiling mask a little bit awry,

Her ivy-wreath aslant across her eye.
In silvery and not too solemn voice
She lauds the object of her latest choice.

   'From these same boards (says she) where in his day
Immortal Shakespeare held unchallenged sway,
Where Wycherley and Congreve flashed their wit,
And Sheridan and Goldsmith did their bit,
And Wilde, and Haddon Chambers, and Pinero,
Today I introduce another hero.
Let all Parnassus with one voice enthuse
For *Coward* and his Talent to Amuse.'

   She ceas'd; and as the air resounds with cheers
From out the wings great *Coward* now appears,
His face and figure young and lithe again
And (so indulgent are the gods to men)
Attired as a Rear-Admiral, RN.
He stands awhile to savour his ovation,
Then answers with a courteous oration.

   'My dears (quoth he) I would have given odds
'Gainst such a warm reception from the gods.
But, deeply though I'm mov'd by your affection,
I'd like to make one overdue correction.
"A talent to amuse" may seem complete
For this nice character in *Bitter-Sweet*
But it's a bore when people will suggest
That it's the only talent *I* possess'd.

   ' 'Twould not have been at all what I was after
If folk had left *The Vortex* weak with laughter,
Or if a giggle were the only meed
The audience offered for *This Happy Breed*.
To make the people sing, or laugh, or weep
Was easy. I could do it in my sleep.
But sometimes, when I got beneath their hides,
I made the darling creatures think besides.

'I haven't dealt, I own without apology,
With current politics or sociology
Like all that clever intellectual crew
Who throng the Court and Centre 42.
Yet in my work I hope you can detect
The simple virtues that I judge correct,
Like patriotism, pride and self-respect.
And while I'm up, I'd rather like to speak
About some subtle points in my technique.'

Here Coward paus'd; and ere he could resume,
A spate of voices echoed round the room.
First, Polyhymnia, Muse of sacred song,
To whom two more accomplishments belong –
One, Mimicry, the other, Eloquence –
Who thus began. 'It clearly makes more sense
If Coward's art's so serious and fine
To move him from Thalia's care to mine.'

But ere she'd well begun, Melpomene
Call'd out, '*Sirocco* was a *tragedy*!'
Calliope now made confusion worse –
'*Mad Dogs and Englishmen* is epic verse!'
Quick to put in her claim, Terpsichore
Cried, '*Dance Little Lady* must belong to me!'
While, as a final damper on the jollity,
Astronomy's Urania claimed *Star Quality*.

Dissent among the Muses grew so rife
That soon all nine were lock'd in mortal strife,
And *Coward* was wisely running for his life.
One last reproof he flung them from the portal.
'None of you knows what made me immortal.
It's none of all th' ingredients of your schism –
It's my immaculate professionalism.'

Tiny Alice

'The play is quite clear,' says Edward Albee in a prefatory note to the published text of *Tiny Alice*. But he is honest enough to confess that this is only his view, and the view of some others. To many, including myself, its clarity is by no means entire.

The subject is faith, a subject that often persuades the faithful that justification is self-explanatory. Brother Julian, the lay priest whose faith is under examination, once entered a mental home as a voluntary patient because he had lost his faith, and while he was there he was subject to hallucinations. These two facts are important to remember.

At the beginning of the play, he is appointed emissary for a cardinal who has been promised an immense sum of money for the Church from a mysterious woman called Miss Alice. Miss Alice lives in a vast castle that has been transported stone by stone from England; in her library is a scale model of the castle, believed to be tenanted by a tiny chatelaine called Alice (not to be confused with Miss Alice). The model shares experiences with the real castle; when Julian calls out that the chapel of the model is on fire, it's a fire in the real chapel that has to be put out.

Miss Alice and her henchmen, a lawyer and a butler named Butler, are engaged in a trial of Julian's faith; they behave towards him with the same other-worldly authority as Sir Henry Harcourt-Reilly and his friends in *The Cocktail Party*. The test involves his marrying Miss Alice and, when he refuses to accept the reality of the Alice in the model, his murder by the lawyer. He dies abandoned, slumped against the model, with the words, 'God, Alice . . . I accept thy will.'

So the main theme of the play isn't hard to understand. There are innumerable other facets, however, that present more difficulty – problems of symbolism, and even problems of casual behaviour. Why do the lawyer and the butler exchange endearments at their first encounter in the play, since there's no question of their having any kind of concealed understanding? Who, or what, are we to associate with these two characters? What does the promise of money to the Church (and to other churches, hospitals, universities, orchestras, revolutions here and there) represent?

No doubt one can find out answers to these questions in time, though certainly not after witnessing one performance. I suspect, though, that a good deal of the smaller fancies are just there to add graces to the dialogue, perhaps to wrench the situation into line when there is a danger of its wandering in the wrong direction.

The result, at any rate, is a play of remarkable poetry and force. Mr Albee is a master of dialogue. He makes what I consider to be tactical mistakes sometimes, the most serious of which is giving Julian such a long and arid dying speech; but throughout most of a longish evening (the cuts that were made in New York have been restored here) there are many moments of matchless wit and beauty of thought.

The production by Robin Phillips bears his characteristic brand of romantic beauty, though it has not yet settled down. David Warner as Julian, in particular, has still a good deal more to give; his performance runs dangerously near to monotony, and he hasn't achieved the ecstasy in his soliloquy on martyrdom, nor the passion in his final speech, that they require. Ray McNally's machine-gun delivery of the lawyer's lines is often effective but could do with more variety. Richard Pearson, with his light, quite uncardinalitial voice, is an unexpected but effective bit of casting as the Cardinal; the donnish chatter coming from such an imposing figure helps him to build up an interesting rendering. As Butler, Frank Gatliff puts over ably the character's blend of kindness and resolution.

Irene Worth played Miss Alice also in New York; one couldn't ask for a more impressive performance than hers, ranging from a young woman's tenderness to a stern dignity fit for a goddess. This is at present the hub around which the evening turns, a performance to be treasured.

Farrah's designs are breathtakingly lovely, and solve ingeniously the scenic problems the author demands. At the back of the stage is a screen of reflecting material through which back projections may be shown. The Cardinal's garden in the first scene needs no more than a suggestion of trees, a couple of chairs and a birdcage; for the second scene, Miss Alice's library, it is only necessary to change the back-projection (which is effectively amplified in more reflecting surfaces in the wings), add some suitable furniture, and lower the enormous model from the flies, so that it can take up a suitable position bang in the middle of the stage, an amenity that the author doesn't seem to have envisaged. Change furniture, change projection, and you have the sitting-room.

The changes are made with dexterity behind lowered curtains, while an eerie electric hum maintains the tension. The hum is also used in one or two places to accompany the action where extra tension is required. The heartbeats and the laboured breathing that fade in during Julian's final speech until they fill the whole house say perhaps more than some of Julian's words do.

This is a difficult play, no doubt about it. I've put in what seem to me two useful clues. Another is the passage in Act 2, Scene 2 about the mouse in the model. But if the difficulties remain unsolved, the magic of the play remains; its problems linger in the mind when the performance is done.

Mr Kilt and the Great I Am

Hampstead Theatre Club   *9 June 1970*

Kenneth Ross's new play contains a lot of wonderfully funny lines, that outnumber the foolishly pretentious lines by about three to one. Of the eighteen or nineteen scenes, half a dozen or more are very amusing indeed. He has created a gallery of fantastic characters who are well worthy of the clever cast that Stephen Hollis, the director, has assembled for them.

Now that Mr Ross has seen his play performed – and performed at a standard that must have pleased him very much – he should sit down and think how to reorganise his materials until they are more than merely comic, until in fact they make the good satirical play that is lurking among them.

He has got a good theme. Beerbohm Kilt, a supremely ordinary young man not much use at anything, murders his wife when her eccentricities drive him beyond endurance. In search of someone to unburden his soul to before he gives himself up to the police, he visits a Roman Catholic Canon, a former showgirl professing a trendy kind of Christian Science, and the Salvation Army, and each turns him away for some specious reason. Finally, he falls into the hands of a Church of England vicar who has gone over to television, and he makes an appearance as a special guest on the programme, 'Get In With God', before he is taken up by the law.

These materials are not wielded as skilfully as they deserve. The first two scenes, showing Kilt (a good neutral performance by Brian Smith) working in a shop and then chatting with his landlady, are much too long. By cutting them down to the very minimum length needed to convey their content, the first two acts could be made into one and the play pitched more quickly into its main stream, which really begins at the fourth scene, an extremely funny seduction scene between a shy teenage boy (Peter Denyer) and a sophisticated fifteen-year-old girl (Clare Sutcliffe) that ends with a smashing curtain line.

The rest of the play tends to fall into a series of vaudeville acts. There are delightful bits for Brian Oulton as a camp churchman, writer of popular romances under a pseudonym; for Peter Bayliss as a police commissioner who enjoys making love to his reflection in a full-length pierglass; for Marcella Markham as the ginger-haired ex-showgirl, Roland MacLeod as (among other parts) a Salvation Army Captain, and John Carlin and Penelope Keith as the television parson and his Girl Guiding wife.

But there's not enough backbone to the piece. In his third act Mr Ross has tried to pull it into shape by recalling the different people we met earlier on, and he too often falls into the trap of repeating a good thing too soon. The best scene in the last act is the one where Mr Kilt finds himself sharing a cell in Brixton with the canon. The canon, as ever, is so interested in telling his own troubles he can't listen to Mr Kilt's; and, in the middle of his recital, Mr Kilt breaks out into a cry of real agony that is the second most effective thing in the evening.

Although I've used so much space pulling this play to pieces, I must repeat that it's very funny indeed, and beautifully played. I laughed almost unceasingly.

Home

Royal Court   *18 June 1970*

For a full half-hour Harry and Jack sit in a garden and exchange small-talk of a smallness seldom encountered in the theatre. Both are middle-aged, and their conversation is not unlike the conversation in many a hotel lounge up and down the country. They discuss the weather, they inquire after their respective wives, they compare their times in the services during the war, they refer rather vaguely to their professions.

There is only this vagueness to suggest that they are not two perfectly ordinary old buffers. Harry confines himself mostly to such remarks as 'Ah yes' and 'Absolutely', and when he has to make a positive statement he does so with as little detail as he can. Jack is more forthcoming, but there is an air of improvisation about what he says. Having revealed that he works in the food-distribution line, he embarks on a fantasy about the relative saleability of jam in glass jars and jam in cardboard cartons.

When they leave for a walk, their places are taken by two talkative working-class women whose conversation is utterly different – vigorous and lewd and absolutely frank about their current situation. They are in a mental hospital.

David Storey never develops a play in any way you could expect. This one he hardly develops at all. Between lunchtime and tea a faint breeze of friendship blows the four together. There are hints of what brought the two apparently respectable old chaps into the 'home'. We are given a glimpse of a pathetic ex-wrestler reduced to semi-humanity by pre-frontal leucotomy. As the lights fade at the end, Harry and Jack stand weeping uncontrollably at their inner thoughts.

I found it heartbreaking. Mr Storey has pitched on the essential truth that the real pathos of madness lies in its incommunicability. He tells us virtually nothing about Harry and Jack (and a good deal of what we do hear about them is probably unreliable), and it is the very unreachableness of their personalities that cries out for understanding.

It cries out also for acting of the very highest quality. How easy it would be to make them funny, or to make them dull. As handled by John Gielgud and Ralph Richardson, they are steered with astonishing skill past any such quality. They are simply wisps of humanity, ashes of burnt-out personality embodied with macabre unsuitability in the bodies of these respectable middle-class men.

Harry (John Gielgud's character) is the more remote. We never learn what has brought him to this state; he seems to be a courteous, friendly man, something has gone wrong with his marriage, he has receded into melancholia. Jack (Ralph Richardson) has been committed because of a weakness for following little girls about; he has a way of taking refuge from the truth in fantasies that vary from one account to the next. There is a remnant of flamboyance about him that Sir Ralph keeps on a tight rein. Sir John has less to work, only murmured truisms and, just once, when he is approached by one of the women patients, a sudden gleam of friendliness that shines like winter sun through rainclouds. The house that he has erected from such fragile cards is a marvel.

Dandy Nichols and Mona Washbourne play the two women. The parts are more conventional and forthright, as it were, to the misty uncertainty of the men. They are admirably done, and none the less pathetic for their outward humour when you stop to consider what their real situation is. Alfred, the ex-wrestler, whose virility has been taken from him to protect him from his uncontrolled aggression, is perhaps sadder than any of them; he has nothing to look forward to but a lifetime of carrying furniture about to remind himself that he was once strong and athletic.

My admiration for Mr Storey's writing goes up with each play I see. He has begun to work quite independently of any stage conventions generally accepted, yet he has an instinctive knowledge of what 'comes off'. I was a little reminded of Marguerite Duras's *The Square* and *Days in the Trees* in the way that *Home* does not develop but is slowly unveiled as a whole that was whole when the house-lights first went down; but in general Mr Storey seems to me a true original, sensitive and poetic and constantly aware of a dramatist's responsibility towards his audience.

Oh! Calcutta!

Round House   *28 July 1970*

The chief difference between *Oh! Calcutta!* and other revues is that it presents in public what is otherwise only done or spoken of in private. This can be a desirable thing to do; it was the principle behind *That Was The Week, That Was* and its successors, and salutary and entertaining programmes they were. I can't see why something funny enough to arouse laughter in a smoking-room (whatever that is) shouldn't be just as funny on stage. I will go further, and add that to my mind a *good* joke can be made about any subject at all without violating the canons of good taste.

But there, naturally, you come up against the unanswerable question, what is a good joke? I can recall two good jokes from *Oh! Calcutta!* though –and this is worth noting – the recognised standards of restraint in the Press deter me from recounting either of them in detail. One was in connection with a scientific investigation into sexual enjoyment, an investigation that has in fact been made on lines not very different from those shown in this sketch; and one was about masturbation images. Throughout most of what I found an unexciting evening, however, the fun was extracted simply from saying, or doing, or describing, in public things that are normally restricted to privacy. This isn't at all the principle I quoted with approval in my first paragraph.

I've noticed before that one sure way of getting a laugh from a West End audience is to have a famous actress say 'bugger'. People laugh, I suppose, because of the unexpected conjunction of the actress and the indecency, on the principle explained (with graphs) by Mr Koestler in his essay *The Cognitive Geometry of the Comic Stimulus.* But a programme of fourteen turns that consists almost exclusively of people saying taboo words, or describing taboo acts, or even simulating their performance (with, I couldn't help noticing, as little effect on the performers as on me) is hardly enough. I simply longed for more jokes.

Anything on the credit side? Yes, indeed. The two dances that open the second half, where artistic instead of erotic advantage is taken of a naked cast, are splendid; I only wished I could hear the words of the song that apparently had something to do with the second one. A pretty song sung by a biscuit-brown girl at the beginning. A promising situation in a piece about Sadesque machines, written in the manner of Wilde; but it oozes away in a morass of sexual description.

Still, I think I can say specifically that *Oh! Calcutta!* is unlikely to have an effect such as to tend to deprave and corrupt persons who are likely, having regard to all the relevant circumstances, including the circumstances that the tickets cost between £1 and £2 10s. to attend it. You can hear similar conversation in a good many public bars – saloon bars too, if it comes to that. A man would have to be made out of stone not to feel an occasional surge of erotic excitement as the company go through their erotic drill. If Kenneth Tynan's object in devising the show was to arouse a transient thrill in his audience, I wonder why he has stopped where he has. There were shows available to the troops in Cairo and Port Said during the war no less artistic than this.

If more sensitive people were to succeed in persuading the Attorney-General that there was a tendency to deprave and corrupt, I think it would be very hard to prove that the performance was for the public good on the ground that it is in the interests of drama. And it contains one incontrovertible defamation.

A Midsummer Night's Dream

What Peter Brook has done in his acclaimed production of the *Dream*, newly arrived in London after ovations in Stratford and America, is to scoop out everything accepted, everything familiar, everything that belongs to what he calls the Deadly Theatre, and replace it with something not only unfamiliar in the context but unfamiliar in the theatre. There's no sign of a wood; the action takes place in a white box surrounded by a balcony. Instead of trees, coils of silver wire are lowered from the end of fishing rods; when they are swished about by their attendant fairies and accompanied by a cacophany of bird-calls, they make as eerie an atmosphere as there ever was in those Athenian woods, in spite of the hard white light that remains unchanged from first to last.

None of Mr Brook's copious invention ever contradicts the text. Sometimes, it's true, it distracts the attention from it; it's hardly possible to concentrate on Oberon's beautiful lines about the bank where the wild thyme blows when he is spinning a silver dish on the end of a wand. I doubt if anyone unfamiliar with the play could safely follow all the convolutions of the plot. But what remains is the powerful magic. The unexpected entrances on ropes and trapezes and stilts; the constant presence of most of the company lurking in the background even when not playing, sometimes changing from one person to another; the unorthodox interpretations of familiar lines – all these help to build up a feeling of uncertainty, a feeling that anything might happen, that fairies and mortals exist side by side and a man might as easily be changed into an ass as miss his train home.

The playing, I have to say, is at the moment not at all good. It was far better when I saw the play at Stratford last year. Now it has become very slow (I never knew the mechanicals' play to take so long) and the speech is full of those wrong accents and misplaced caesuras that used to be the Royal Shakespeare Company's hallmark. Alan Howard as Oberon and Theseus is much the worst offender; how he has the impertinence to mock at a man for 'making periods in the midst of sentences' I don't know, for he makes them in the midst of almost every line. At one point he reverses the meaning of the words when he says, 'Death, counterfeiting sleep, with leaden legs, etc.' instead of 'Death-counterfeiting sleep'.

He is closely followed in his vice by John Kane's Puck, whose broken-up lines suggest to me that too many accretions have attached themselves to his playing during the run. 'Up! And! Down!' Indeed! Sara Kestelman's Titania, too, in most ways the strongest performance of the play, is not immaculate; 'Oh, how I love *thee*,' she says to the transfigured Bottom. Let her listen to the next two young people she encounters making love and see whether they say that. Even Quince's prologue, where the misplaced pauses are deliberately put there by the author, is spoiled as the otherwise admirable Philip Locke speaks it with some of the pauses corrected.

It is in the visual realisation that the production excels, and the greatest credit is due to Sally Jacobs for the designs. The mysterious appearance of the coloured worms heralding the arrival of the fairies; the sudden streams of silver darts across the black sky when Oberon and Titania make their first appearance; the coloured streamers and confetti of paper roundels that accompany a loud and unlooked-for performance of the first bars of Mendelssohn's Wedding March when Titania goes to her scarlet feather-bed to couch with Bottom – these are brilliantly inventive. So indeed is much of the 'business' that accompanies the tagmatch in the woods; and the young lovers, having less chance to suggest their importance than those orotund fairies – being in fact pretty well confined to the job of chasing one another about in three dimensions – give performances that I find much more acceptable. Frances de la Tour, as long and thin as a Modigliani, is as funny a Helena as I have ever seen, once she's got going, and Mary Rutherford keeps her on her toes with her firebrand Hermia.

'Every action is an analogy of something else,' Peter Brook wrote in *The Empty Space*. There is hardly a movement in this *Dream* that could be considered a straightforward illustration of the text; yet there is hardly a movement that is irrelevant. The Deadly Theatre, the theatre of accepted traditions, is completely exorcised for the evening, and the *Dream*, potentially, shines out fresh and new. Only potentially at the moment; but for all its defects this production is still the most exciting in London.

Plays for Rubber Go-Go Girls

Hampstead Theatre Club　　　　　　　　　　*11 August 1971*

There are four of these short plays by Chris Wilkinson, plus a kind of coda in which a kind of collage of elements from all of them is wildly assembled. The company performing them is called The Portable Theatre and the designer and director is Malcolm Griffiths. They are only playing until the end of the week, and they richly reward the journey to Swiss Cottage.

Each play deals succinctly with some matter currently the subject of attention in the mass media. Mr Wilkinson's line is that the highly-coloured treatment accorded, by Press, television and films, to these matters turns them from fact into legend while they are still happening, so that it's hard to get a solid black-and-white view of them. The relationships between the US forces and the Vietnamese, between the Hippies and the fuzz, between the guerillas and the South American Governments, have acquired such a fictional character that we see them only in terms of James Bond or Modesty Blaise or (for the cognoscenti) Jerry Cornelius.

So these plays are written and performed as elaborately animated comic strips. There are short, sharp scenes with dialogue suggesting speech-balloons, and with taped sound and voice-over to represent the written connecting narrative. Not only are they very funny indeed, they have a refreshingly neutral side towards the unhappy obsessions of our time, like sex, cruelty, drugs, the generation gap and so on. This is how it is, they say; how do you like it?

The acting style also derives from the comic strip, with much use of conventional poses held briefly in tableau to express the emotion of the moment. In my experience, The Portable Theatre is of all the young avant-garde troupes easily the most adept at doing efficiently what it sets out to do, and these plays are presented with a briskness and a vivacity that gave me the greatest pleasure. They use a minimum of clobber; a couple of plain screens behind them, a scarlet circular mat to play on, a chair and a handful of simple props and there you are.

All the members of the company play several parts during the evening, and their teamwork is immaculate. The six young people involved are Patricia Hodge, Diana Patrick, Emma Williams, Mark Penfold, Paul Seed and Colin Stepney. If you miss them at Hampstead you may be able to catch up with them at the Edinburgh Festival.

CHAPTER FOUR

More Change

The time came when Tony Curtis decided that five days a week in the office were not helpful to a young man anxious to write original work of his own. One day in October 1971, Sir Gordon Newton summoned me to his office. It was possible, he said, that he might think about making me Arts Editor after all. He thought, moreover, that there was no reason why I shouldn't go on doing the theatre reviews as well.

A few days later I saw Lord Drogheda, the Chairman, in his office on the sixth floor. He didn't see why I shouldn't edit the page. Would I, he asked, give more attention to arts coverage in Europe in view of our membership of the EEC, and would I fill a little more space on Saturdays (I never did, but that was not my decision), and would I try to keep the music critics in order?

He added in a 'Droghedagram' a couple of days later that the visual arts needed more attention.

Nothing else happened for three weeks.

Then Tony asked me to lunch with him, on 4 November, and confided that he was giving up the arts page and confining himself to the books page, which up till then had been an arts pages responsibility. The Editor was going to ask me to take it on. The same afternoon, the Editor did indeed ask me to take it on, starting the following week. 'I've only one thing to say,' he said. 'Run that page and run it yourself!'

So I ran it. I was fifty-nine. I wish I had been thirty-nine.

*

Long Day's Journey into Night

New Theatre   *22 December 1971*

Eugene O'Neill drew on nothing for this play but the raw material of his life. There is no added sentiment or extra emotion or concession to dramatic tradition. There is only the merest semblance of a plot. All he shows us is one day in the life of the O'Neill family – rechristened the Tyrone family, though there is no attempt to hide the identity of the characters. It is the day when Mary Cavan Tyrone reverts to her morphine addiction after the false dawn of a cure, and Edmund Tyrone, her youngest son learns that he has tuberculosis and must go into a sanatorium.

Edmund, who represents the author, is at the centre of a wild cat's cradle of family relationships. His father, James Tyrone, is a famous actor – famous not so much for being good, in spite of a youthful promise that led Booth to say that he played Othello better than he did himself, but for having anchored himself to a profitable production (*The Count of Monte Cristo* in James O'Neill's case) which he played season after season for the greater part of his career, long after his real merit was forgotten. His mother has delusions of gentility not borne out by fact; but she was a good Catholic girl when she married James.

She bore three sons, James Junior, known as Jamie, Eugene and Edmund. Jamie has become a drunk and a womaniser who, at nearly forty, exists for half the year by playing in his father's company and for the other half by sponging on his father. Eugene died in infancy. (In the O'Neill family the middle child was Edmund, the youngest Eugene.) The youngest, Edmund, has spent a year or two as a seaman, but is now working on a local newspaper, where his contributions have earned some approbation.

Both sons rail constantly at their father for his parsimony; he rails at them for their idleness and their preference for modern degenerate poetry (Swinburne yet!) instead of Shakespeare. In spite of a superficial comradeship, Jamie resents Edmund because at the time of his birth a doctor (a cheap doctor, miser James's choice) dosed his mother with morphine which became an addiction. At the time of the play's beginning she has lately undergone a cure.

In Constance Cummings's glittering performance – a performance to travel across the country to see – you see the return of the craving suggested with the most delicate artistry. At first there is a faint obsession with the tidiness of her hair, a forgetfulness about where she has left her glasses. But her hands pick at each other nervously; she is clearly not a well woman. During the morning she makes an excuse to go up to her room, and when she comes down it is clear she has succumbed to her addiction. James, gentle and tender in the face of all his torments, refrains at first from saying anything; but left alone with her, Jamie, the outspoken, unsympathetic one of the family, charges her directly. From that time on the secret is out and Mary gets worse and worse, giving way to endless bouts of talking, feeling herself receding into her past.

Two such simultaneous misfortunes as Mary's addiction and Edmund's consumption might be bearable in a normal family; but the Tyrones are anything but normal. The long evening continues in scene after scene of scarifying interchanges, accusations, deceits. O'Neill makes little attempt to refine it into conventional drama. Edmund has a phrase that tells how O'Neill felt about his own writing; 'I did just stammer,' he says about his early work, 'it is the best I'll ever do.'

So the talk goes on, much as it must have done in that haunted family, trimmed only as necessary to keep the progress of the tragedy before us. It ends with a scene of utter misery; father and two sons, all either slightly drunk or very, quarrelling at midnight in the shabby sitting-room, interrupted by the figure of Mary, quite reverted now to her childhood. Ends? But, of course, it doesn't, this is the real tragedy. The play ends, but the Tyrones' life goes on.

With anything less than first-rate acting the play could be tedious. In this fine production by Michael Blakemore, it is monumentally grand. Laurence Olivier gives one of his noblest performances as James, completely the prosperous Irish-American householder, and – a much harder feat – completely the actor off duty, an ordinary man following his needful daily activities, only occasionally allowing his 'glorious voice' to come into action, when, for example, he shouts at Jamie, 'It was in those days I learnt to be a miser' after recounting the penurious circumstances of his youth. The hard line of his mouth has begun to relax too often into a gape of defeat, but there is strength in every movement and every word.

Ronald Pickup is excellent too as Edmund – wafer-thin, stoop-shouldered, enormous eyes flickering above the projecting cheekbones, he confirms the outstanding impression he made as St Just. Denis Quilley has not quite the panache for a Broadway butterfly, but he is a pretty fair Jamie in this distinguished company. The excellent representational set is by Michael Annals.

London Assurance

As once before with *After Haggerty*, Eddie Kulukundis has rescued a favourite Royal Shakespeare production from its impending disappearance to give it another showing. This time it is Boucicault's *London Assurance*, the great popular success of the summer season at the Aldwych in 1970. Except that Dinsdale Landen has replaced Barrie Ingham as the dashing but rootless adventurer Dazzle, cast, décor, and production are exactly reproduced. I was away when it opened last time, and I am delighted to add my voice to the chorus of approbation it earned then.

London Assurance was Boucicault's first play, written when he was twenty and at a loose end in London. It is closely modelled on Sheridan in style and in plot. The London fops who descend on the country house of Max Harkaway in Gloucestershire are matched in their assurance by the author himself. He is prepared to allow Sir Harcourt Courtly to believe that his scapegrace son Charles is actually a stranger named Augustus Hamilton and only to recognise the boy when, following the needs of a plot that suggests *The Rivals*, he goes off-stage, changes his clothes, puts on a pair of silver-rimmed glasses and then admits his paternity, though his looks must then have been far less familiar to Sir Harcourt than Augustus Hamilton's were.

Still, no one minds this kind of absurdity in this kind of comedy, which never pretends for a moment to be anything but artificial. The story, as usual, depends on the wooing of a rich heiress. Harkaway, for what reason one need not enquire, has arranged that if Sir Harcourt marries the eighteen-year-old Grace, his only child, he will come into the estates and £15,000 a year. When Sir Harcourt arrives at Harkaway's place he finds Charles and Dazzle already there (this is where Charles has to make his quick exchange of personality). Charles, naturally, has already fallen for Grace, and Sir Harcourt switches his affection to Lady Gay Spanker, a hard-riding country lady of the neighbourhood. No need to go into detail; Charles gets the girl and the estates, Lady Gay remains ultimately faithful to her dotard of a husband, and it is left to Sir Harcourt to make a curtain speech (addressed rather unfairly to Dazzle) extolling the virtues of true gentlemanliness over mere assurance.

Ronald Eyre directs in what must be condemned as a thoroughly impure style, though it may be in the same breath praised as a thoroughly amusing one. There is more than a hint of mockery of the dramatic conventions of the time, with its innumerable asides explaining the plot in the way that the old Punch joke-captions used to explain the jokes, and its sharply overdrawn characters. No one, I think, would play Sheridan this way, though too often one sees the melodramas of the mid-nineteenth century similarly mistreated. Still, Mr Eyre may be forgiven; the result is exceedingly comic, and it's clear that, for all the re-writing that has been done, Boucicault's play is fundamentally respected.

There is a gallery of splendidly entertaining performances. Glittering at their head is Donald Sinden, who has made Sir Harcourt a close relation of Lord Foppington. His ludicrous curled black wig, his rouged cheeks, his sleek clothes, his carefully-held classic poses are a delight, and his range of disparaging expressions at the multitude of things that displease him is something to be treasured. 'Am I the thing?' he asks his valet, Cool, quizzing himself in a mirror before he goes in to meet his intended. He definitely is.

There is lovely playing, too, from Judi Dench as the blue-stocking Grace, forever encouraging Charles with simulated discouragement; Elizabeth Spriggs, horsey yet ever ladylike, given to addressing her friends as if they were horses; Jeffrey Dench as Harkaway, Michael Williams as Charles, Derek Smith as Meddle, the lawyer permanently in search of a case, Sydney Bromley as Spanker, seldom able to remember the end of a sentence when he begins one. It is all great fun.

Kaspar

Almost Free Theatre   *10 February 1973*

You taught me language, said poor Caliban, and my profit on't is, I know how to curse. Peter Handke in *Kaspar* takes a Calibanian attitude to language. His hero, if that is the word, is based on the historical Kaspar Hauser, a sixteen-year-old boy who in Nuremburg in 1828 turned up out of nowhere with nothing in his mind but the memory of having lived in a wooden cell and the ability to speak one sentence, in broken German, 'I want to be a horseman as my father used to be.'

He used this sentence indiscriminately to express all needs and all emotions. What Peter Handke has done is not to show what life was like for the actual Kaspar on exposure to 'civilisation', but to imagine what the impact of language might be on someone in Kaspar's condition. Originally the play was to be called *Speech,* and Handke says in his introduction that it might be subtitled *Sprechfolterung* – speech-torture.

All that the play shows is the rise and fall of Kaspar as he is subjected to the discipline of speech. When we first see him at the Almost Free Theatre (played by Henry Woolf in what must be one of the finest performances to be found in London at the moment) he is a disorganised, inarticulate monster. He has to experiment with each step in order to find out how to walk. He discovers the properties of the miscellaneous objects that surround him – chairs, table, wardrobe – by playing with them as apes do. After a few experimental sounds he speaks his only sentence, which as Handke has it runs, 'I want to be someone like somebody else once was.' He says it with no understanding of its meaning, he tries it in a dozen different ways and still gets nowhere.

Then begins the speech-torture. From a loudspeaker the voices of three instructors ruthlessly educate him in the nature and use of language. First he learns the proper use of his single sentence; then he is told the use of language in establishing order, initiated into the mysteries of conceptual thought, evaluation of ideas. By degrees he assimilates the rules of conduct, until he proudly presents himself to us, the complete self-satisfied bourgeois.

But his perfection is unstable. Identical reproductions of himself flake off and wander independently about the stage playing id to his ego. They become increasingly unruly, and Kaspar's newly achieved respectability crumbles until at last he is reduced to repeated cries of 'Goats and monkeys!' He has been taught language, and he knows how to curse.

A play with so little action in it might be expected to be hideously dull. Robert Walker's production, bolstered by Henry Woolf's superb playing, is anything but that. As the Almost Free did before with Naftali Yavin's productions of some of Handke's shorter pieces, they have allowed themselves some freedom in the interpretation of the stage-directions and added a visual element necessary to keep the attention focussed on the stage. Mr Woolf is not handicapped with a mask, for instance. I found the evening enormously exciting; but I suggest that for the uninitiated some preliminary reading might help.

Kaspar is published by Methuen (hardback, £1.65, paperback 65p) and there is a good book about Handke by Nicholas Hern published by Oswald Wolff in their series of Modern German Authors (£1.15).

The Misanthrope

Old Vic   *23 February 1973*

This is the gayest English-language Molière I ever saw. It's played in a stunning new version by Tony Harrison set in 1966, though the time-travel does no violence to the text. The verses, in springy rhymed pentameters avoid too much commitment to poetry on the one hand and too much freedom on the other. Malraux and de Gaulle pop up quite logically in the dialogue. While never renouncing their claims as verse, the lines are so practically conversational that I sometimes resented the actors' interpretations of them, for spoken exactly as they come off the page it seemed to me they would have needed no extraneous accenting. They read delightfully: Rex Collings, paperback, £1.00.

There is an enchanting set by Tanya Moisewitsch, Celimene's drawing-room framed by great silver drapes hung carelessly around the proscenium arch, a tiled floor flanked by two noble windows, furniture from the advertisements in the Sunday colour supplements, a hi-fi, champagne and caviare in wait for anyone who comes in. Alceste wears a green velvet suit with a loose tie; Celimene the loveliest long-skirted dresses; Arsinoe loose gowns of immense smartness but appropriate severity over trouser suits that give her away. The whole thing has immense style.

Style, in fact, is written all over the production. The director is John Dexter, the most stylish director we have, and he has conjured up this precious world of amateur *hommes de lettres* and fashionable lovers with loving imagination. After all, there is little enough in the story; Alceste, the blunt devotee of truth, quarrels with the flatterer Oronte over a matter of literary criticism and has a confrontation (offstage) with the Academie; he is concerned with a lawsuit of which we hear hardly anything; he suspects Celimene his freewheeling mistress of deceiving him. What is important is the subtlety in the characterisation, the *pétillant* wit of the conversation. This is so exactly displayed in this production that it matters not at all whether the current monarch is Louis XIV or Charles de Gaulle. If Acaste and Clitandre had called Celimene up on the telephone my eyebrows would have stayed unraised.

Alec McCowen's abruptness with society as Alceste is not Puritanical but intellectual; he is in fact rather an attractive young man, but impatient at the inability of the rest of Paris to think exactly as he does. Mr McCowen ranges the emotional gamut with a great display of vocal flexibility, hurling a commination at faithless Celimene in a sounding fortissimo, dropping a moment later to a courteous murmur as he confidently invites God to take his side. He is well matched with, or rather against, Diana Rigg's coltish Celimene, as tall as he is, her splendid clothes topped with a curly wig that really makes her look like the twenty years old she claims.

There are no other parts in the play to compare with these, but the rest of the cast are by no means overshadowed even by two such likeable performances. Alan MacNaughton gives Alceste's confidant an exact blend of staidness and humanity, and looks very distinguished in his silk suit. There is a nice oily Oronte from Gawn Grainger and a suitably respectable Eliante from Jeanne Watts. Gillian Barge is immensely funny as Arsinoe; her big scene of insult-swopping with Celimene is one of the funniest things in a very funny evening.

The conclusion is entrancingly pretty; Celimene, shipwrecked on her devotion to fun, walking up the deserted stage towards the window, all her friends gone about their own amusements. This is an evening not to be missed at any cost, the National Theatre at its peak.

Little Hopping Robin

Almost Free   *19 March 1973*

A key to Paul Ableman's new play lies in his clever first novel, *I Hear Voices*. A young man suffering from a mental breakdown is involved in a series of illusory adventures. In one of them he is in his brother's office. An enormous desk, cigars, buttons to press. 'Here's authority. Here's dominion.' 'You can sit here at this desk,' says the narrator, 'and direct all sorts of things, plan and scheme – can you move mountains?' 'I'm only a clerk,' says the brother irritably.

Robin, in *Little Hopping Robin*, also has delusions of grandeur. He seems to be a senior executive of Power Fuel, about to present an important report. But his life is a sequence of curious happenings. His secretary sometimes turns into his mother and he into a small child. He finds himself in the Garden of Eden, where his father-in-law has become a pine-tree; or squatting on a pyramid in the desert awaiting a secret agent; or lying among expensive rugs and cushions, challenged to demonstrate his virility. Doubts about his virility obsess him, and doubts about his wife's faithfulness, and worry about his poor degree at Cambridge and his seniority in the firm and where to have a pee. Twice he actually delivers his report. The first time it is gibberish; the second time, read by a herald to the sound of trumpets, it is an encomium of his own excellence.

These dream-images are convincingly presented by Mr Ableman, who knows only too well how what seems to be a favourite situation in a dream can suddenly turn to one of awful embarrassment. Often they seem hilariously funny; but one must treat the humour with reserve, for it is all mobilised against Robin's self-respect. Twice the dreams turn to storms of childish tears, which I found heartbreaking. Tony Robertson plays the part remarkably well, blending his borrowed dignity with his ant-like physique (displayed with some courage in the scene where he appears wearing only a bowler hat and an umbrella).

Mr Ableman's final scene shows Robin, real, awake Robin, getting up in the morning with the dreadful sounds of the commercial world ringing in his ears as he shaves. It is, I think, a mistake; we know by then that Robin has been dreaming, and why, and the 'And then I woke up' theme is too obvious a way to end so inventive a play.

The director is Jim Hiley. He is clearly handicapped by the spatial shortcoming of the Almost Free Theatre in dealing with so many changes of scene and costume, but pace is maintained admirably in the circumstances. There are worthy performances by Malcolm Ingram as Charles, Robin's junior colleagu e and possibly the seducer of his wife; by Liz Munday and Valerie Lush as his secretary young and old; by Bruce Purchase as the head of Power Fuel, and others. I particularly commend the play to busy company directors.

Savages

Royal Court   *13 April 1973*

Christopher Hampton's theme in his new play is the 'Indian question' in Brazil. His aim is to persuade us that the preservation and rehabilitation of the handful of indigenous inhabitants (for whom he claims no special merits) is more important than the conflict between the Government of Brazil and the insurrectionaries who are trying to overthrow it by guerrilla activties. It is a sentimental view, but happens to be one I share, for although I know nothing more about the Brazilian Indians than I have learnt from a television programme some time ago, I have encountered the Bushmen of the Kalahari Desert, who are fundamentally the same kind of people.

The difference is that the Bechuanaland Protectorate, and now the Republic of Botswana, regard the Bushmen as worthy of help and encouragement, whereas the Brazilian industrialists regard the Indians as a damn nuisance, to be obliterated as quickly as possible by poisoning, infecting, shooting, bombing or other useful methods. I must take Mr Hampton's documentation on trust, though there are many references given in the programme, but his case is a formidable one, and formidably presented.

He keeps two stories running in parallel in alternated scenes. In one story, a British diplomat has been kidnapped (the date is 1970–71, when diplomats from Japan, Germany and Switzerland were so treated) and is shown handcuffed to a bed exchanging views and playing chess with one of his kidnappers. In the other, barely coherent enough to be called a story, we are shown various examples of the treatment of the indigenous peoples – by the Government, by the Indian Protection Service and the National Indian Foundation, by the guerrillas. In some of them the diplomat is present as an observer, in others the scene is shown without comment. The picture they present is appalling. Alan West, the kidnapped Briton, is played by Paul Scofield at the top of his form. Mr Hampton has made him a characteristic example of how we like to see his type, with his liberal views and his amateur indulgence in the arts (he has published 'slim volumes' of verse). The conversation is basically small-talk, and it is a delight to see how Mr Scofield so times it, so points it, that the most unimportant observation ('oh', for instance, or 'No') takes on a patina of breeding and sophistication.

The conversation of the others, whether well-intentioned anthropologists or Government officials or guerrilla bandits, has neither breeding nor sophistication, but tends to long declarations of policy of manifesto quality. The only people never given a voice are the Indians. Instead, we see them, between scenes, carrying out their native rites far upstage, while Mr Scofield, downstage, tells us some of the native legends he has learnt.

During the last of the rites, a funeral ceremony, the Indians are bombed by a Government aircraft intent on making more room for industry. At the same time Carlos, the guerrilla in charge of Alan West, learns that there has been a hitch in the plan to return him and, albeit unwillingly, shoots him at point-blank range. The indignant comment of the world's Press on this murder is shown on a screen lowered to the stage. There is no comment in the Press about the bombing of the Indians.

Carlos is sympathetically played by Tom Conti, and there are good cameo performances by Michael Pennington as a young anthropologist, Geoffrey Palmer as a missionary, Terence Burns as a tame Indian, Rona Anderson as Mrs West, and half a dozen more. The imaginative direction is by Robert Kidd.

Equus

Old Vic   *27 July 1973*

'The laws of God, the laws of man,' wrote the tortured Housman, 'let them keep that will and can. Not I : let God and man decree Laws for themselves and not for me.' Alan Strang, the subject of Peter Shaffer's new play, has committed a crime that by accepted standards must seem appalling, but a liberal magistrate has succeeded in having him committed to the care of a psychiatrist instead of a gaoler. The psychiatrist can 'cure' him; that is to say he can bring him to a condition where he will be amenable to the laws of God, the laws of man. At the same time he will deprive him of the one passion that makes his life worthwhile.

The play encompasses no more than the duration of the boy's treatment, though of course it doesn't consist of scene after scene of physiatric examination. In John Napier's austere set, the consulting room occupies an island stage in the middle of the stage proper. Its only

furniture is a few benches. But there are more benches outside the
island, and on these the characters wait until they are wanted. Whenever the dialogue between doctor and patient requires an illustrated
recollection, a new dramatic scene springs into being, sometimes with
the doctor or the boy commenting from the sidelines. There are more
sinister characters, too – the inhabitants of the boy's nightmares.

At the start of his treatment, Alan won't answer questions. Instead,
he sings television advertising jingles, and this gives Dr Dysart, the
psychiatrist, his first clue; one, or both, of the parents will not allow
him to look at television. It is a slender clue enough, but Mr Shaffer,
with an expertise that suggests a lifetime spent overhearing the traffic
in psychiatrists' consulting-rooms picks out the faint track and follows
it to its dreadful conclusion. The crime for which Alan has been
arrested was blinding six horses in a riding-stables with a hoof-pick.

Little by little the details come out. At six years old, Alan had
been given a ride on a horse by the seaside which had ended in a tiny
drama making the horse look majestic and Alan's father ludicrous.
Six years later, the father had torn down a picture of Christ on the
way to Calvary that hung in the boy's bedroom and replaced it with a
photo of a white horse looking over a gate. This it was that clinched the
aberration in Alan's mind; he was already 'mad about' horses, but
they now took over from Christ as the object of his worship. His simple
mind devised flamboyant myths and liturgies, extrapolated from the
stories and the Bible readings his mother fed him; and later, when he
was doing weekend work at the stables, he had secret physical contacts with the horses which (though it is never specifically stated)
appear to have been partly sexual.

Simple question and answer is succeeded by hypnotism by 'truth
drug', or rather by the administration of a placebo masquerading as a
truth drug. Abreaction follows, and Alan re-enacts the whole story of
his last evening. A girl working at the stables led him to a 'skin-flick'
in the neighbouring town. In the middle of the performance, Alan's
father (claiming only to have come to see the manager on business)
interrupted them and ordered them out. Alan, seeing his father for the
first time as contemptible rather than only dull, refuses to go home,
and the girl Jill takes him to the barn at the stables. They fall eagerly
to sex, but Alan can't function; the image of the horse imposes itself
over the reality of the girl. The horse is God, and God sees everything.
He sends the girl away and blinds the Gods that watch over him.

The treatment cures the boy, but to the doctor the cure is like an
emasculation. In a final speech of great power, he voices his doubts on

the value of the 'normal'. Which is better, to live a full and passionate life on unaccepted lines, or to be condemned forever to satisfaction with the trivial, spiritless things of the normal world? Of course Mr Shaffer is not arguing about worshipping horses but about all the common abnormalities of our day. His call is an attractive and sympathetic one; but it overlooks the fact that though making love to horses on dark nights may be harmless, there are other deviations, like raping old women and assaulting children, which are less so, and he offers us no guidance as to where we should draw the boundary line.

It's a fine, thought-provoking play all the same, and John Dexter's production ensures that the excitement is electrifying throughout. The first scene, where from pitch black a spot comes up to show the boy embracing his horse – an actor, Nicholas Clay, in brown tights and a metal horse's head designed by John Napier that mysteriously suggests the pagan godlike quality Alan ascribes to it – starts the pulse racing at once. The climactic scene, the naked boy striking out at the six horses as they threaten him from every side with the astonishingly equine movements Mr Dexter has devised for them, is at once terrifying and desperately pathetic.

Alec McCowen never puts a foot wrong as the psychiatrist, suppressing the private anguish of a loveless marriage as he tries, against his inner convictions, to bring back to the grey world this boy who had known a glimpse of paradise. Peter Firth plays the boy, an actor new to me. The insolent stare, the gradual melting in the consulting-room, the rapt glory of his terrible love are wonderfully expressed in his face, while his voice remains, in touching contrast, the voice of a simple country boy; they go to make a memorable performance. In the scene where he and Jill (Doran Godwin) undress for their first love-making, both of them are enviably unselfconscious.

Alan McNaughton and Jeanne Watts play the parents, he stern and unimaginative, she indulgent but ignorant, and there is a good performance by Gillian Barge as the woman magistrate. A credit must go to the lighting by Andy Phillips, who has to cope with a kaleidoscopic series of quick scene changes in a non-realistic set, and never (the highest praise) makes us conscious of his work; and a credit, too, to Claude Chagrin for movement.

Ashes

Open Space   *10 January 1974*

Near the end of his long one-act play David Rudkin broadens the poetic view he takes of his two main characters with a long soliloquy for both of them. Colin, the married and determinedly paternal homosexual, tells how he went home to his family in Derry and was prevented from following the bomb-shattered remains of his Uncle Tommy to the grave but made to stay at home with the women. His wife Anne, a decent ordinary girl prepared to make him a complete wife whatever his shortcomings, saw the world poisoned with filth and encountered a featureless child that terrified her.

These two speeches are no more than the ornamental capital that completes a plain, sturdy column; for the story tells, almost without relief, of the long and unsuccessful attempts of Colin and Anne to have a child.

The long, hard road is charted from the initial sound of offstage copulation through every stage that follows. The two provide a postcoital sample for a seminologist; they consult a gynaecological surgeon. At every move they are assured that there is no reason why, if instructions (sometimes grotesquely humiliating) are followed, they should not have a child. But when pregnancy is at last achieved, it ends in disaster. Anne begins to have haemorrhages, which become more and more persistent. But she reaches her time, and is delivered of stillborn twins.

At first I found the insistence on medical detail, much of it faithfully represented on the stage, repellent. After a while, the pathos and the poetry of the situation took hold of me, and as the progress towards the final tragedy went its inexorable way I became more and more deeply involved.

Mr Rudkin's method is to juxtapose simple, naturalistic scenes with soliloquies that not only help one to grasp the whole dimension of characters who, in their unexceptional lives, talk only in terms of daily cliché, but also promote them to their status as characters in a poem. Conception and pregnancy and childbirth are, after all, poetic things, in whatever circumstances they occur, and the biological side of them, tactfully handled, can be as poetic as another. What thought could be more poetic than Huxley's in his 'Fifth Philosopher's Song' – the single survivor from the million million living spermatozoa that chose to be himself?

One touch of vulgarity would have brought Mr Rudkin's structure crashing to the ground. But he treads his dangerous ground with infinite care, and he is aided by two wonderfully sympathetic performances by his two principals.

Colin and Anne are unremarkable people. Colin is a schoolmaster, perhaps a shade trendy, but not colourful, not flamboyant. Peter McEnery displays his bewilderment, his impatience, his kindness in simple terms; and when he moves from simplicity into a speech that is full of the author's poetry he does so without change of personality; we have only begun to look a little more deeply into his head. Anne, played by Lynn Farleigh, is a similar character. There is nothing heroic about her; when her endless bleeding irritates her beyond bearing, she is cross and tiresome. She is not even, as she confesses to the visitor from the adoption society, terribly fond of her husband; they have set up a home and they want it to be complete. Miss Farleigh's undemonstrative display of everyday emotion is a touching match for Mr McEnery's devotion.

Two other players fill the other roles in the play. Ian Collier encompasses a variety of doctors with a subtle variety of personalities, and throws in a fascinating cameo of an ambulance man (not, at that moment, on strike). Penny Ryder is a nurse, a receptionist, the adoption society's visitor, and touches them off with economical exactness. The scenes in which they appear are written with delicate certainty.

It is very easy to imagine that people will say, 'Who wants to see a play all about our horrible intimate functions?' I beg such people not to allow such a thought to deter them. The play is as truly poetic as the subject of human birth deserves; it is played with appropriate excellence, and deftly directed by Pam Brighton, though she is a bit optimistic about the sight-lines from the back row.

The Norman Conquests

Greenwich Theatre   *10 May 1974*

Alan Ayckbourn is an unpredictable writer; the only thing you can forecast safely about any play of his is that it will be hilariously, and never cheaply, funny. It may have a plot of hair-raising complications; it may have hardly any plot at all. *Table Manners*, which is the first play of a trilogy, *The Norman Conquests*, has a plot of the utmost conventionality, a story of multiple seduction that might date from the seventeenth century.

The scene is a country house in which Annie, played by Felicity Kendal with a fine blend of comedy and pathos, is looking after her widowed mother. Annie has arranged to spend a weekend with her sister Ruth's husband Norman, and for this reason, suitably disguised, has asked her elder brother Reg and his wife Sarah to mind the house for her. As it happens, the seduction never occurs. Norman, and subsequently Ruth, join the family party and an even sextet is completed by the presence of Tom, an amiable but extremely thick vet practising nearby.

The action all takes place around the table in the dining room of Alan Pickford's pleasant cottage set; it rises to a climax at supper in the first scene of Act 2 that is as funny as anything Mr Ayckbourn has written.

So much for story. How dull it might have been in other hands! But in this writer's it provokes an almost unbroken obbligato of laughter. He is our greatest master of situation comedy today. There are not many actual jokes in the play, certainly nothing like an epigram; but Mr Ayckbourn has such a precise knowledge of how we behave that he can always present it to us at once familiar and mistreated, so that a conventional line of action leads to a ludicrous consequence.

The director, Eric Thompson, also knows the secret of presenting natural action that inspires laughter by its very normality rather than any kind of distortion. The company at Greenwich could hardly be better. Tom Courtenay's Norman, certainly an unusual character with his extrovert ebullience (and hardly recognisable under his bushy beard) never angles for any laugh that could not result from his entirely possible behaviour. Penelope Keith as the bossy Sarah is remarkable too; she can rouse the house to hilarity with a straight delivery of a simple line like 'I've had a lot of nervous trouble', polishing the dining table as she speaks. Michael Gambon as the humourless Tom, Mark Kingston as the cheerfully vulgar Reg, Penelope Wilton as Norman's sour intellectual wife Ruth, complete the assembly, as faultless a bunch as you could ask.

The Norman Conquests

Greenwich Theatre   *22 May 1974*

At the start of *Living Together,* the second part of Alan Ayckbourn's comic trilogy, Tom Courtenay, who made a very late entrance in the first play, appears at once, a blue woollen cap over his head, looking like Clement Freud disguised as a garden gnome. The play follows exactly the same plot line as *Table Manners,* but does not at any point present the same events, which we see this time taking place in the sitting-room while *Table Manners* showed us only the happenings in the dining room.

It is quite unnecessary to know about what goes on elsewhere; this is a complete play on its own. All the same, there are some extra depths to be got by mental reference. The dreadful Sunday supper of the first play is replaced by an appalling session at a home-made game on Saturday evening as the highest point of fun in this second play.

No need to repeat my praise of the company, who are if anything even better than they were before. The author's scheme involves some enlargement of the characters; Penelope Wilton in particular, as Norman's wife Ruth, has a bigger part and a bigger personality. My admiration for them all – Mr Courtenay, Michael Gambon, Penelope Keith, Felicity Kendal, Mark Kingston – is undiminished; the direction is immaculate; the intricate mechanics of the writing more impressive than ever.

The Norman Conquests

Greenwich Theatre   *7 July 1974*

Round and Round the Garden takes a third look at the amorous affairs of Norman, Tom, Sarah, Annie, Reg and Ruth, this time from the garden we have only glimpsed before through an open door. The overall plot remains the same, of course, but some of the incidental detail is quite unexpected, notably Tom's assault on Ruth, whom he believes has been leading him on when she has only been advising him on a proper approach to Annie. There are comic climaxes as good as any in the other plays – Sarah's half-hearted resistance to Norman's first approach, Penelope Keith at her best, snapping a diminuendo refrain of 'That's enough!' as she fails to fight him off; the game of catch, devised by Reg, that leads only to one successful and one unsuccessful clinch.

No need to repeat my admiration for the company, Tom Courtenay, Penelope Wilton, Michael Gambon, Felicity Kendal, Mark Kingston and Penelope Keith; and for their director, Eric Thompson, the designer Alan Pickford, the lighting man, Nick Chelton. But it is interesting to consider the value of the plays more closely before leaving them for the West End transfer that must inevitably await them.

The fact that they fit together so ingeniously that they could, given enough room and enough stage-hands, be played simultaneously by a single cast is more than a mere curiosity. Though each piece is a perfect work of art, the three form a serial of an original kind, in which the entire story is presented not in three consecutive instalments but in three instalments that show the same sequence of events from different angles, and by doing so add something each time to our knowledge of the characters and their motives.

Mr Ayckbourn's choice of middle-class domestic trivia for his experiment doesn't mean that there is anything unimportant about it. The domestic trivia of his middle-class families are material as valid as the trivia of Molière's middle-class families, or Congreve's, and the observation of family ties in *The Norman Conquests* seems to me no less important (or funny) than that in *George Dandin* or *L'Ecole des maris*.

Comedy rivals tragedy throughout the history of drama (and indeed Mr Hovhannes Pilikian wants us to believe that Sophocles' and Euripides' tragedies were really meant to be played as farces). When serious social commentary is involved, comedy is frequently the chosen medium, as in *The Recruiting Officer* or *The Inspector General*. Social commentary is not as it happens a major factor in Ayckbourn, but it is clear from *Time and Time Again* and *Absurd Person Singular* that it could be if he wanted it.

Mr Ayckbourn's dramatic technique in his chosen field is unrivalled at the moment. As is generally known by now, the three *Norman Conquests* plays were composed together, the three scripts laid out side by side. In *How the Other Half Loves* Mr Ayckbourn out-Goldoni's Goldoni by presenting simultaneously two scenes taking place at different times. His scripts are as full of scrupulously detailed specification as Feydeau's. They use few of the clichés of farce, they do not depend on seasoning with epigrams, they do not call for star performances.

They are situation comedy of the highest and most valuable quality, and some of our theatrical whizz-kids, with their apparent belief that audiences must defer to them, not they to the audience, would do well to study them. But if all this suggests that Mr Ayckbourn's work is intellectual, let me say as plainly as I can that his plays, among which *The Norman Conquests* rate very highly, are as accessible and enjoyable as any I can think of over the last twenty years.

Fanshen

ICA Terrace   *22 April 1975*

The Joint Stock Company worked for months to produce a dramatic version of William Hinton's book *Fanshen*, an account of how Communism came to a little Chinese village. Finally a definitive script was written by David Hare, and this is what they now play.

The play, the programme note says, is a historically accurate note of what happened in one Chinese village less than thirty years ago. Many of the characters are still alive. 'Fanshen' means turning the body over – revolution, in other words.

We first see the villagers working on their land and they are introduced to us one by one, peasants, landlords, revolutionary leaders, bandit, labourer, beggar. An imperious voice offstage calls 'There will be a meeting!' and the process of redistributing wealth begins.

Introducing equality into a community that has never dreamed of it, where poor peasants live off the fruit of half an acre of infertile land and girls are sold as wives at four years old, is an uphill task. David Hare has not tried to introduce any kind of dramatic narrative beyond showing in a series of short scenes how the process goes. The first reaction of the newly-liberated peasants is to exact revenge on those who have oppressed them, or who have collaborated with the Kuomintang, or who have otherwise appeared to work against the general good. Soon one kind of tyranny is replaced by another kind of tyranny as the strongest and most ambitious jostle for power in the new regime.

The ensuing developments reproduce in miniature the progress of communism as one has seen it elsewhere. There is a 're-classification' of the peasants so that 'the fruits', as resources are called, may be more equitably distributed; then another re-classification to correct the errors of the first. There are endless meetings at which members are asked to criticise themselves for their performance. A Work Party descends on the village to ensure that they are on the right lines; then the Work Party goes back to headquarters and is told it has got it all wrong. At the only truly dramatic point of the play, they have to return to the village and explain that all the reclassification done so far has been a mistake.

The final scene is the same at the first. The peasants till their land as they have for hundreds of years past and will no doubt for years to come. Have all the meetings and the reclassifications and the self-criticisms made any difference?

The play is a human rather than a political document. No one is asked to feel elation at the arrival of the Communists or the display of the slogans on their blood-red banners. One is asked only to understand what the imposition of new, strange standards on people accustomed to centuries of tradition can do to them. The simple, low-coloured performance, with little in it in the way of theatrical excitement, shows us the picture without chiaroscuro. I found it extremely interesting; but moving, no.

Travesties

Aldwych   *30 May 1975*

Tom Stoppard says that his play is 'A work of fiction that makes use, and misuse, of history'. It also makes use, and misuse, of literature. What it does not do is point a moral or offer a commentary on the state of the world. It is pure comedy in which the facts of history and the stuff of literature are assembled like the glass fragments in a kaleidoscope to produce new and unexpected pictures, not intrinsic in themselves.

The facts of history on which it draws are that James Joyce, Vladimir Ilyich Lenin and Tristan Tzara were all in Zurich in, or about, 1917, that Joyce organised an amateur theatrical company in which the part of Algernon in *The Importance of Being Earnest* was

played by Henry Carr, an official of the British Consulate; that Tzara
is credited with having invented the word 'Dada' in a Zurich cafe;
that Lenin left, after the Russian revolution had begun, to make his
journey to the Finland station. The literary references are more widely
scattered, but are attached most to *The Importance*, though they
range, often with delightful inconsequence, through a broad spectrum
of English drama.

The times are seen as remembered by Henry Carr in his old age,
about to embark on his memoirs. John Wood's performance as Carr
is a dual miracle. He is first discovered sitting at his upright piano,
playing with some accuracy but little talent, a cigarette constantly
dropping from his mouth, or held, ready for inhaling, in his right
hand, never more than a foot from his lips. In an old cracked voice he
tells us about his forthcoming recollections, trying one phrase after
another as he conjures up those Zurich immortals. Then a remarkable
thing happens. He has begun to talk about the time he played Ernest
– no, not Ernest, the other one – when he draws off his slippers, slips
out of his long overcoat, throws away his shapeless hat, raises his voice
half an octave and is revealed as the elegant young vice-consul dressed
to kill, an Edwardian man-about-town.

He crosses from one personality to another several times during the
evening, though this is the only time he does it in public. Having
shaken off the years, he moves upstage into his sitting-room, where
Bennett, his manservant (or sometimes Algy's manservant) is attending
him. Significantly, the director, Peter Wood, has draped a mock curtain round an inner proscenium at the front of this room, for what
takes place in it is not real, it is only the fantasy of Carr's restless mind.

So when Tzara and Joyce arrive, they are music-hall parodies of
humanity, and the initial conversation is carried on in the form of
limericks. Later, Carr's memories become more restrained, and there
is some approach toward genuine traffic between real people. But
events have a habit of slipping into the plot of *The Importance*, and
the conversation of turning into Shakespeare, or even into popular
song. The brilliance of the writing is amazing; there is a literary allu-
sion in every other line – until we come to Lenin. Lenin is never
properly absorbed into the story; there is little contact between him
and Carr, only a reconstruction of how things might have gone as he
prepared to leave for Germany and embark on his sealed train. I
found the passage concerning him frankly dull.

Tzara, the happy, boyish Dadaist, is given a sparkling performance
by Robert Powell, and John Quentin puts a good visual resemblance

to Joyce on to Carr's recollection of the writer as a quarrelsome Irish-man. (Their relationship was, in fact, littered with lawsuits over trivial disputes.) Harry Towb cannot contrive to make Lenin interest-ing when the author has not, but he does what there is to be done. The girls – Carr's sister, Gwendolen of course, and Cecily Carruthers, a handy librarian – are prettily done by Meg Wynn Owen and Beth Morris, and Frances Cuka gives a solid Russian personality to Lenin's faithful Krupskaya.

And always in the background is the changeable personality of the manservant Bennett, sometimes servile, sometimes autocratic, some-times even *au fait* with official correspondence. It comes as no sur-prise in a final coda in which Carr discusses the old times with his ageing wife (Cecily), to learn that Bennett was actually the name of the Consul. Joyce put him into *Ulysses* as the sergeant-major. Carr only became one of those foul-mouthed soldiers.

Travesties is a comedy for sophisticates. The more allusions you can spot, the more fun it is. But there is nothing intellectual or diffi-cult about it. It is a very funny play indeed.

No Man's Land

Old Vic   *24 April 1975*

Two men in Pinter's new play inhabit No Man's Land, that region defined by one of them as a land that never moves, which never changes, which never grows older, but which remains for ever icy and silent. One of them, Hirst, is the dipsomaniac remains of a man of character and dignity. Endowed with wealth, he is able to retain a comfortable home and two menservants to look after him, to keep him properly dressed and fed. Spooner, the other, who may or may not have known Hirst in other days, this being a Pinter play, is a seedy intellectual nourishing the remains of his education on pub culture. Both are given performances of an astonishing excellence such as we seldom see.

Their relationship is charted in a script that contains all Pinter's familiar formulae. There is an intruder in a self-contained house; Spooner has inveigled Hirst, after a chance meeting at Jack Straw's

Castle, to ask him home. 'I never stay long with others,' he says apologetically. 'They do not wish it,' but he stays the night and most of the next day and is still there when we are shown how inextricably the house is engulfed in a No Man's Land from which it will not emerge.

There are two mystery men, Hirst's servants Foster and Briggs, radiating an aura of menace. There is a relentless interrogation on matters not susceptible of answers : 'Tell me,' Spooner asks, speaking to Hirst of his wife, 'with what velocity she came off the wicket, with what speed she swung in the air, whether she was responsive to finger-spin, whether you could bowl a shooter with her, or an off-break with a leg-break action.' There is a bravura speech about the best way to drive to Bolsover Street.

Plot there is none, only a sketch of the developing relationship between the two men, and that examined only as far as is required to summon up the spiritual wilderness in which the men live. The play is a concert-piece for four actors. As Pinter has repeatedly demonstrated before, it is possible to create both music and tension on the stage without the need of an anecdote; he has created both in abundance in this play. The subtle antithesis in his dialogue of pompous formality with sudden descent into demotic crudity : the artful changes of pace : the insertion of clichés and familiar phrases into speeches of orotund propriety – these, and a dozen other devices, go to make a quality of dialogue that is both literary and fluently speakable.

We have been warned often enough, by the author himself, against looking for inner meanings in his plays. I do not think there is an inner meaning in *No Man's Land*; the meaning is what you see and hear. And what you see and hear in this production, directed by Peter Hall and designed – a great semi-circular salon dominated by a big table laden with bottles and glasses – by John Bury is truly memorable.

For some time we see only Hirst and Spooner. Hirst, played by Ralph Richardson, is of military cut. He is tidily dressed in casual clothes and wears a grey moustache that gives him the look of an Edwardian general. His conversation is monosyllabic and terse, and he is probably half-drunk from the start, though he holds it in until he suddenly falls on the floor. Sir Ralph's performance of this scene is almost entirely the product of suggestion rather than demonstration, and it is masterly. Later, after Hirst has slept off his problem overnight, we see him in better shape, in a blue suit with a Leander tie, capable of dominating the nimbler-brained Spooner in an extraordinary discussion of their respective sex-lives, much of it, in characteristic Pinter vein, apparently referring to quite other people.

Spooner, played by John Gielgud, begins intensely nervous, unaware how long he can contrive to be asked to remain. He presents only the tatty remains of a once tolerable man. Sir John's observation of the tiny details of his behaviour is infinitely acute – the way he holds his cigarette or speaks with it in his mouth; the way he hitches up his long-unpressed trousers belted round a cheap orange-coloured shirt loosened at the neck; the nervous movements of the hands that disguise their natural grace; the shuffling walk with the sandalled feet. When, after he has been sleeping all night in the room, he rises to investigate the daylight, his stiff walk and his revulsion from the sun are masterpieces of invention.

As we saw in *Home*, these two players react on one another to magical effect. The scene in the second act where Hirst and Spooner exchange reminiscences of juvenile infidelity is spectacular, each side gaining a faint mastery over the other, losing it as another strange reminiscence is brought out. When it ends, Spooner has gained a slight lead, tenuous but enough to embolden him to try and get rid of Hirst's secretary (or whatever he is) and take over his job himself.

It is Foster, the secretary, who settles the question, and brings the play to an end by insisting on a literal interpretation of Hirst's bad-tempered request to 'change the subject for the last time'. If the subject can never again be changed, then things must always stay as they are. 'I'll drink to that,' says Hirst appropriately in the play's last line.

Foster and Briggs are played by Michael Feast and Terence Rigby; they are the new characters but clearly derived from *The Birthday Party* and other earlier pieces. Mr Feast, young and good-looking, with curious tales of women and guns in the East, is the secretary; Mr Rigby, burly and loyal, is the manservant. Both players give performances that are worthy of their fellow-actors on the stage, and I can't offer higher praise than that.

Comedians

Old Vic   *25 September 1975*

The uncomfortable truth that Trevor Griffiths demonstrates in this fascinating play is not the truth he is after. The play ends with a philosophic discussion between Eddie Waters, a veteran comedian, and Gethin Price, one of his pupils at night-school (brilliantly played by Jimmy Jewel and Jonathan Pryce respectively). The younger man has just junked the act he had got ready for an audition and substituted a grotesque display by which he hopes to reform society by hatred.

Mr Griffiths appears to concede that the young man's belief is true, though he is fair enough to leave the issue unresolved. The fault in the argument is that the new act has quite failed to interest the audience – the invisible audience in the play, that is – and therefore can carry no message at all. There is, though, another truth that Mr Griffiths reveals conclusively, that an audience does not really know a good joke from a bad one.

The author, fortunately, knows very well. The first of his three acts shows six ambitious amateurs under Eddie Waters's instruction in the secondary school classroom where the course takes place. Waters is an old school man, and he instils in his pupils the established principles of his craft. This is the last night of the course; in half an hour all the students will play before the frequenters of a bingo hall where an agent awaits them with blank contracts in his pocket.

The next act shows with much subtlety how the auditions go. The first aspirant (Jim Norton) gives an intimate, sophisticated monologue filled with jokes about Roman Catholics. He is followed by an ambitious young Jew (Louis Raynes), whose smart white tuxedo fails to cover floundering with his script. Two brothers (James Warrior and Dave Hill) cannot agree on what they should be doing. A bright, forthcoming young Irishman (Stephen Rea) is restless but attractively confident. Finally comes the disaster of Gethin Price – a few moments stolen from Grock, some violence derived from the karate cult practised on a pair of dummies in evening dress, representing the rich, an out-of-tune rendering of 'The Red Flag' played on his toy violin.

Mr Griffiths supplies his characters with good jokes and bad jokes, with jokes that are well put over or fumbled. In between, he demonstrates that laughs can be extracted by the simplest statements of fact. 'They've gone bloody mad down there, that karate lot,' the caretaker moans, dropping some pieces of wooden desks. 'This'll take half an hour at most,' the MC at the bingo hall promises. Lines like these raise laughter that any comic would envy. So do the students' good jokes. So do their bad jokes, laughter, it appeared to me at the bad jokes themselves, as jokes, not at Mr Griffiths's subtlety in grading them.

Because I have written so much about the quality of the fun it may seem that I have underestimated the earnestness of Mr Griffiths's plea. He is always a writer of great earnestness, and it does not fail him here; what is more, his characters are most subtly drawn and acted with exemplary skill by the members of the Nottingham Playhouse company. The play is directed by Richard Eyre, and the designer is John Gunter, who has made the classroom and the bingo hall seem in some incalculable manner equally bleak.

The Bed before Yesterday

Lyric   *10 December 1975*

Exquisitely comic as it is, there is a solid core of pathos in Ben Travers's new comedy, though not a touch of sentimentality. It is about the sexual education of a middle-aged woman so scared by her experiences on the first night of her honeymoon decades ago that she has never had intercourse with a man since. Both in situation and dialogue, it is much more outspoken than Mr Travers's earlier plays, though it is perhaps to his credit that the four-letter words he ascribes to young Aubrey so often sound unconvincing.

Alma, the middle-aged woman, is in every sense the heroine of the play. When we first see her, she is remote, dignified, irritable, twice married but now alone, brooding on her inability to induce friendships with men. Joan Plowright keeps her right away from farce territory, playing her – quite rightly – as if she were a character from Chekhov. A chance encounter in a hotel has led to an acquaintance with Victor Keene, who is poor, wet and well-bred. Within twenty minutes of her pouring out the first cup of tea, they are engaged. Not, though, with any idea of a honeymoon; on both sides one of the main attractions is that the contract will be social but not sexual.

But successive encounters with less restrained people arouse a new curiosity in Alma. She talks with Victor's son's girl-friend Ella (Helen

Mirren), whose permissive ideas must have been explosive in 1930, the date when this was happening. She talks with her déclassée cousin Lolly (the engaging Patsy Rowlands). New horizons appear before her, especially after some practical tuition by an eminent actor (Royce Mills), who is also an eminent ram. Victor, alas, is no longer a young man. But Alma has heard tales of young men in Italy. . . .

No point in following the details of the story to its conclusion. It is packed with good fun, but it is also full of understanding of the sadness of unfulfilled mature women. The Travers style in the dialogue is as fresh as ever. Mr Travers seldom writes a witty line; there is hardly ever any memorable repartee. Each exchange in the dialogue is a microcosm of situation comedy. 'She was Australian, you see.' 'Oh, how sad.' Or the unexpectedly frank : 'So that's where your tastes lie.' 'Yes.' Out of context there is little point to be seen in such lines; as Mr Travers manipulates them, they sparkle like gems.

John Moffatt has an ungrateful task with Victor, a man notable, if notable at all, for his lack of personality; but Mr Moffatt can be trusted to make the most of anything he is given. Frank Grimes, his hair an improbably auburn, did not persuade me as his son Aubrey; nor did Royce Mills, with his solid build and Charlie Chaplin moustache, recall the matinee idol of the nineteen-thirties vividly to my mind. Helen Mirren, on the other hand, could have stepped straight out of *Vile Bodies,* and there are able sketches by Gabrielle Daye as a charwoman and Leonard Fenton as a croupier from a dodgy gambling club.

Alma's Brompton Road house is a taking design by Alan Tagg, and the women in their pretty thirtyish dresses by Beatrice Dawson adorn it pleasantly. The director is Lindsay Anderson, whose firm hand is apparent until the end, when, rather than bring the curtain down on the curtain-line, he launches the company into a song-and-dance routine of contemporary songs.

I like to think that he mainly did this on the first night in order to give Mr Travers time to come down from his box and take a bow with the players, which Mr Travers did to thunderous applause in which I heartily joined.

The Ik

Round House   *16 January 1976*

Peter Brook's production of *The Ik* is extracted, with a creditable absence of subjective interpretation, from Colin Turnbull's book *The Mountain People*, about which a few words to begin with. *The Mountain People* (Pan, paperback, 70p) is a remarkable book by an anthropologist about an African Nilo-Hamitic tribe, the Ik, who live in the northern heights of Uganda. They were hunters until in 1946 a Government edict turned their hunting-grounds into a game reserve.

The endemic starvation that resulted turned the Ik into a people lacking most normal human characteristics. They lived like chickens in a barnyard, foraging for whatever food they can find, snatching it if convenient from the hands or even the mouths of their weaker members. The old and sick, being useless, are left unfed and die. Children are turned out of their parental home at three years old. Nothing survives of tribal organisation or of religious or ceremonial practices.

The Mountain People is not an anthropological textbook like Hollis on the Masai or Peristiany on the Kipsigis. It is a descriptive travel book of great evocative power, and Peter Brook has done no more – has had no need to do more – than dramatise passages from it exactly as Dr Turnbull has presented them. Any subjective element in *The Ik* comes from Turnbull, not Brook. The English text (the play was previously done in Paris) is by Colin Higgins and Denis Cannan, but overlaid with the contributions of the actors, whose task has been not to represent the Ik physically but to devise ways of showing the Ik's situation in a manner capable of immediate digestion by a European audience.

It is the very simplicity of the result that made it, for me, both so evocative and so affecting. There is no scenery; before acting begins the company cover the acting area with earth and site a few white stones. Some cut sticks, clearly raw material for a hut, are dumped on one side. An actor tells us who the Ik were, and another actor, representing Colin Turnbull, plays a game of driving a Land-Rover on rough African tracks. Turnbull makes tea on a Primus (a proceeding that for some reason indiscernible to me struck the audience as comic). An Ik man approaches with the usual greeting – not 'Ida piaji', which is a courtesy, but 'Brinji lopot', give me tobacco.

Pictures follow of tribal life, insofar as it can be called either tribal or life. A hut is built. Losike, the woman potter who still remembers the days when men were kind, tells her tale. Lolim, the old priest, shows how to divine with the aid of his sandals and tells about Didigwari, the God who made the Ik and lowered them from the sky on a vine. Two catechists from a neighbouring mission promise food in exchange for a well-sung hymn (but no food comes: for the Ik, it never does). A child reaching for meat burns his hand in the fire and sets the company laughing – the Ik, like the green men of Barsoom in Edgar Rice Burroughs's fantasies, laugh only at pain and cruelty. A half-witted child is shut away in a compound, being useless, and dies of starvation.

It is all represented with total simplicity. One soon forgets that the players are wearing European clothes with, at best, a monkey-skin to imply that they are Africans. Some scenes, Miriam Goldschmidt's scene as the mad child for example, are almost unbearably moving. Some, like the vomiting of the villagers who stuffed themselves with the food sent for famine relief, are both physically and morally revolting.

The six-strong company, most of whom play several parts, are Malick Bagayogo, Michele Collison, Miriam Goldschmidt, Bruce Myers, Andreas Katsulas (who plays Turnbull) and Katsuhiro Oida (who plays his Ik guide Atum). They are augmented by some black children recruited from an Islington school, who seem already to have learnt how to act, or rather not to act, in the Brook manner.

Tamburlaine the Great

Olivier   *5 October 1976*

Andrew Porter once dismayed the operatic Establishment by beginning a review of *Der Rosenkavalier* with the candid judgment that the story was 'tedious tosh'.

The story of Marlowe's *Tamburlaine* is tosh too. It tells only of a string of conquests studding the career of the Scourge of God, with special attention to the dreadful cruelties he inflicted in winning them. Each conquest is ritually achieved, by a formal announcement of its imminence, followed by an account of the subsequent fate of the victims. The relationship with Zenocrate is no more than a formal concession to the need for love. There are small sub-plots that deal with such affairs as the escape of Bajazeth's son Callapine and his later destiny, and the unsatisfactory nature of Tamburlaine's own son Calyphas, but these are no more than milestones along the bloody path to world domination that ends with Tamburlaine's death from an unspecified sickness.

The play, however, is written throughout in some of the most wonderful language ever put down on paper, glowing verse that smoulders and glitters with unceasing invention over the whole of the play's two parts with hardly a moment's respite. There is little in the way of characterisation; everyone has his share of the mighty lines, and it is on the speaking of the verse above all else that a production of the play must depend. There is little scope for acting in the Shakespearian mode, and little opportunity for a flamboyant production, since there is only a modicum of action.

Peter Hall, in the production with which he opens the Olivier Theatre, has chosen exactly the right path. The characters are confined to the circular, undecorated stage, the groupings predominantly symmetrical. The emotional content of the narrative must be gleaned almost entirely from the speech, and this is not such an easy matter as it sounds, for few of the characters are allowed more than a single quality apiece – indeed many of them are virtually interchangeable, including Tamburlaine's three principal cronies, Theridamas, Usumcasane and Techelles.

Visual excitement is ensured by the splendour of the costumes (John Bury is the designer) and the horror of the gruesome inventions Marlowe puts in – Bajazeth in his cage, Tamburlaine's chariot drawn by two captive kings with bits in their mouths, the Governor of Babylon hung on the walls of the city and shot to death by Tamburlaine's musketeers. There are no battle scenes such as we see in *Henry V*, but the dialogue encompasses some of the most terrible things in drama.

What adds to their dread is the beauty of the language in which they are narrated. The Governor of Damascus believes that his city may be spared if he sends a bevy of virgins to plead with Tamburlaine. Tamburlaine shows them his sword: 'There sits death, there sits imperious death, Keeping his circuit at the slicing edge.' But rather than have them so conventionally butchered, he will have them impaled on the lances of his horsemen.

Marlowe has given Tamburlaine a macabre humour. Albert Finney, who speaks the verse both with an acute understanding of the pitiless fury of the man and the fine music of the poetry, catches this humour effectively. Of the other characters, only Zenocrate (Susan Fleetwood) has room for subtlety, for Zenocrate is afflicted with a divided loyalty, to her father, Tamburlaine's enemy, and to Tamburlaine himself, and she must indicate both sides of it.

Denis Quilley speaks Bajazeth's lines splendidly, though I felt he might have exhibited more signs of exhaustion after being starved in his cage. He dies horribly, but reappears in the second part of the play as Bajazeth's son Callapine and plays him equally well, though without making any more difference between them than Marlowe has provided for, which is not much. Michael Gough speaks beautifully as Zenocrate's father, the Soldan of Egypt; and Robert Eddison, as one of the finest verse-speakers we have, is rightly given the first lines on the new stage as Prologue. Later he gives a moving performance as Orcanes, one of the 'pampered jades' that pull the chariot.

Brian Cox, Gawn Grainger and Oliver Cotton play Tamburlaine's 'contributary kings'; there is a tender performance by Diana Quick as Olympia, who kills her son to some of the loveliest lines in the play; of a dozen effective images, I recall Mark McManus looking pathetically boyish under Tamburlaine's great crown as his father sits dying at his feet.

Musicians sit on either side of the stage, sharpening the emotions of the words with Harrison Birtwistle's music. Beyond them there is only a black surround that opens for entrances and exits.

Privates on Parade

Aldwych   *23 February 1977*

Here is life in an Army entertainment unit in Singapore in 1946. Half the unit is gay. ('You dare to speak to an officer like that,' says Acting Captain Terri Dennis, 'and I'll scream the place down.') There is no discipline except on the stage. Major Flack, the Regular officer in charge, is so devoted to his muscular Christianity that he has no idea of the men's real interests, and the Staff Sergeant-Major is shoulder-deep in smuggling and selling small arms to the Chinese revolutionaries.

Peter Nichols did some of his National Service in a unit like this, and *Privates on Parade* (a title whose ambiguity is exploited at every opportunity) is a kind of sequel to his *Forget-me-not Lane*. It's *Forget-me-not Lane*, as it were, crossed with *Virgin Soldiers*.

I can't pretend that it is actually a good play. It is a sequence of mostly good numbers, and some of the jokes are so funny, especially to anyone who has ever encountered, however remotely, the kind of life it illustrates, that a lot may be forgiven. In so far as it has a plot, it is crude melodrama. SSM Drummond, the smuggler, believes that the newcomer, Acting Sergeant Flowers, must be an MI6 man, since he wears an Intelligence Corps badge ('a pansy resting on its laurels,' as we used to say). So he organises a raid through his Chinese contacts, in which it appears that he has been killed and beheaded. Actually, of course . . . but there's no need to go on.

However unlikely the plot, it is no more unlikely than the plot of a pantomime, and since it is only used to show the behaviour of this curious unit in various kinds of emergency it is not worth denigrating. Aside from the actual entertainment performances, the routine of the men, and their attached women, often burst into a kind of music-hall turn. Nothing is to be taken seriously.

What commends the evening is the excellence of the performances, directed with much versatility by Michael Blakemore. Denis Quilley as the Acting Captain not only adopts the stereotype mannerisms of the flamboyant homosexual with total persuasion, he reveals an unsuspected talent for cabaret, in impersonations of Marlene Dietrich, Noël Coward and Carmen Miranda. Very well-written numbers, these are, with admirable music by Denis King.

No one else is given quite such opportunities, though Joe Melia as the foul-mouthed Birmingham sergeant and Tim Wylton as his mate do a good Flanagan and Allen. But many of the unit are reasonably normal men, though they have moved into abnormal spheres in abnormal circumstances: Kipling knew the temptations that beset 'single men in barracks'.

These are what I call one-quality men. Ian Gelder as young Stephen Flowers is innocence seduced; it is bad luck that the 'Anglo' girl he falls for should also be the Sergeant-Major's bit. The girl, half-Welsh and half-Indian, is brilliantly played by Emma Williams. David Daker is the SSM, half-crook, half-bully. After the raid he is lost from the plot, save for a couple of appearances dressed unconvincingly as a Chinese, and then attention is focussed more on the real commander, the Major, whom Nigel Hawthorne plays with a blend of comedy and truth that works out to perfection.

The elaborate sets are the work of Michael Annals; they enable scene-changes between the twenty-two scenes to be made smoothly and fast. A pianist sits on the stage, and there are five more musicians in the orchestra pit.

On the debit side, there is no doubt that more than three hours is too long for a show of this kind. The production is self-indulgent; with so much good material to turn to, Mr Blakemore has decided on an *embarras de richesses* instead of sorting out only the best of it. There comes a time when one feels that some kind of resolution is due. Well, too much of a good thing is not such a serious fault.

German Skerries

Bush   *26 January 1977*

Not quite a still life, Robert Holman's tender one-acter, more a landscape with figures. There is action in it, quite violent action, a man mortally wounded by the explosion of a pipe carrying boiling water, strikers demonstrating outside a factory. But the action is kept off-stage, and the function is not to form part of a plot but to help in describing the central characters : for the description of young Jack Williams and his newly-married wife Carol is what the play is about.

We first see Jack bird-watching on a cliff at the estuary of the River Tees that overlooks the German Skerries, the sharp rocks that stand in the mouth of the river. In conversation with a fellow-enthusiast he paints the first strokes of the picture : he works for ICI, he would like promotion but doesn't take life seriously enough, he has a small tatty sports car he can't afford, when he and his wife set out for their honeymoon they never got further than Carlisle.

Anything else we must learn from his reactions to others. He is still childishly in love with his young wife, though he can't be as serious as she would like him. When an injured driver needs help, it is she that drives him into Redcar. The colour is added little by little until we know Jack intimately; Paul Copley's sensitive performance brings Mr Holman's beautifully observed speech into glowing life.

The other characters, even Carol, are called on only to complete the picture, but they too are drawn with the same eager truth. Carol (Caroline Hutchison) will be motherly one day, for all her present youthful gaiety : she serves to indicate Jack's fundamental weakness. John Normington gives a sharp performance of the ageing schoolmaster who shares the cliff in search of cormorants and oyster-catchers; his occasional fun is delivered in stern tones, as if he were dealing with nine-year-olds who mustn't be given too much chance to laugh. Mark Penfold as the diver has only one scene that matters, and that is short and played in the dark; yet each word of his dialogue is as carefully moulded as the rest.

Frankly, I thought the play was going to be dull at first, when so much went by without development. But it's not dull, not at all; it is a happily composed scene of life whose every lack of excitement is part of its attractive quality. Seldom do you find a play nowadays that you might call gentle; yet gentle is above all what *German Skerries* is. Even the demo at the ICI works was there only to force the firm to move their hot-water pipe, which seemed likely to interfere with the bird-life.

The director is Chris Parr, the designer Miki van Zwanenberg.

Tales from the Vienna Woods

Olivier   *27 January 1977*

Though Odön von Horvath lived most of his life in Germany, and was educated there, *Tales from the Vienna Woods* is a very Austrian play. In the tradition of Schnitzler, it examines what to other minds would be a romantic situation and reveals the worm in the wood. Only incidentally is it an anti-Nazi play. It is an anti-hypocrisy play.

It is set among the bourgeoisie of Vienna. Marianne, the young daughter of the Zauberkönig, the proprietor of a toyshop, is on the point of becoming engaged to Oskar, the butcher in the shop next door. In the course of a picnic in the Wachau, Oskar surprises her dallying with Alfred, a young man of easy morals who has just concluded an affair with Valerie, a middle-aged lady of similar disposition who owns the tobacconist's shop on the other side of the Zauberkönig.

The result is disaster, for when Marianne breaks off her engagement and goes to live in poverty with Alfred, she is cast off by her father and he is cast off by the grandmother from whom he cadges pocket-money; and Alfred, no man to sustain a situation of no advantage to him, persuades his mother to care for Marianne's baby and then walks out. The story is told with much detail and involves a great number of characters, all depicted completely in the round. It leads to what appears from one angle to be a happy ending; but by a master-stroke of irony, the bolt that would have secured that situation, makeshift as it is, has been removed, and the ending is desperately bleak.

The production, under the direction of Maximilian Schell (himself a Viennese) is masterly. Everything takes place on the revolving stage. Its surface is bare planks; there is one main item of scenery, a rectilinear mansion that can show the street of shops on one side and Alfred's mother's house in the Wachau on the other, but can also be turned into something like the tiring-house of the Jacobean theatre, with an inner stage and a balcony. The designers are Timothy O'Brien and Tazeena Firth.

On this system, scene-changes are instant. It is even possible, at one exhilarating instant, to move directly from the street to a glamorous evening at Maxim's with diners at a dozen tables, a bar on one side, a curtained recess for the cabaret. The cabaret is a splendid example of expensive vulgarity; first a bevy of dancers go through a tired can-can, then there is a little set-piece glorifying the Graf Zeppelin airship (which is last seen floating up to the ceiling) and ultimately a scene called 'Search for happiness' features half-a-dozen nude girls. One of these, alas, is Marianne, who has found herself unfitted for life on the streets; and in the restaurant are her father and all the society of Vienna.

Marianne is played by Kate Nelligan in a subdued humour. This is a girl without much expectation from life; she has worked in her father's shop since she was a little girl, she has no pretty clothes, she moves without grace (though surely Miss Nelligan need not make her so bow-legged). A spark of life flares up at her meeting with Alfred by the Danube; a spark of pride as she tells her father at Maxim's 'I can't afford shame'; and a tremendous surge of anger after she learns of the death of her child and curses God for the life he has given her.

Stephen Rea turns Alfred, most effectively, into an Austrian Playboy of the Western World, a man for ever playing a part. He has some good scenes with his grandmother (Madoline Thomas), an ill-tempered old harridan who can still be persuaded to lend some money or to sew on a button. He can never have had to face much competition from Oskar, whom Warren Clarke makes a plump, expressionless man capable only of elementary feelings.

Valerie, the tobacconist, is a variation on the familiar theme of the tart with the heart of gold. Splendidly played by Elizabeth Spriggs, she devotes herself to seducing the young men and putting right the short-comings in other people's lives. Paul Rogers plays the Zauberkönig with a kind of vulgar panache, as if he were always conducting an orchestra; indeed, he tends to use phrases like '*Da capo!*' when he means 'Do it again.' There is a wealth of good work among the many supporting characters, who include such players as Ellen Pollock (the manager of Marianne's dance-troupe, who has a great moment when she bursts through the curtain at Maxim's at the height of the trouble); Sybil Coleridge (her blind sister, who plays Wagner on the harpsi-chord); Struan Rodger as the pro-Nazi Erich; Nicholas Selby as a re-tired captain; and many more, including some beautifully unself-conscious children.

CHAPTER FIVE

Final Change

The fatal calendar struck me on 20 January 1977, my 65th birthday. By British tradition, you retire from your work at the age of 65. Sir Gordon Newton had. So had Lord Drogheda. I could not withstand such examples.

Antony Thorncroft took my chair. I went on covering the theatre. The Ph.D. theses of those American students will find that the notices are on the whole a bit shorter than they had been, but this is nothing to do with Tony Thorncroft's policy or my own. There was a higher policy that decided to put more advertisements on the page.

I moved out of the office on 1 April, hoping that perhaps the whole thing was a hoax. I bought three dozen bottles of red Italian wine from the canteen and three dozen glasses from Woolworth's in Cheapside, and asked anyone who felt like it to come to the office and see me off. To my embarrassment, the Editor, Fredy Fisher, came and made a flattering speech. He presented me with a folder, beautifully illustrated and signed below a generous message by an enormous number of colleagues. There was also a cheque that I have never declared to the Inland Revenue. I felt very happy to know so many nice people and be liked by them as much as I liked them.

*

State of Revolution

Lyttelton   *26 May 1977*

Robert Bolt introduces us to the events of the Russian revolution of October 1917 by way of Lunacharsky, who became Commissar for Education. He is addressing a gathering of Young Communists on the anniversary of Lenin's death, and his talk materialises into the events themselves, beginning with a conference in Capri in 1910, where he has submitted a paper to a meeting of Lenin, Dzerzhinsky (later head of the Cheka), Kollontai (Commissar for Social Assistance) and Maxim Gorky.

Anyone who believes that the revolution was splendid under Lenin and only went wrong under the brutal domination of Stalin will have his ideas corrected by Robert Bolt, who has been both a schoolmaster and a Communist. The Lenin presented to us in this play is very different from the benign figure the Russian theatre offers us. He is a foul-mouthed bully capable of ordering the most heartless atrocities in support of his theories of Communist government. If the inauguration of the New Economic Policy in defiance of his convictions demonstrates a touch of humanity after the rebellion of the Kronstadt Council, it is followed at once by his order to Stalin (who was known to him then as he is known to us now) to 'purge' the Party in Georgia, knowing well what that means.

Michael Bryant gives a most convincing performance in the part, his gravelly voice and bright eyes dominating any assembly where he is present, his small frame topped with a close likeness of his original. In the scene near the end of the play, after Lenin has suffered a stroke, Mr Bryant is outstanding both in the detailed observation of the crippled walk and in the faulty speech.

Mr Bolt's selection of highlights from the seven years of Lenin's supremacy gives a sharp impression of the times as they affected the leading participants. This is not a political play, it is a play about people who work in politics, and the people are given vivid life. The acting is fine throughout. The extent to which the players resemble their models physically matters little. In fact, they are given as much resemblance as possible, but what is more important is that they are consistent characters capable of doing what history tells us they did.

Lunacharsky was the idealist of the Party, a genuine believer in the possibility of universal brotherhood. Stephen Moore, scholarly in look and in speech, contrives to suggest both the devotion to Marxist ideals and distress at the means sometimes called in to impose them. John Normington gives a finely graded performance as Dzerzhinsky, a Polish nobleman by birth appointed against his will to lead the Cheka, and receding further and further from humanity as his sense of duty leads him into excess, until he becomes a prototype of Himmler.

The rivalry between Stalin and Trotsky is dwelt on throughout the play until it reaches its final resolution. Trotsky, the potential Bonaparte, is given a dapper personality by Michael Kitchen, his sour wit expressed with a Voltairean self-confidence. Stalin, on the other hand, played by Terence Rigby, is a big coarse figure with a touch of provincial accent from his Georgian origin. His eventual victory is the product of his willingness to take on any job that was offered. In the early scenes he is shown as having only a superficial knowledge of Marxian dialectic, and Trotsky rags him for this. Then all the phrases that he has picked up from his comrades in conference come tumbling out in his final speech to win him an ovation.

The director is Christopher Morahan. With the use of an ingenious set designed by Ralph Koltai he keeps the action moving fast, each scene melting into the next. When stage properties must be moved, this is done in an urgent hurry by soldiers or peasants who form part of the scenery.

History may find in the distant future that the October revolution was the most important event since the happenings of the New Testament (if we are saved). Mr Bolt has written what is in its way the Passion Play of the occasion. I found it rivetingly interesting, and its cool unpolitical neutrality enables the content to be fitted into whatever historical slot the viewer may wish to put it.

The Madras House

Olivier   *24 June 1977*

Granville Barker's wonderful Christmas pudding of a play is crammed full of ideas packed in with apparently reckless disregard of their ultimate concord. The overall theme is no more than what used to be known as 'the battle of the sexes' but now has an ism attached to it; that is to say, the proper relationship of men with women and vice versa. But in pursuit of it, Barker touches on the duties of children to parents, the 'living-in' system in shops, the rights of unmarried mothers, the function of women's fashions, the absurdity of suburban small-talk, the education of children, and other things besides.

The result is a sprawling, extravagant, hugely enjoyable play, calling for all the resources of a company as rich as the National. In the first act, played on a lavish set designed by Hayden Griffin representing the big L-shaped drawing-room of Henry Huxtable's Denmark Hill home, we learn that the Madras House, a big dressmaking concern, is to be sold to an American exploiter, Eustace Perrin State; but in the course of such discussions as take place between the ageing Huxtable and his partners Philip Madras and Major Hippisley Thomas we learn more about the life of the six unmarried Huxtable daughters and the tragedy of Philip's mother Amelia, long deserted by Constantine, her husband, than we do about the business.

The second act shows us young Philip in action, resolving a scandal among the staff – Miss Yates (a magnetic performance by Dinah Stabb) is 'in trouble' and there has been a false imputation of paternity. The various trails converge in the third act, where discussions about the sale are made over a parade of new dresses, and where, a deus ex machina, Philip's errant father, appears for the first time to put forward his predatory notions about women, in pursuit of which he has gone to live in Arabia and become a Mohammedan. This is Paul Scofield, playing a deliberately flamboyant eccentric on whom he has poured all his most precious essences of comedy. He uses a dark velvet voice with a hint of foreign vowels ('my grandfather was a Smyrna Jew') and wears green velvet with a polychrome waistcoat.

In a final act, affairs are concluded, if not exactly solved, and this big play ends in an intimate talk between Philip and his wife Jessica covering a variety of matters not necessarily even suggested in what has gone before, as if a great piano concerto were to conclude with an extemporisation by the soloist.

Barker was not a great reformer like Shaw – Philip proposes to do his share of putting the world to rights by resigning his directorship and standing for the London County Council – but he writes beautifully provocative and entertaining dialogue, and he creates the most totally actable characters. Even such stage-dressing as the Huxtable girls are designed with built-in personalities, and under William Gaskill's minutely detailed direction they emerge as real individuals. The major characters, apart from the colourful Constantine, show the same cunning construction; they are basically representative members of their kind but so deeply explored through their conversation that they may stand as archetypes. Paul Rogers as Huxtable, with his pathetic sniff, is the pattern of modern suburban shopkeeper risen above his natural station in life (and it is fascinating to see how Barker and Mr Gaskill have suggested his origins in little Mr Belhaven, the office-boy at the Madras House). Philip and Jessica are given sterling individuality by Ronald Pickup and Helen Ryan, though they are only quite ordinary folk.

Constantine has nothing in common with such people; and yet Mr

Scofield touches muted chords of pathos at his meeting with his wife Amelia in the last act – a sad figure in whom Jane Hylton truly suggests that she has spent the thirty years of desertion in the hope of reconciliation.

There are telling performances by Joss Ackland as the American, State – whom Barker, unfashionably for his time, provides with a suggestion of wide reading and culture – and by Oliver Cotton as Philip's accountant, Major Thomas, a smooth, flirtatious figure with black patent leather hair. Michael Medwin's dress designer is a seminal example of high camp. One would like to run through the whole great cast-list with a word for each, for there are indeed no bad performers.

The four sets, in the design of which Hayden Griffin was assisted by Peter Hartwell, are evocative as well as intrinsically interesting, and as full of observation as the characters themselves.

Writer's Cramp

Bush   *2 November 1977*

Writer's Cramp by John Byrne was the hit of the 1977 Edinburgh Fringe. It professes to give an account of the life of F. S. McDade, a Scottish polymath who died in Nitshill, Glasgow, in 1976 – a leaf, as the commentator says, from 'the deciduous tree of Scottish literature'.

McDade was a writer, poet, painter and sage. His first poem was for his school magazine, but he seems not to have added anything at Oxford. Here he pursued with moderate success a girl called Pam, his other girlfriend, Anne, having had a misfortune – 'Dickers got Anners preggars at Twickers', his friend tells him cheerfully. During the war, McDade was at an Officer's Training Unit, leaving it only to become a driver's mate in REME. His war diaries, to be called *The Khaki Titfer*, were interrupted when Security discovered that he was not the son of his alleged father, but, illegitimately, of a German, so he had to be rushed off to internment.

While 'inside' at Albany in the Isle of Wight, he wrote his first novel to be published, *Pass the Buns, Dolly,* on two rolls of toilet paper. After the war was over, he married his Pam and spent five years in the Talks Department of the BBC. ('The vultures on the

cookhouse nest, Like poets on the BBC,' Roy Campbell wrote prophet-
ically in the war.) When even that spewed him forth, he gave up
literature and took to painting. He had a brief success at this until the
critics got tired of him and boosted someone else instead.

All this is told in hilarious detail by Mr Byrne with a cast of three.
Bill Paterson takes on McDade from schooldays to deathbed. He is
flanked by John Bett, whose main function is the recounting of narrative, mostly in the language of old-fashioned Scots critics; but he also
copes with a variety of parts, from Pam to an RC padre who falls
asleep in the middle of administering extreme unction; and Alex
Norton, charged with the reading of some of McDade's work, including one of his rare poems in Lallans, and with such characters as
McDade's schoolfriend Double-Davies, who grows up to be a small
crook, and his amorous landlady.

Mr Byrne's invention is not only generous, it is also notably ob-
servant. Given the necessary element of parody, it's remarkable how
close to accessible types his characters come. Even the list of McDade's
casual journalistic pieces given in the programme is cruelly familiar
to anyone who has trodden that path. There is hardly a moment in
the evening when some target is not hit squarely and embarrassingly
on the button; and the three players take on their various incarnations
with great skill.

There is nothing highbrow or private in the floods of fun that fill
the Bush in Robin Lefevre's witty production, and nothing vulgar
either. The evening is a solid heap of laughter.

Bodies

Hampstead Theatre   *21 February 1978*

James Saunders's new play consists mainly of philosophical discussion
of a purely intellectual question. David (David Burke), who has had
a nervous breakdown, finds salvation in a new therapy that he has got
from a book which he chanced to find on a bookstall. His salvation
lies in the belief he has gained from it that the physical is all that
matters in this world, that 'There is only the body, with no outside
reference,' and that consequently such conceptions as love, morality,
happiness are no more than neuroses.

The theory is brilliantly discussed by him in the second act with his old friend Mervyn, a headmaster. Mervyn is full of whisky, and his own 'neuroses' are readily near the surface. He has much material to fall back on, for eight years before, he and David had exchanged wives and later returned to their original partners; and at his school a boy has just attempted suicide on a motor-bike, a boy he particularly disliked, and is now surviving only with life-support mechanism. Dinsdale Landen plays Mervyn so vividly, deploying his forces more and more dangerously as the emotions become less and less under control, that what might otherwise seem a long and wordy exchange of dialectic with the placid David acquires a flashing interest.

The armoury from which he draws his ammunition is built up in the first act, written in a different style from the continuous development of the second. (Development of argument, not of situation, I must point out.) Soliloquies or short conversations, in no chronological order, reveal why Mervyn's wife Anne (Gwen Watford) should have fallen in love with David, why David's wife Helen (Anne Stallybrass) should react by falling in love with Mervyn, and what kind of people they are when they are free of emotional strain.

Mr Saunders's object, however, is to establish a single situation that is only to be allowed one piercing development. This is reasonably achieved, with talk that is salted with some dry humour, and it is only in this first act that the ladies are able to offer performances to equal the men's. Robin Lefevre, the director, and Tanya McCallin, the designer, have kept this act as purely diagrammatic to look at as the dialogue is to listen to. Even in the second act they have only permitted the lightest suggestion of a sitting-room.

The author has not chosen intellectual means only to hold the tension in his big argument. Mr. Landen flourishes a flick-knife (confiscated that afternoon) to elucidate one of his arguments; and the long-awaited telephone call that is to let him clinch his argument is preceded by some tactical wrong numbers and one ring that I suppose to have been an accident. If such devices are felt needful to hold the attention to all that philosophy, well and good; it is no more than academic of me, I am sure, to find them out of place.

Robert Wilson

Royal Court   *6 June 1978*

I Was Sitting on my Patio This Guy Appeared I Thought I Was Hallucinating (the opening line as well as the title) is called a play by its author, Robert Wilson, but it is not a play in the sense that we understand it, however broadly. Mr Wilson has assured me that if you want to leave for a while and come back later you won't have missed anything. The work does not develop; it simply is. You don't examine it from end to end any more than you examine the Venus de Milo from top to bottom.

It is not one work of art, moreover, but several. There are five elements in it that I could discern – script, décor, music, costume and lighting. They are almost independent, only clamped together like the layers in a club sandwich. Mr Wilson plays the first act by himself (and I suppose his playing is another element in the whole). When the lights go up he is lying on a rectilinear chair before a black curtain pierced by three big openings on to a bright white backdrop. His words are of little importance; they consist of loose conversational phrases that do not supply a continuous story, though in general they suggest a man in a state of tension about something, not always the same thing.

They are accompanied by a taped score of music by Alan Lloyd using Mozart's vocabulary more or less, though with no discernible objective but accompaniment. The lights change independently of any action in Beverly Emmons's plot; halfway through, the windows on to the patio are obscured by blinds. At one point Mr Wilson throws off his long black cloak; he attends, or fails to attend, to a constantly ringing telephone. On a small screen, various films are projected, usually of penguins.

Lucinda Childs, who is the co-director with Mr Wilson, plays virtually the same lines in Act Two. She plays them quite differently. The lighting plot is different too. The piano is replaced by a harpsichord. Instead of doffing a black cloak, she dons a white one. Swimming ducks replace the penguins on the screen. As in the first act, there is no overt meaning or development. The meaning is what you see. The nearest we have to it in our recent experience here is probably the living sculpture of Gilbert and George.

Did I enjoy it? Well, I didn't laugh, or cry, or flinch. Was I interested? Yes, absolutely fascinated, mostly of course by the second act, observing the variations. I can only recommend it as a quite new experience; and as that I recommend it to anyone interested in the collection of novelties.

American Buffalo

Cottesloe   *10 October 1978*

David Mamet's fascinating play contradicts what I have been saying lately about the new American writers. There is nothing overtly poetic about it at all; the two hours of conversation between three small-time Chicago crooks is hard and brutal, and the story of the set-up to rob a man of his coin collection, which goes wrong because the intelligence of the participants is not enough to cope with it, would barely fill an hour of *Z Cars*. Yet there is no doubt in my mind that is a very good play indeed.

Beauty is truth, truth beauty; but there is more than the jagged, everyday truth of this dialogue to give it the beauty it undoubtedly possesses. Mr Mamet plays with words as a musician plays with notes in a fugue; subtle relationships are constructed from the simplest, grubbiest phrases to chime and echo in a rough resonance that is almost poetry, and yet is still convincing gangster chat.

The overall shape of the play, moreover, is most exactly calculated. It begins with the lightest of exchanges between Don the junkshop dealer, who is setting up the job, and Bobby the boy who lends a hand in the shop (a glorious mass of rubbish assembled by the designer, Grant Hicks). Bobby, eager to play a modest part in the hit, is so stupid that he can't be trusted to do anything, especially as he always lies to cover up his mistakes or, even worse, makes things up to add interest to his routine reports.

With the arrival of a gun-happy hit-man, Teach, the feeling grows tenser, until ultimately it explodes in a climax of violence. The character of each of the men is brought to its individual peak; Bobby reaches a peak of stupidity, Teach a peak of mindless violence, Don, faced with the collapse of his plan, calls in violence or anything else that is necessary to keep life from boiling over, yet stays calmly in mindless charge.

The players are Anthony May as Bobby, Jack Shepherd as Teach and Dave King as Don, fine performances all and, to my ear, honed on the television, convincingly American, though none of them is. For this and the other excellences we must thank the director, Bill Bryden.

Wheelchair Willie

Royal Court *11 December 1978*

Those who prefer not to see the unbearable represented on the stage can write off Alan Brown's *Wheelchair Willie* at once, and need read no further.

Mum – given a performance by Frances de la Tour that I shall never forget – has two children, Willie and Sue. Willie is paralysed from the neck down; though he is good-natured and intelligent, he has no control over his sphincter muscle and his pants are generally filthy. By the end of Act One, he has had his tongue torn out, probably by the television fitter Teddington Ted, and been abandoned on the motorway.

Sue, a schoolgirl when we first see her, looks after Willie with devotion. When we last see her, five years on, she has had three bastard children by Ted – Kojak, four, who has his head kicked in by his father; Columbo, one, who is incinerated with a blowlamp by his grandmother when he won't stop crying; and a third, nameless, baby who has survived a miscarriage in the lavatory pan.

Besides being Sue's common-law husband, Ted is a repressed homosexual who is reported as having sex on the landing with a young West Indian boy, and makes his last entrance in drag, though wearing the steel-capped boots he has killed Kojak with. Mum and Janet (Sue's schoolfriend who, after teaching Willie the joys of sex, makes a fortune on the streets) would have emasculated him with a flick-knife if Sue had not started her miscarriage at that moment.

There is also Aberdeen Angus, a fly-by-night lorry driver who is a former lover of Mum's but now prefers shop-window dummies.

As all these horrors are at their climax, Willie, who has disappeared between the acts, descends from Heaven in a golden wheelchair and takes possession of the new baby, while the flat is consumed by fire.

Now the odd thing is that, ghastly as all these matters are, and presented in appropriately disagreeable language, I found the play compassionate and even poetic, though Mr Brown's lack of economy in his second act, where too much outrage is piled together, blurs what ought to be an impressive culmination. Mr Brown displays these things as unemotionally as an alien scientist examining the life system of the earthman. He shows no more disgust than I suppose Dr Harker of Cambridge showed when he cut off a cockroach's legs and grafted its body on to another cockroach to see if there would be any change in its daily rhythms. Nothing that Mr Brown records is beyond belief but the concentration of so much horror in so small a household.

Why he should choose to deal with such things, not only in this play but in his other writing, is another matter. He will give no one any pleasure; the titters of laughter I heard sounded self-defensive to me. He offers no remedies. If, like Terence and the *News of the World*, he believes that nothing is alien to him, I only ask myself why he chooses only the bestial to show us.

The production by Max Stafford-Clark is outstandingly good. Miss de la Tour's iron-voiced Mum battles against visible hunger and fatigue to maintain a home; Tony Rohr, reciting *Finnegans Wake* in his sleep, and Carrie Lee-Baker play her two children; Alfred Molina and Robert Walker are the two men. Willie's jet-propelled heavenly wheelchair brings the only touch of glamour to Peter Hartwell's distressful sets.

Empress Eugénie

May Fair   *5 February 1979*

When the Empress Eugénie was ninety-three, she travelled by public transport, alone, to the Château de Compiègne. Once she had lived there, wife of the Emperor Napoleon III of France and holder of a dozen Spanish titles of her own. Now she joined the line of tourists, paid her admission fee and began to follow the guide with the others. In her old bedroom, she made an excuse and sat alone, recalling more prosperous days. This is where we see her.

The long solo by Margaret Rawlings is a remarkable feat simply as an achievement of memory by an actress who makes no secret of her age, which is seventy-two. But it is much more than that. It is a truly lovely performance, full of sudden changes of mood, subtly varied pace, truthful assumptions of regal dignity alternating with quick darts of salty humour.

Jason Lindsey's words and Miss Rawlings's interpretation of them suggest that Eugénie was not as good as she was likeable. Her extravagance was astonishing. Why shouldn't the ladies of her court bring ten to fifteen trunks for a two-day visit? They set the fashion, herself in the lead. Of course it was wasteful to burn three hundred thousand candles a night at the Tuileries, but oh, what fun to see the chandeliers burst into light!

She seems always to have been playing a game, and no doubt this accounts for her responsibility (which she admits) for the tragedy of Maximilian and Charlotte in Mexico. Perhaps even by encouraging the regal panache around her husband she helped to push him into war with Prussia in 1870 – but in this she admits nothing.

The second half of the evening deals mostly with the darker things in her life. She gives a breathtaking account of her escape from the mob-threatened Tuileries, through the Louvre, to take refuge with her dentist. She tells with great pathos of the death of her husband and her son. Yet she is always the same vigorous lady who remembered with the same excitement the opening of the Suez Canal and climbing Vesuvius at the age of eighty and making her first aeroplane flight on her eighty-fifth birthday.

The director of this most enjoyable perfomance is Marianne Mac-Naghten, and a delightful introduction, with all the Spanish titles in it, is given by Vernon Dobtcheff.

Bent

Royal Court   *4 May 1979*

Bent is really two plays about the same man, a young German called Max. We first meet him in Berlin in 1934, a homosexual playboy living with a young dancer, Rudy. After they have carelessly picked up one of Karl Ernst's SA boyfriends in a gay club, they have to go on the run, but ultimately they are arrested by the Gestapo. On their way to Dachau, the guards make Max help them to beat Rudy to death.

In the second act, Max is in the concentration camp, where he has cunningly arranged to be a Jew instead of a homosexual. Here, in spite of the ferociously restrictive regime, he starts an affectionate friendship with Horst, who is a registered homosexual. Horst develops tuberculosis, so Max, always a bit of a fixer, gets him some medicine by pleasuring an SS captain, pretending that he needs it for himself.

When the captain finds out that he has been conned, he kills Horst by means of a Gestapo game known as the 'hat trick', which finishes with the victim against the electric wire. Left alone with the body, Max changes coats with his dead comrade and, proudly revealed with the pink triangle of a homosexual on his breast, electrocutes himself.

Martin Sherman, the author of this play, clearly has a generous theme in his mind, that homosexuals are as capable of love and self-sacrifice as heterosexuals are. This theme has long ago become a cliché in the theatre, especially in the American theatre, and it is not illuminated by this series of stereotype situations peopled with stereo-type participants. The only novelty Mr Sherman offers us comes in the Dachau scenes of the second act, where Max and Horst, during the periodical three-minute breaks in their labour, show the depth of their mutual love by bringing one another to orgasm by talking about it.

Everything else in the play has been gathered up from existing documentation about Nazi Germany, in magazines, films and so on. As these predigested thoughts are presented in predigested dialogue, it is hard even for an actor as good as Ian McKellen, who plays Max, to persuade us that we are seeing human beings in action. Little Rudy is rather touchingly played along well-established lines by Jeff Rawle, and Tom Bell does what he can with Horst – little enough in a part where thought is so shallow and action so firmly circumscribed by prison routine. The other characters are really little cut-outs from films and books.

The director, Robert Chetwyn, has evidently given up hope of breathing life into the script except by cheating, so the three-minute intervals in the very slackly supervised labour camp last at least twice as long, and the fiercely monotonous work of moving rocks about is so idly performed that Max and Horst have lots of time to chat with one another, and are never checked for it. The SS isn't what it was.

Amadeus

Olivier   *5 November 1979*

Peter Schaffer has retold the story of how Antonio Salieri poisoned Mozart, with some romantic variations of his own. This is how it goes in his version :

Salieri is Court Composer to the Emperor Joseph II. In 1781, Mozart arrives in the capital, having sacked his Archbishop (or vice versa), and Salieri, overwhelmed by the sounds of the wind serenade K361, begins to see him as a possible rival. More than that, however : he had dedicated his talent to God, and when he sees that the talent of this vulgar little whippersnapper is greater than his own, he accuses God of ingratitude and dubs him *nemico eterno*, the eternal enemy.

A curious enemy, for Salieri triumphs both at court and in the opera house while Mozart, denied promotion by Salieri's machinations, dwindles into a squalid poverty that his concerts and his exiguous pay as *Kapellmeister* do little to alleviate. Salieri is not concerned to wreck his rival's prosperity so much as his talent. As Mozart struggles to finish his Requiem (and who was the mysterious stranger who commissioned that ?) Salieri haunts his lodgings in a black mask and leaves poisoned wine on his doorstep. Mozart goes to his pauper's funeral, and Salieri progresses to the guilt-ridden old age in which we find him as the play begins.

Despite a commanding performance by Paul Scofield as Salieri, on stage for virtually the whole three hours of the play, there is no life in Mr Shaffer's story. Salieri recounts it in the manner of an illustrated lecture. Discovered in old age in his apartments, crying 'Pieta, Mozart!' to the world, while the world, represented by two *venticelli*, little breezes that blow the rumours and look like a couple of Mad Hatters, comment on the tale Salieri is said to have told.

Salieri goes to his fortepiano to conjure up an audience (us) and, rejuvenated, recounts the story himself, occasionally concealing himself in a high-backed easy chair to allow episodes from Mozart's more intimate life to be presented while he remains unseen.

The decorations of Peter Hall's operatic production do little to invigorate this unimaginative piece. Mozart himself is shown as a macedoine of the qualities we know about – conceited, ambitious, frivolous, given to coprophilous fantasies. Simon Callow gives a bird-like performance of this ultra-lightweight figure, adding a high-pitched giggle that I can't accept. Was there no more to Mozart? It can be argued that this is only Mozart as Salieri saw him, but the point of the play is that Salieri recognised Mozart as a transcendent genius, and Mr Shaffer might surely have tried to work this side of him in somewhere.

Other characters are little more than scenery. As the Emperor, John Normington elegantly spreads his hands and proclaims, 'There it is!' whenever he makes a decision. Andrew Cruickshank as the Director of the Imperial Opera and Nicholas Selby as the Prefect of the Imperial Library, as well as Salieri himself, help him to make the decisions. Constanze Weber (Felicity Kendal) larks about with Mozart on the floor and says, 'Ta very much' to show how common she is. Philip Locke as Salieri's servant loyally brings him cream cakes at all hours, but can't stretch his loyalty so far as to go and haunt the desperate Mozart in his lodgings.

The production, as I have said, is decorative, and needs to be. John Bury's handsome set, radiant with the cultured elegance of the period, has a proscenium arch at the back and makes me think, not for the first time at the Olivier, that the play is better suited to the Lyttelton. Behind the proscenium, a line of Viennese citizens appears now and then to express approval, curiosity, alarm or some other public emotion, a happy extravagance only a big permanent company like this can afford.

Behind the decorations, both of the text and the production, I thought *Amadeus* as hollow as a strip-cartoon. Only once, when Mr Scofield gave his long speech about the ingratitude of God, did I feel that I was truly in the presence of masters.

Duet for One

Bush   *18 February 1980*

One of the two characters in this duet is confined to a wheelchair for most of the evening. The other confines himself to his own armchair, remaining silent a good deal of the time, even when speech seems to be urgently called for, and gazing absently at his shoes. The play is one of the most exciting to be seen in London at this moment.

Stephanie Abrahams, played by Frances de la Tour, has been urged by her husband to consult a psychiatrist. She is a world-famous violinist, and she has contracted multiple sclerosis. When we first see

her, she is gaily dressed and talks optimistically about what she will do
when she can no longer play, about taking pupils, about doing secretarial work for her husband, who composes atonal music.

Sometimes, she confesses, she feels 'a bit low', but the face she presents to Dr Feldman is confident and brave. Dr Feldman, cryptically
reticent, prescribes tablets for her depression.

In the following five scenes, Tom Kempinski charts the conflicts
between the patient and the doctor. The patient seems to grow steadily
worse. She sends her pupils away on the ground that they are useless
material. She relinquishes her intention of doing secretarial work. She
loses confidence in her husband's music, which before she had spoken
of with exaggerated praise. She exchanges her public charm for a
vulgar manner and boasts of a squalid sexual affair with a rag-and-
bone man.

In the final scene, there are hints that the psychiatrist's angry out-
burst at her helplessness – his only exhibition of feeling during the
evening – may have had some effect. She is a little tidier, a little more
polite. But she has only come to say that she will not come again.

'Shall we resume next week at the same time?' says Dr Feldman
conventionally as his patient leaves.

This is a wonderfully sensitive play, positive and optimistic. Miss de
la Tour's performance, which spans the whole range of emotion between bumptiousness and breakdown, is as good as anything of its
kind that I can remember, and confirms my opinion that she is one of
the very best actresses we have today. David de Kayser, projecting the
doctor's resolute humanity through a modicum of action, is remarkable too.

No one seriously interested in the theatre can afford not to see this
production. The excellent direction is by Roger Smith, and the evocative set that tells us so much about the psychiatrist through his choice
of surroundings, is the work of Caroline Beaver.

Doctor Faustus

Lyric Studio, Hammersmith   *26 February 1980*

Marlowe's *Faustus* is a difficult play combining a true philosophy
with a curiously naive idea of what can be done with power when
you have it. It is immensely exciting up to the arrival of Lucifer in

Faustus's chamber. The final scene is one of the most moving in all English drama. But in between, when Faustus's more elaborate requirements are met, in Rome, at the Emperor's court, and so on, the play can seem childish.

This excellent production under Christopher Fettes is set in a mood that integrates the serious concern with sin and damnation and the simplicity of the central scenes, and so the central scenes retain something of the serious character of the beginning and end. Yet Mr Fettes has introduced comic touches even in the most serious moments, and they work well; for instance, when Mephistopheles first appears (as 'a Devil') he wears a funny hat and is accompanied by the music of the Golden Calf song from Gounod's opera.

So later, when the Pope appears in the person of David Rappaport, an actor some three-and-a-half feet tall, the presence of a joke is not a new element. Helen and Alexander are more than mere sideshows; they are made to illustrate the thoughts of those that watch them, and when at the play's end the devils come, who should they be but Helen, Alexander and the rest.

In spite of the few resources available in this little theatre, I liked the production better than any I have seen before, even the Oxford production with Richard Burton and his then wife. It is set in a room furnished only with a long table with chairs and forms around it. There is an inner stage, covered with a transparent traverse, wherein other-worldly scenes may be disclosed.

The small, all-male cast conjure up the pictures by their admirable speaking of Marlowe's splendid poetry. They are helped by a variety of ingenious ideas. The good and evil angels (John Sommerville and Simon Cutter) are fellow-students at the table with Faustus, and when they speak, their voices seem like disembodied thoughts in his head. When the boy Robin (Mr Cutter again) tries his hand at magic, in a much cut scene, there is a sound of off-stage weeping. Mr Cutter also represents Helen of Troy, an idea that may sound unlikely, but in practice, with the imaginative use of drapery, works well.

The two main parts are splendidly played. James Aubrey is a romantic young Faustus, curly-haired and dark-bearded, and though at his heights he never shows quite the arrogance that Faustus's pranks suggest, he is fine in the early parts and superb in the marvellous last scene. Mephistopheles is played by Patrick Magee, his deep, vibrant voice emerging with gentle intransigence from the dignified figure of a grey-haired old friar.

The other parts are shared by Garry Cooper, Roger Frost, James

Griffin and those I have named already. Most of the time they all wear long black Wittenberg students' cloaks, but Faustus has modern clothes on underneath, and there are various suggestions that the play may be taking place as much in our time as in any other.

Only one thing displeased me in this notion. The recorded voices of the astronauts that sound over the magical final lines broke the spell. There, more than anywhere, our minds must concentrate on Faustus's fate, and potentially our own.

Nicholas Nickleby

Aldwych   *23 June 1980*

For its latest Wagnerian cycle, the Royal Shakespeare Company has gone to Charles Dickens, and come up with a two-part play lasting altogether nearly eight-and-a-half hours and containing 136 parts. It gives you two long evenings, or one long Saturday, of extreme pleasure; and as it is only scheduled to run six weeks, bookings for every civilised family should be made at once.

David Edgar's adaptation keeps amazingly near the original, even including some of the original prose lucubrations ('There is a dread disease which so prepares its victims, as it were, for death, which so refines it of its grosser aspect' and so on for fourteen lines) to serve as connecting passages. This they do effectively as they are orchestrated between the voices; but I was not so much convinced of the need to give characters little quotes in the third person to describe the expression on their own faces or the sound of their own voices when they are actually showing them to us.

Perhaps they are sops to avid Dickensians, but if they are, they are not needed, for Dickens's tale and Dickens's people are there in faithful detail. Only once do we leave the Master, when a performance by Vincent Crummles's company of *Romeo and Juliet*, with the many-talented Nicholas (Roger Rees) in the lead, is extended with a new happy ending – by Nahum Tate, perhaps? or John Barton? – and followed by a patriotic song in the manner of Charles Villiers Stanford sung by Mrs Crummles.

No call to recapitulate the plot, which everyone knows, or thinks he knows. The three most memorable episodes come in the first play.

Nicholas, having failed to find a job with Sir Matthew Pupker, is taken on by Squeers and sets off for Yorkshire, where he has his brief career as a pedagogue and begins his ambiguous relationship with Smike, once he has chastised the headmaster for his cruelty. Meanwhile his sister Kate (Susan Littler) goes to work for the Mantalinis (Thelma Whiteley and John McEnery, who addresses his wife somewhat uncanonically as 'my little *apfelstrudel*') and becomes exposed to Sir Mulberry Hawk (Bob Peck) and Lord Frederick Verisopht (Nicholas Gecks). How the idiotic Mrs Nickleby (Jane Downs) could have had such children, heaven only knows.

Mrs Nickleby exposes her daughter still further after she has become companion to Mrs Wititterly (Jane Dale); and by this time Nicholas and Smike are walking to Portsmouth for a theatrical career. The great 'bespeak' performance for Miss Snevellicci (Suzanne Bertish) brings the first half to an end.

The second half is perhaps less interesting, just as the second half of the book is, sorting out problems raised earlier and introducing a rather overdue love-interest for Nicholas. Dickens seems to have forced this in reluctantly at the end, being perhaps content to leave his hero with Smike (a sentiment echoed here by the directors, Trevor Nunn and John Caird, who at the final curtain have Nicholas pick up one of the runaway boys from the now dispersed Dotheboys Hall and carry him off to his new happy home life, from which Smike is the only missing factor).

Well, it gives us a pretty Madeline (Juliet Hammond-Hill); but even though she has five other parts she is given none of the chances of the less romantic ladies, like Miss Bertish, who is not only Snevellicci but also a ginger Fanny Squeers and Peg Sliderskew and a milliner, or Julie Peasgood, who is both Tilda Price and the Infant Phenomenon. Multiple casting is the rule rather than the exception; some of the boys at Squeers's academy are girls in breeches, and some of the milliners at the Mantalinis are boys in drag.

It is really astonishing to find on reference to the programme that what looks always like a crowded stage is peopled only with forty-four players altogether. You will want to know who is in the main parts besides those I've chronicled already. John Woodvine is the sinister Ralph Nickleby; Edward Petherbridge is Newman Noggs; Ben Kingsley is Squeers (among other people); David Threlfall is a very crippled Smike; Bob Peck, when he is not Sir Mulberry, is John Browdie; Graham Crowden is Crummles; the Cheeryble Brothers, grownup Tweedledum and Tweedledees, are David Lloyd Meredith and Hubert Reed. Had I but world enough and time, I would tell you what is specially good about each of them; instead, I can tell you only that they are all good and all genuinely Dickensian, though Mr Petherbridge's Noggs is not quite so run-down as I have always imagined him.

The direction, by two directors and an assistant, is tirelessly inventive, on a stage transformed from its usual aspect. A catwalk runs in a circle across the back of the stage and around the circle in the auditorium, and what the Japanese call a *hanamichi* cuts across the middle of the stalls. Scenes are played downstage on the bare stage, or on trucks that are brought on obliquely from either side of the upstage area. Lots of old railings and things flank the walkways to give an overall feeling of squalid nineteenth-century London.

The whole thing is a triumph. If this is the kind of thing the company invents to save money (as they say it is), may they long remain in financial peril.

The Romans in Britain

Olivier   *18 October 1980*

Each time I see a new play by Howard Brenton I feel a slight sense of reassurance. Could *The Churchill Play* have been quite as appalling as I thought? Why, yes – here is *Sore Throats* to confirm my judgment. But suppose *Sore Throats* was really a little better than it seemed to me? Well, there is nothing in *The Romans in Britain*, which opened on Thursday at the Olivier, to suggest any such thing. Its three hours are devoid of wit, beauty or drama, and the message it appears to offer us only surfaces in the closing scenes. Whatever weaknesses there may be in Mr Brenton's writing, inconsistency isn't one of them.

He begins *The Romans in Britain* in characteristic vein. Two ragged Irish peddlers slink timidly through the sturdy bare tree-trunks of Britain (north of the Thames) to speak to us from downstage. 'Where the fuck are we?' one of them asks in the argot of 54 BC. They are looking for the sea, but before they ever reach it they are overrun by a party of blond-haired naked Britons (*non Angli sed angeli*) who hang one of them upside-down from a tree and cut his throat.

The Britons in their turn are scared of the Romans, big metal men rumoured to be in the neighbourhood; and soon enough the Romans appear. 'Three wogs!' they cry, spotting the Britons. They quickly subdue them, and the leading Roman buggers one of his captives, who claims to be a priest. Julius Caesar himself comes with his staff and demonstrates his bent for authority. When they leave, their influence is well expressed: 'They have struck a spring in the ground under your feet. It will never dry.'

Nor indeed has it dried in the second act, which takes place simultaneously in AD 515 and the present day, when on the one hand we have the British fighting the Saxon invaders as the last vestiges of Roman colonisation fade away, and on the other a British officer in the SAS setting up an operation in which he appears to be offering to supply the Irish with Czech small arms, but is naturally shot by the Irish as soon as they find out who he is. This episode is written with such profound disregard for truth or probability that it can't possibly convey any message to anyone.

Colonisation is the theme, the conquest of indigenous people by newcomers, and the resultant effect on the peoples even when the conquerors have gone. There is a poetic coda. One of the slaves of a Roman matron who has just died of plague sits down and extemporises a tale about an imaginary king who never lived, a king with an ordinary, everyday name, like Arthur.

The action all takes place in forest or in field, set for us by Martin Johns. There is little chance for creditable acting, but Michael Bryant, in a few minutes only, gives a most memorable portrait of Julius Caesar. His staff historian is called Asinus, which I hope is not meant as a reflection on the *Commentaries*.

Stephen Moore plays the SAS officer, but the part is written with such abject ignorance of how such a man would behave that there is nothing he can do with it. The legend of the non-existent King Arthur is attractively told by John Normington, who earlier in the evening has been one of the Irish peddlers. There are some magnificent dogs – Irish wolfhounds, are they? – who behave impeccably.

The director is Michael Bogdanov.

A Chaste Maid in Cheapside

Theatrespace   *12 February 1981*

A Chast Mayd in Cheape-side is the way they spelt the title on the programme in some year between 1611 and 1615; they spelt the author's name Thomas Midelton. We know what they meant, for we've seen the play since then, both at the National and the Royal Court. There's no point in my telling the story point by point, but it's easy to say what it's about: it's about love and fornication.

Young Touchwood is in love with Moll, daughter of the goldsmith Yellowhammer, but she is plighted to marry the rich Sir Walter Whorehound. Sir Walter has a mistress, Mrs Allwit, with a complaisant husband. Sir Oliver Kix has been married seven years but has fathered no children, and Touchwood's brother claims to have a tonic that, in the right circumstances, will put this matter right. Take it from there.

The Cherub Company give the play a suitably uproarious performance on the dishcloth-size stage at the Theatrespace (which you will find in William IV Street, near the Strand). They play it straight through like real Jacobeans, allowing characters to ignore one another if business demands. We don't look for polished acting from the Cherubs, but what we get is pace, vigour, clarity and understanding.

The plot calls for thirty-six characters, but it is played here, under Andrew Visnevski's ingenious direction, by six boys and four girls. Upstage they have a small platform, and beyond this is a small frame carrying a traverse curtain split in the centre to form an entry. You can see the players changing their costumes (which, as you can imagine, they have to do quite often) at the back.

I found it immensely enjoyable. Vicky Ogden, who is not only Lady Kix but also a Welsh whore, speaks fluent Welsh; Yellowhammer's son (Anthony Wise), has just become a Bachelor at Cambridge and chats away with his Tutor in Latin, in a very un-Jacobean pronunciation. Young Touchwood (David Acton) plays the 'cello. There is delightful pseudo-17th century music by Peter Fincham.

Let no one feel that because this is an old play there is anything stuffy about it. It races along from one wanton situation to the next at a great lick. There was standing room only at the first night in this funny little cellar, but that's just how it ought to be. This is Jacobean pop.

CHAPTER SIX

Change Down

Conscience kept urging me that I must sooner or later make way for a younger person. I went to see the Managing Editor one day in the spring of 1980. He suggested I should begin to ease myself out the following year.

This I did rather pleasantly. If I were to be second string, while Michael Coveney, the current second string, moved up to my place, I wouldn't have to live in London any more. On 16 March I moved into a minute house in Cheltenham, which had always seemed to me a good place to live (and still does). On 19 March, before I had even sorted out my furniture, I flew to Louisville, Kentucky, for their annual festival of new American plays, as enjoyable a festival as there is. On 28 March I flew home. I was now second string.

I didn't have the same freedom to make my own choice of plays. On the other hand, I went to a lot of plays that I shouldn't otherwise have been able to see. In a lot of ways, life was much the same.

*

Translations

Hampstead Theatre   *14 May 1981*

The plot is simple and familiar. A foreigner comes into a tight-knit community and falls in love with a girl who is already promised elsewhere. Brian Friel hasn't even rounded it off; he leaves the story with an open ending. It's the evocation of the sight and the feeling of the time that makes *Translations* so wonderfully moving.

The community is gathered around a 'hedge-school' in a County

Donegal village in 1833. Hedge-schools were amateur ventures run by the Irish peasantry to atone for the total lack of education provided by the British government. Typically, they taught reading, writing, arithmetic, Latin and Greek; and the education was carried on not in English but in Irish. This particular school is run by old Hugh, himself a hedge-school graduate, whom they call 'Master'; Ian Bannen plays the Master with a battered topper on one side that makes him look as well as sound like W. C. Fields. He is helped by his son Manus (Stephen Rea), a cripple from birth. Classes are held in a barn, finely designed by Eileen Diss.

To them comes a little miscellany of students ranging from Sebastian Shaw as the almost neolithic Jimmy Jack, whose mind wanders among Greek, Roman and Irish gods, to little Sarah (Maire ni Ghrainne), who is barely able to speak at all. Their chatter is of the new National School, of the possibility of blight in the crops (not at that time an actual threat), and the antics of the English soldiers (which are).

It's an English soldier who tries to pierce the shield of the Irish community. George Yolland is a young officer attached to the Royal Engineers to record the local names and, with the help of a local assistant (Tony Doyle), turn them into something like English. George likes the Irish and they like him; but between them there is a great gulf fixed – neither can understand a word the other says.

Both the English and the Irish dialogue are spoken in English in the play, and Mr Friel has mingled them very ingeniously. When George goes with pretty Maire into the barn after a dance, the gulf shrinks visibly. Though George knows only a few Irish place-names and Maire a single sentence, learnt parrot-fashion, about the maypole in Norfolk, there comes a point where it matters no more and they kiss in the universal tongue. They are seen by little Sarah, and she goes at once to tell Manus, for Maire was to have married Manus when he got his job in the new National School.

So next day Manus packs his books and goes; and George is nowhere to be found. If he isn't found within forty-eight hours, says his commanding officer, all the livestock will be shot, everyone evicted and their buildings levelled to the ground. At this point, the play virtually ends.

I can't bring myself to talk about the rights and wrongs of Irish politics. Call the two parties Montagues and Capulets if it makes things easier. This is as tragic a play as we are likely to see for a long time, and the acting and production under Donald McWhinnie are faultless. Shaun Scott and Bernadette Shortt as George and Maire are a beautifully mismatched couple, and Stephen Rea's Manus, culture and ambition loyally confined, his lame leg keeping him from outside work, is a symbol of the people he lives with. Besides those I've mentioned, there is good playing from Anna Keaveney and Ron Flanagan.

The Witch of Edmonton

The Other Place, Stratford-upon-Avon   *8 August 1981*

Elizabeth Sawyer was hanged at Tyburn for witchcraft in April 1621, having made a full confession. This play, described on its first edition title-page as 'A known true story', appeared the following December. Many actual details from Mother Sawyer's confession were used, and her confession is combined with a conventional Jacobean romance about marital infidelity. The playhouse was clearly anxious to get the play on quickly, and employed three of its stable of writers on it. For what it's worth, it is thought that Dekker wrote the scenes about Mother Sawyer, with their social comments; Rowley wrote the comedy scenes for the clown Cuddy Banks; and Ford, perhaps with Dekker's assistance, the scenes of domestic infidelity.

This story runs along fairly normal lines. Frank Thorney secretly married his fell-servant Winnifrede in the first scene, and in the second scene is persuaded by his old and debt-plagued father to marry Susan Carter for a rich dowry. Discontented with the double life he tries to lead, he murders Susan and throws the blame on his former rival, Warbeck.

There are two minor plots. One concerns Cuddy Banks, who is after Susan's sister Catherine. The other is about the poor old woman Mother Sawyer, who is commonly thought to be a witch because she is ugly and bad-tempered; and it is she that brings the special interest to the play, for one day when she is sitting cursing, she is visited by a diabolical familiar in the shape of a dog.

The use of the devil in the play is subtle, and can't have been stuck on the Thorney-Carter plot as an afterthought. The dog, who can talk, explains that a devil is always available when someone is in the mood for it. 'Thou never art so distant from an evil spirit but that thy oaths, curses and blasphemies pull him to thine elbow.' Mother Sawyer is easy meat.

Later, when Frank is running away with Winnifrede and his second wife comes on the scene, the dog appears and brushes against him; it is at that point that Frank decides to solve his problems by murder. Cuddy also chats with the dog; but Cuddy is a decent man, free from wrong thoughts, and the dog can't influence him.

The excellent production under Barry Kyle reeks of evil. It is played against a farming background (designed by Chris Dyer), where there is little courtesy, though much kindness. From the moment the dog appears, bursting out of a sack as Mother Sawyer sits swearing, an atmosphere of uneasy tension builds up. Evil is abroad. The scene of Susan's murder, where the dog unexpectedly appears and surrounds the players with an invisible barrier before providing Frank with the weapon he needs, is breathtaking.

It would be easy to make the dog seem funny or silly, but as Miles Anderson plays him, blacked all over with a curly spaniel wig and a black harness incorporating a tail, he is a true menace, no less one for his enticing personality. Miriam Karlin plays the witch without any exaggerated witch-like characteristics, no doubt to emphasise how prejudice rather than bad works were the basis of her reputation. She makes a fine thing of her defiance of the accusing Justice, 'What are your painted things in princes' courts?'

Gerard Murphy's Frank begins as a proper young man forced into wrong by the bad influence of his elders. Once he has made contact with the dog, he turns evil, and he is evil until the scene of universal forgiveness in his cell at Tyburn (at the end of which, after they have all sung a hymn, the director gives the dog an uncanonical entry at Winnifrede's side.) Harriet Walter is Winnifrede, her rustic accent rather a trial, but otherwise a convincing victim – though she couldn't have had a real chance against Juliet Stevenson's tender Susan.

Anthony O'Donnell is a pleasant, humorous Cuddy Banks, and George Raistrick stands for all that is good about farmers except their treatment of witches. The near-lynch that follows the interval is as socially interesting as the scene with Cinna the Poet in *Julius Caesar*, where also a mob is ready for violence on no better ground than an unconfirmed rumour.

The Little Foxes

Victoria Palace   *12 March 1982*

Lillian Hellman's *The Little Foxes* was a good choice for Elizabeth Taylor's debut on the stage. It is an eventful, rather melodramatic piece of about the same brow-rating as *Dallas*. As Regina Giddens, the ambitious Southern lady who will stop at nothing to become rich enough to enter high society in Chicago, Miss Taylor has opportunities to show her talents for charm, for cunning, for anger, for power, without overstepping the limits of emotion further than her author has intended. But in this play she is flanked by other characters who are also given such chances. Oscar Hubbard and Ben Hubbard, her brothers, are both slightly larger than life in their capacity as small-town swindlers; her nephew Leo is a high-grade little waster, Horace her husband is always effectively on the edge of death (until he is over it).

Miss Taylor herself is bound to seem larger than life to the packed audiences waiting to see her, advance bookings having already passed the million-pounds mark; yet in *The Little Foxes* she need not overtop her colleagues. Indeed I'm prepared to say that the company is on the whole a well-matched team.

The story deals with the attempt of Oscar and Ben to cheat poor ailing Horace out of his Union Pacific bonds so that they can invest them in a scheme to build a cotton-mill on their cotton-plantation and make a fortune. There are as many unexpected reversals of fortune as Dame Agatha Christie could have dreamed up for them, each one revealing a fresh facet of Regina's nature. Miss Taylor plays her part with a kind of Southern whine, the vowels she wants to emphasise prolonged with a little upward or downward slur. All the speech, incidentally, is amplified; I heard perfectly from Row J of the stalls, but some people at the back reported difficulty.

Miss Taylor plays as many scenes as she can in profile, and very fine she looks in her 1901-fashion dresses by Florenz Klotz. She is admirably restrained until Horace (J. D. Cannon), whom she has repeatedly wished dead to his face, has a heart-attack in front of her and gives her a chance not to pass him his medicine. Surely, though, when he scrambles upstairs to get it he ought to collapse on the handsome staircase in Howard Bay's set, rather than go on out of sight round the corner? If he doesn't, daughter Alexandra's line, 'What was a man in a wheelchair doing on the staircase?' loses point: who besides Regina knew he was on the staircase?

Nicholas Coster and Robert Lansing as Oscar and Ben shout endlessly at each other or their children or their wives; you don't wonder that young Leo is anxious to get away from them to his woman in Mobile, stealing if necessary to help. William Youmans as Leo is wonderfully shifty; it's almost as if his makeup has been able to move his eyes closer together to give him the right look. Ann Talman keeps Alexandra very placid, even when she is firing her last charge of hatred against her mother Regina, who has lately fired a far stronger charge against her over the banisters of the staircase, one of Miss Taylor's better moments.

There are two good little performances by the black players Novella Nelson and Hugh L. Hurd as the family servants, and the evening's only other suggestion of gentlemanly behaviour comes from Humbert Allen Astredo as the Chicago businessman who is going to build the mill. He regards the Hubbards and the Giddenses as Southern aristocrats, and treats them so, though, as they are honest enough to tell him, the only Southern aristocrat among them is Oscar's ill-used wife Birdie (Sada Thompson), and she has no real function except to confess to her secret drinking.

The direction by Austin Pendleton contains some well-thought-out detail, but he is too prone to stationing characters lurking in doorways to create melodramatic effects.

CHAPTER SEVEN

Musicals

'There ought to be different critics for different sorts of plays,' Peter
Bridge said once at a meeting organised by the Critics' Circle. 'For
instance, B. A. Young ought not to be allowed to go to a musical.'

I can't imagine what it was that led him to such a sadistic decision.
My trouble is that I enjoy musicals so much that I keep saying they're
the best there ever was. I found myself in trouble when I went to see
the National Theatre's production of *Guys and Dolls*, because I had
said that *My Fair Lady* was the best musical there ever was so recently
that people would have remembered it. Without looking it up, it may
be said that I said the same thing about *Oklahoma!* I am quite un-
repentant. 'Do I contradict myself?' Whitman asked. 'Very well then
I contradict myself. (I am large, I contain multitudes.)' I do not feel
so multitudinous as Whitman, but if I feel on my arrival at Bracken
House that the performance I left a quarter of an hour before gave
me more pleasure than anything of its kind had ever done before, I
should like to convey that feeling to my readers so that they may have
the chance of experiencing the same kind of joy. Anyway, I don't say
that *every* musical is the best I have ever seen.

The criteria by which I judge whether a musical is the best I have
ever seen or not are these :

The songs should contain some genuine musical intrinsic interest
and not simply be tunes over rum-ti-tum tonic-and-dominant accom-
paniments. At least one of them, but preferably all of them, should
have tunes that you can remember next morning.

The lyrics ought to contain enough wit, either in the form of
jokes or word-play or both, to stand as comic verse when detached
from the notes.

The story should be reasonably interesting in itself, and the
dialogue should have at least a tinge of dramatic worth. The songs
should amplify or continue the dialogue, not simply interrupt it.

If such requirements are reasonably met, the production is no more than a bonus, as anyone will remember who saw *Pal Joey* at the Half Moon Theatre.

I once wrote that the story of a musical ought to be about love, but I'm not so sure about that. The story of *My Fair Lady* is only marginally about love, and *My Fair Lady* is the be . . . what am I saying?

*

Little Me

Cambridge *19 November 1964*

Some fair old liberties have been taken with the life of Belle Poitrine in its journey from page to stage. Her origins have been transferred from Venezuela, Ill., to Camden Town, which gives Eileen Gourlay a chance to graduate from poor cockney commonness to rich Californian commonness as she follows her fortune. It's perhaps even more of a wrench to find Belle fitted out with a One True Love to whom she remains mentally faithful while she runs through the gamut of her husbands. These include an aged miser, a French cabaret singer, an American doughboy and a German film director, with a near-miss on a central European prince, and they are all played by Bruce Forsyth.

This unexpected accession of constancy in a character whose basic principle of behaviour is simply to rise on stepping-stones of her dead husbands, doesn't matter very greatly, and it adds a backbone to what is a loosely episodic story. The casting of Mr Forsyth in seven different parts no doubt has the same object, but it has disadvantages to which I'll come in a minute.

The adaptation has been done by Neil Simon, and he has included Patrick Dennis, who wrote the original book, as a character in his play, trailing around behind Miss Poitrine with a tape recorder; so we may take it that Mr Dennis has no objection to the changes made. Certainly the spirit of the book is well preserved; the ludicrous episodes follow one another with the right heartless comedy, and in its superior Light Programme way I found the evening amusing with hardly a serious break.

I am bound to say that Bruce Forsyth is not my cup of tea in this kind of thing, though. There is a coarse music-hall quality about his work that stands in his way when he tries a bit of character acting, and all the line of lovers turn out only to be that ingratiating old compère of *Sunday Night at the Palladium* in fancy-dress. They even drop their respective accents in moments of stress and return to basic vaudevillese cockney.

Mr Forsyth has a fund of high spirits that sees him through, all the same, and there's no doubt that his clowning was greatly to the taste of the audience.

Belle Poitrine appears in two incarnations. Avril Angers plays her in maturity – an admirable but unrewarding performance, since she always appears in her little linking scenes on the tail of someone else's applause. She has a duet with her younger self, Eileen Gourlay, at the end, to show what a talented performer she really is when she gets the chance.

Miss Gourlay, whether as a London slum child, a famous film star or a *grande dame*, is always delightful, and as Miss Poitrine on the way up, she sings like a non-U angel. It's a shame that the songs aren't better worth singing. They are momentarily funny, and momentarily tuneful in a tonic-and-dominant kind of way, but they don't offer anything to remember afterwards, with the possible exception of a cynically romantic number in waltz-time called 'Real Live Girl'; and that goes on for much too long. So does the death-scene of Prince Chermy, surrounded by the tributes of his loyal subjects.

The chorus is wonderfully drilled by Bob Fosse, the costume and the numerous sets (which include a shipwreck) are charming and witty, and the direction of Arthur Lewis is quick and certain. Altogether it's a thoroughly enjoyable show, and I don't see how it can fail to run for a long time.

Hello, Dolly!

Drury Lane   *3 December 1965*

Hello, Dolly! is an unquestionable smasheroo, to my way of thinking, and oddly enough its success depends largely on the economy with which it's put together. Although based on a straight play (Thornton Wilder's *The Matchmaker*), it is primed with no more than the mini-

mum amount of plot to keep a musical in motion. There are only a
dozen songs. Although there are fifteen scenes, a lot of them are provided by the use of drop curtains and just enough props to furnish the
scene. There are no serried ranks of boys and girls in the chorus, only
a body of skilful dancers used in routines that never depend on quasi-
military drills but make points witty in themselves and apt to the
occasion.

This kind of economy lets us focus our attention more firmly than
usual on its separate constituents, and to stand up to that kind of
inspection the constituents must be extra good. So they mostly are.
True, the score doesn't provide a great run of hit tunes like we used
to hear in the old days (shall we ever have another *Oklahoma!*?). But
the songs are tuneful and the lyrics blandly amusing, and the one big
number, already so familiar to us at the hands of Louis Armstrong,
Frankie Vaughan and other improbable executants, is reserved for
the middle of the second act, where it makes its best effect. Music and
lyrics are both by Jerry Herman.

The sets are designed by Oliver Smith; and when I said they were
economical I didn't mean they were parsimonious. A truly splendid
locomotive steams out of the wings to bring a train into Yonkers
station, and the 14th Street parade that brings the first act to a rousing
conclusion is a riot. The scene changes are managed with exemplary
smoothness, seldom interrupting the onward flow of the action; and
where backdrops are employed they are particularly pleasant ones,
mostly showing street scenes in detailed photographic realism.

Gower Champion, the director, is his own choreographer. His
dances are as witty as they are good to look at, and he has an excellent
corps of dancers at his disposal. The waiters' gallop at the Harmonia
Restaurant is the funniest thing of its kind since the Shriners' dance in
Bye, Bye, Birdie.

In order to accommodate routines expansive beyond the ordinary,
the stage has been extended with a curved platform over the orchestra
pit. It doesn't allow much more than an occasional single-file procession, though some of the bolder dancers are allowed to jump from
the main stage across Alyn Ainsworth's orchestra on to the extension.
But it also allows Mary Martin to come forward and give us more of
her confidence than we can normally hope for at Drury Lane.

How good it is to see Miss Martin here again! When, in her character of Dolly Levi, she counted 'one, two, three' as she taught a stiff
young man to waltz, I thought of her twenty years ago at this same
theatre in something called *Pacific 1860.* Then the dance was the

polka : 'The fascinating rhythm of the one, two, three – One, two, three and a hop.' There's a polka in *Hello, Dolly!* too, but a much livelier affair. Even Miss Martin couldn't enliven *Pacific 1860* much; but she made up for that in *South Pacific*.

In some mysterious way the commanding figure of Dolly Levi, marriage-broker, dance-teacher, attorney-at-law and anything else you care to mention, seems about three inches taller than Ensign Nellie Forbush; but she hardly seems a year older. Miss Martin knows exactly how to speak the basic musicalese dialogue so that it never sounds dull or silly or pretentious, and that is a gift all too few actresses possess. And she sings with an effortless magnetism that made me want to rush out when the curtain fell and destroy every microphone in the land.

Dolly's matrimonial prey is Horace Vandergelder, a rich misanthropic dealer in hay and feed, who is played by Loring Smith in the great American tradition of middle-aged grouches that perhaps reached its acme in W. C. Fields. I found it an altogether delightful change to be asked to concern myself with the affairs of two mature people instead of the tiresome teenagers that take up so much of our time nowadays; and if anyone deserves to win Mary Martin on the stage, then it's Loring Smith, who can be romantic in spite of his balding head, his swelling stomach and his rasping voice.

The younger generation is taken care of in a sub-plot about two of Vandergelder's employees, breezily played by Garrett Lewis and Johnny Beecher. One of those, even, finally gets stuck with a widow, whom he woos with the second-best song of the evening, 'It only takes a moment.'

Curiously enough, it's the familiarity of all the characters and situations that made me feel so warm towards *Hello, Dolly!* Only the other day I was crabbing an American comedy for using prefabricated personages in prefabricated affairs; but a musical is a musical, and old ideas can be very welcome if they're used as a peg to hang new routines on. Too many recent musicals have run into plot-trouble through the use of unorthodox subjects for the libretto. Michael Stewart's adaptation of Mr Wilder's play shows how adequate a simple book can be when it is expertly trimmed.

Charlie Girl

Adelphi   *16 December 1965*

There's no secret about the fact that Miss Anna Neagle is a veteran of the musical comedy stage, and in any case she is the prettiest girl to be seen in *Charlie Girl*, whatever her age may be. But once it had been decided that she should make a come-back, there was surely no need to dream up a show for her that would have seemed old-fashioned in the 'thirties. *Charlie Girl*, which has a book by Hugh and Margaret Williams and Ray Cooney, based on an original story by Ross Taylor, looks far more like a veteran than Miss Neagle does, and a creaking veteran at that, which she most certainly isn't.

This story of Mr Taylor's is about a well-born girl who falls in love with a footman, or anyway some vague kind of servant. It's written *de haut en bas;* we are supposed to identify with the newly poor aristocracy who suffer agonies as they shepherd inquisitive crowds round their stately homes, and laugh indulgently at the comical antics of the lower classes. We are also expected to laugh at American millionaires marrying into Debrett, at the idea of anyone enjoying motor-bike scrambles, at people being hit over the head with framed pictures, and (rather unexpectedly) at girls taking off their dresses in the middle of a deb dance.

Well, I couldn't laugh at any of this, but after all, musicals are commonly expected to have silly plots, though no one could expect them to have one quite so full of glaring loose ends as this. So how about the music and the dances?

The bad old traditions of the 'thirties raise their ugly heads again. The songs, of which there are, as usual, too many are simply grafted on to the story without any real cues. They are not very catchy songs, by and large, and the words, when I could hear them, struck me as below the average, though there seemed to be a funny patter song for Joe Brown about fish and chips. It came as something of a relief, for Mr Brown (the comic cockney servant) appeared lost without his guitar and his Bruvvers, and this gave him a chance to do the kind of thing he knows how to do. He did it quite nicely. As for the dance routines, they were even more inappropriate than the songs, and strikingly free of anything in the way of inspiration. Only David Toguri, a lithe and amusing Japanese dancer, ever brought any inspiration into this department; the dance he does with Miss Neagle in the second act, though perhaps more blatantly shoved in than any-thing else in the show, is a charmer.

One thing that would never have done for the 'thirties is the pusilanimous dependence made by almost everyone in the cast on electrical amplification. From my seat in the dress circle all the voices except that of Hy Hazell, who plays an American millionairess, came to me as thin metallic ghosts through the loudspeakers. In the second half I moved down to the stalls, and there things were a little better. All the same, when I think of the intimacy forged between herself and her audience by Mary Martin in a theatre far bigger than the Adelphi, and compare it with the remote non-communication of the stars of *Charlie Girl*, I can only think that the director of the latter show (Wallace Douglas) has been too easily satisfied.

As a matter of fact almost everything about the production seemed to be obstinately second-class. When the curtain went up on the visitors to Hadwell Hall and they all came down to the front of the stage to sing their first chorus I knew we were in for an evening of cliché direction, and I wasn't wrong. Whenever anyone has a solo number the lights go down and he, or she, sings it bathed in a spot; song over, the lights come up again. There are blackouts at the end of scenes that seem almost accidental, so ill-prepared they are in the dialogue. As for that bit where the girls take their dresses off, it reaches a pitch of vulgarity I was unprepared for.

The reason why they take their dresses off is this : Lady Charlotte, or Charlie (Christine Holmes, who hits a top E in 'Like Love') is so poor she's had to hire a dress for the party. The hirer comes to collect it before the party ends. Joe, the comic servant, who has just won £367,000 on the Pools and has a pocket full of fivers, calmly insists on her giving it up, though he is head over heels in love with her. This kind of slipshod carelessness is characteristic of the entire show.

Funny Girl

Prince of Wales   *14 April 1966*

Barbra Streisand, to begin with.

The legend that preceded her was so overwhelming that it hardly seemed possible that any ordinary mortal could live up to it. Could she really be as good as all that? There were the records (the music of *Funny Girl* has been in all sophisticated households for quite a time now); but you can do all sorts of things in the recording studio. Was she as funny as they said, though? As kooky? As fascinating?

Well, as far as I am concerned the legend can only have erred on the side of conservatism. Miss Streisand is a miracle. She isn't pretty, she isn't even *jolie laide*. The shortcomings in her looks are all frankly summarised in one of the songs she sings, and she accepts them cheerfully and turns them into virtues with a wave of her hand. She has skinny legs, a tubular figure, a 'nose with deviations'; and she is enchanting.

Energy spurts out of every inch of her like electric sparks. She is hardly ever still, but she never makes a conventional movement; every gesture is new and original and unexpected. She can be limitlessly comic in a comic song, deeply sentimental in a sentimental song, poignantly sad in a sad song. How glad I am that I never saw her until now; to have all this talent unleashed on one at the very moment that one has been brought to the highest pitch of expectation is something to remember all one's life.

However, *Funny Girl* isn't by any means only a vehicle for Miss Streisand. It has a plot based on the early life and unsuccessful marriage of the American comedienne Fanny Brice (the character is given her real name), and as Fanny Brice appeared in many of Florenz Ziegfeld's spectacular shows this gives an opportunity to provide Ziegfeld-type numbers for Miss Streisand – a 'glorification of the American bride', for instance, in which she appears amid the orange-blossom sentiment about seven months pregnant, and a wonderfully embarrassing number from the 1917 Follies in which the chorus are dressed as Doughboys.

The book, by Isobel Lennart, is wittier and better-written than any I can remember since *Guys and Dolls*, and the lyrics, that stumbling-block over which so many musicals have stumbled lately, are very expertly written by Bob Merrill, who can fit Jule Styne's gay and tuneful music with something almost worthy of the name of light verse.

The story is told in a succession of short scenes that, in the current fashion, are played against small sets that can quickly be changed in full view of the house while the action continues. Fanny at the start is the gauche little daughter of the keeper of a saloon on Henry Street, on the Lower East Side of New York. The first part we see her in is as a dancer in a second-class vaudeville show (watch her counting the beats with her fingers), and it is while she is playing here that she meets rich gambler Nicky Arnstein. Her rise in the theatre and Nicky's increasing fortune are simultaneous but unconnected until suddenly, on Baltimore railway station, she decides to leave the Ziegfeld company and get married.

Nicky's deviation into dishonesty and consequent imprisonment, and the resulting collapse of their marraige, fill the second half of the show; after such a feast of comedy in the first half the more serious atmosphere after the intermission casts a tiny shadow over the proceedings, but they enable Miss Streisand to show what she can do in more serious vein, and she gets her best song, 'The Music that Makes Me Dance', at the saddest point of the story. This and the already best-selling 'People' in the first half mark Miss Streisand's highest point as a singer; they were rightly received with roars of acclamation.

A somewhat unexpected piece of casting puts Michael Craig in the part of Nicky. He has a musical, if rather small voice (I need hardly say that most of the sound throughout the evening came to me through a battery of loudspeakers), but hardly seems as yet sufficiently romantic. If he can let himself go and add the touch of vulgarity that this part requires, I think he will fill the bill more completely.

There are two delightful comedy performances by Kay Medford as Fanny's poker-playing mother and Stella Moray as her friend, Mrs Strakosh, and an energetic display by Lee Allen as Fanny's childhood friend and helper, Eddie Ryan, who progresses to the post of dance director to Ziegfeld. In the vaudeville show we visit at the beginning Eddie's act which starts with him singing 'Mon coeur s'ouvre à ta voix' while standing on his head on a tub but goes on to a very fine display of tap-dancing.

All the dancing in the show is good and exciting, and it is not surprising to find Jerome Robbins's name on the programme as the 'supervisor' of the New York production. This production is directed by Lawrence Kasha, and the designer of the ingenious sets is Robert Randolph. A word too for Irene Sharaff, who has provided Miss Streisand with a set of costumes that make a perfect match for her off-beat personality.

Fiddler on the Roof

Her Majesty's   *17 February 1967*

There is literally a fiddler on the roof when the curtain goes up on Boris Aronson's first set – a half-symbolic village musician squatting on the raggedy tiles of Tevye's cottage in Anatevka and playing a saucy little tune. We're all fiddlers on the roof here really, Tevye explains, keeping our balance by optimism and good-nature and above all our faith in the old traditions of the Jewish people.

Tevye is the milkman, and he is also the village philosopher, friends with everyone, even the Constable, the instrument of Tsarist oppression. Tevye is also Topol, the Israeli actor making his first appearance on the English stage in this production. He is a thousand times welcome, a comedian with restless friendly eyes peering out of the stubble of his beard and restless hands always ready to help him to argue a point with God when he feels he has not quite had a square deal. He is one of those people that establish an instant atmosphere of warmth and companionability.

The story of *Fiddler on the Roof* is mostly concerned with the marriage of Tevye's daughters. The eldest, Tzeitel (Rosemary Nicols), is first pledged to Lazar Wolf, the butcher, but later allowed to marry the man she loves, little Motel the tailor. Motel is played by Jonathan Lynn, who still has too much of Cambridge left in his voice, but who radiates a pleasant personality and sings a charming song called 'Miracle of Miracles' most attractively.

The second daughter is Hodel (Linda Gardner), and she marries Perchik, the radical student, who gets arrested and sent to Siberia, taking her with him. Sandor Eles gives Perchik a nice strong performance. Chava, the third daughter (Caryl Little), marries a goy, Fyedka, and so becomes dead to the Jewish community, this being one of the traditions they are so immutably devoted to; but at the end, when all the Jews are moved out of Anatevka by a Tsarist ukase (the date is 1905) she is recognised for just as long as it takes to say good-bye.

This persecution of the Jews is the only other theme present in the play, and it is used to give it an unusual downbeat finish, with the exiles trudging round and round the revolve, bent beneath the weight of their possessions, until no one is left but the fiddler, playing his little tune to the deserted scene but ending it on a new, anguished cadence with the second and third of the scale unexpectedly flattened.

It is a daring way to finish a musical, especially one so full of high spirits as this; but it didn't at all diminish the euphoria with which I emerged into the Haymarket.

The fact is that this is a very Jewish play in plot and character and atmosphere, and an ending like this is entirely appropriate. Jewish stories almost always seem to contain a large helping of persecution; it is as much part of their artistic heritage as Merrie England is of ours, and it doesn't seem out of place in what is by and large a happy show.

The show is drenched, too, in Jewish schmaltz, perhaps the most endearing, certainly the most universal, kind of schmaltz. We fall up to our necks in sentimentality, and love it. We love it partly because it is a good, honest kind of sentimentality presented by its practitioners with pride; and partly, on this occasion, because it is so very expertly distilled.

What a pleasure it is, and what a change, to go to a musical where every department seems to be functioning exactly as it was meant to. The music by Jerry Bock, strongly tinged with Jewish and Russian influences, is tuneful and apt, and the kind of music, I believe, that one will like better the more one hears it. The lyrics by Sheldon Harnick are so well attuned to Joseph Stein's book – archetypal Yiddisher comedy – that they might have been by the same hand, and the songs never seem to interrupt the flow of the action.

As for Jerome Robbins's choreography, it is matchless. Mr Robbins is director as well as choreographer, and he gives us a series of lovely stage pictures and vivid and graceful action. Much credit here to Boris Aronson for the sets, Patricia Zipprodt for the costumes and Richard Pilbrow for the lighting.

Topol's performance stands out above any other; it is very much a one-part play. Miriam Karlin works hard as his wife, Golde; but in a community where, we are repeatedly told, the duty of a woman is simply to obey a man, it is hardly surprising that the women's parts are on the whole uninteresting.

Miss Karlin gives us her familiar tigerish domesticity, and her daughters are all charming, if a little too reminiscent, vocally and facially, of Kensington rather than Kiev.

However, I certainly don't feel inclined to pick holes in a show like this. It is the most enjoyable and heart-warming musical I've seen for ages, and I hope it stays with us for a long time.

Sweet Charity

Prince of Wales   *12 October 1967*

Let's get the credits over first with a whacking great alpha plus to everyone concerned : Bob Fosse, who had the idea of adapting Fellini's film play and did the staging and choreography; Neil Simon, for a book that actually has wit on its own and adds a positive charm between the musical numbers; Cy Coleman for tuneful music and Dorothy Fields for lyrics that have wit and a smooth flow and never do violence to the English language; Irene Sharaff for the pretty costumes and Robert Randolph for spare, strong sets with a sense of humour; not forgetting Bernard Delfont and Harold Fielding for presenting this bundle of charm to us.

Sweet Charity, in spite of its sardonic non-ending, which really works round to the beginning again, leaves you with a heart full of the joy of living. The story is a simple one, exactly the right weight as it happens for a musical. Charity Hope Valentine (Juliet Prowse) is a taxi-dancer, available for $6.50 per half-hour to any lonely male who comes into the Fan-Dango Ballroom. As one of her colleagues tells her, she runs her heart like a hotel; she has guys checking in and out all the time.

When we first meet her, her current guy has just stolen her handbag and pushed her into a pond in Central Park; but her insatiable zest for romance lands her almost at once into the apartment of an ageing film lover, though circumstances decree that she will have to spend the night in a closet while the lover passes a night of reconciliation with a quarrelsome mistress.

In the 92nd Street YMCA she gets stuck in a lift with a nice, shy, but neurotic, young man (Rod McLennan); they fall in love, there are the usual kind of obstacles to be overcome. Neither Charlie, who pushed her into the pond, nor Vittorio, who pushed her into the cupboard, ever turns up again; there is simply the question of her past in the ballroom between them, and since it is not surmounted in quite the expected way I shall not reveal how it affects their final happiness.

The story, in fact, is what the story ought to be in a musical, a peg to hang the music, the dancing and the décor on, only this time it happens also to be told with an acid sophistication that it gives it an intrinsic interest of its own.

There's nothing very special about the music. The first half has one good number, 'If my friends could see me now', and one very good number, 'There's gotta be something better than this'. The second half contains a magnificent production number, 'Rhythm of Life Church', a sardonic commentary on the religious aspirations of the San Francisco hippy cults, which is put over with rare energy and precision by the excellent chorus, but on the whole it tails off rather. On the other hand, the music is never dull, and it always fits neatly into the production.

And it's all so well performed. I haven't seen so slick and polished a show for a long time. Although Juliet Prowse is the only star name in the cast, the whole company sings, dances and speaks excellently. Josephine Blake and Paula Kelly head a tough bunch of dancers with a kind of gritty attraction; they combine with Miss Prowse in a wonderfully pretty dance in 'There's gotta be something' – simple pastel-coloured dresses swirling against a plain red-lit backdrop. Mr McLennan has an attractive and reasonably strong baritone voice and a nice line in boyish charm.

As for Miss Prowse, she checked into my heart in the first minute and is likely to stay there for as long as *Sweet Charity* remains at the Prince of Wales, which I hope will be a very long time. She is small and rather cylindrical under her little black mini-dress. An untidy crop of ginger hair tops a face with vast eyes, a short nose, and a wide mouth that readily turns up to become a comic mask or down to represent a tragic one. She hurls herself into dance routines like a mad ballerina and (with the help of the inevitable microphones) sings like a pop angel.

She and all the company gave me an evening of sheer enjoyment such as I haven't had for some time.

Hair

Shaftesbury Theatre   *28 September 1968*

Outwardly, *Hair* at the Shaftesbury Theatre, is just a rock show of the kind we used to see on television on Saturday evenings. It is more lively than anything that even Jack Good produced at his best, but what really distinguishes it from other rock shows is that this one has a point of view.

Before discussing the point of view it's best to describe the show. It has virtually no story and very little dialogue, just enough to link the succession of songs and dances and put them in focus. A couple of girls are about to have babies, neither with the father they'd have liked; the boys are all in danger of the draft, and some burn their draft cards and some turn up in GI uniform at the end. But the principal material of the show is the music and the movement – and of course the point of view.

Anyone who has seen a show directed by Tom O'Horgan before will have some idea of what goes on on the stage. The boys and girls, dressed, when they are dressed at all, in the conventional hippy dress as familiar now in the King's Road as it is in Greenwich Village, are kept ceaselessly, restlessly on the move. And when I say this goes on on the stage, I should add that it also overflows all over the theatre. The Shaftesbury is not an ideal theatre for this kind of thing, but there seemed constantly to be some young thing trotting about somewhere in the house. Sometimes they shower the audience with leaflets; one character takes his jeans off and throws them to someone in the stalls to mind for him. Audience participation is intense; and last night's audience rose to it creditably.

The songs are based musically on the usual pop formulae, with harmonies that reveal their origin in the neck of a guitar, but the lyrics arc less conventional. It's not always easy to hear the words, as a matter of fact, but you can hear enough to know that moon, spoon and June are not likely to be the kind of rhyme you're going to encounter. The first line of one song runs 'Sodomy, fellatio, cunnilingus, pederasty'; the lyric of another (most tenderly performed by Vince Edward and Leighton Robinson) consists of Hamlet's soliloquy, 'What a piece of work is man'.

This comes at the end of a long passage in the second half in which the 'tribe', having come to what one of them describes as turny-onny time, have a marijuana dream culminating in a vision of the Vietnam war; the comment is piercingly apt.

Even more lively and imaginative than the songs is the dance movement, in which Mr O'Horgan has had choreographic help from David Toguri. It is strikingly imaginative. Sometimes it consists of simple, joyful communal dancing; sometimes the characters are grouped into patterns suggesting, though not literally representing, action. Fascinating use is made of big sheets of fabric; people climb under them, turn them into a shelter, batter them in search of freedom. And, as everyone must know by now, at one moment the tribe, who have been lying on the floor out of the lights, suddenly rise to their feet as naked as jaybirds. The effect, which arises logically from what has gone before, is of a primal innocence that flatters the outlook of any hippies I've encountered.

The white members of an integrated cast are almost all British, though they assume their transatlantic nationality with conviction. The coloured members are, of course, mostly West Indian. I felt during the first half of the evening that there was a certain self-consciousness, a lack of spontaneity about the company; and with a show like this, lack of spontaneity could be fatal. By the time the interval was over it was evident that the audience, with the exception of a vocal few in the gallery, were very much with them, and spontaneity was achieved, to the enormous improvement of the performances.

It's not easy to pick out individual work for special praise; this is teamwork of the kind we constantly read about but seldom encounter. But Paul Nicholas is an invigorating Claude, the boy who (though he claims to come from Manchester, England) is the first to get a draft card; Oliver Tobias is strong as Berger, the one that throws his pants into the stalls; there are three smashing girls – Linda Kendrick, Annabel Leventon and Liz White (whose singing of a sentimental song, 'Frank Mills', is outstanding). But one's standards, when judging from the pop-music outlook, must be modified. No one tries to do more than belt their naked emotions over the footlights.

Sticking out uncomfortably all the time is this point of view, an outlook no one over thirty is very much accustomed to. Here we have the permissive generation, and they see nothing wrong with smoking pot or even taking 'acid', with promiscuous sex, with dirty language, with disobeying the laws of the land when the laws seem not to make sense. The only authority they have for believing that these things are wrong is the word of an unsympathetic generation.

On the other hand, they are extremely unpermissive about some other things which their elders take in their stride. They see no virtue in serving in an army, to kill foreigners with whom they have no quarrel. They do not notice any difference between the black, white, yellow or red races. At the end of the evening, after we have seen some of them turn into soldiers, the company comes down to the front of the stage and sings a song called 'Let the sun shine in'. It is not hard, after the conditioning one has had all the evening, to see that their point of view, by and large, makes at least as much sense as, say, President Johnson's.

The audience was clearly in two minds about it. There was some

booing from the gallery, but it was swamped by the cheers from elsewhere; and within a few minutes of the end of the last song members
of the audience were being hauled up on to the stage to join the
company in a general paean of rejoicing. I am only sorry that the
need to write this notice prevented me from joining them; *Hair* seems
to me not only a wildly enjoyable evening but a thoroughly moral one.

The responsible moralists are Gerome Ragni and James Rado, who
wrote the book and lyrics; Galt MacDermot, who composed the
music; Julie Arenal, dance director; and Jules Fisher, responsible for
the prodigies of the lighting.

Godspell

Round House   *18 November 1971*

The Godspell according to St Matthew, to be exact, the King James
version basically, but paraphrased most of the time into simple
language to make it easier for today's young people to understand.
There's no question of acting out the Bible story realistically; only
Jesus is personified consistently, and even in this case the identification
is kept so delicate that the character is as much a symbol as a person.
He is played by David Essex, a likeable, roundfaced young Londoner
who gives himself a faint suggestion of a clown's make-up. It's not a
bad way to present Jesus to modern young children, and to suggest
miracles by the use of simple conjuring tricks is a pretty idea.

All the same, this isn't a conventional Jesus, a fact I attribute to
the Jewish influence in the writing of Stephen Schwartz and John-
Michael Tebelak. Jesus's words at the Last Supper are spoken in
Hebrew, for instance, and there's no mention of the Resurrection.
Instead, when Jesus has been taken down from the Cross and borne
away in triumph by the crowd, there is a dreadfully weak finale sung
to the words 'Long Live God!'

Most of the songs are rather nice, though. Tuneful and adequately
sung, they puncture the series of little playlets through which the
Gospel is presented, the sort of thing that children might extemporise
at Sunday school. I found it rather heart-warming and happy.

Anyone sold on what I have written so far had better stop reading
here, however for the rest of this notice will treat the production less

kindly. Indeed, there hardly seems to have been any production; they all (except David Essex and Jeremy Irons, who progresses from John the Baptist to Judas Iscariot through a dozen incarnations) seem to have been let do what they please. Adult actors are seldom attractive playing children especially when, as in this case, their material is supposed to have been made up by children too. No doubt it's very hard for them; but there's no need for the Godspell company to rush at it like bulls, exaggerate everything wildly, drown every action with extraneous business, put on endless funny voices and accents and generally go on as if the whole thing had been made up during rehearsal.

What's needed is a strong director to sift the good from the bad and build a production worthy of the subject. The Gospel according to St Matthew is a cast-iron script, and last night it produced laughs and cheers and weeping in plenty. But the children I saw at Sheffield last week could have performed as well as this company now does. Several of them I know to be young players of talent and personality, and it's sad to see their qualities so little exploited.

Jesus Christ Superstar

Palace   *10 August 1972*

Librettist Tim Rice, the one that doesn't get written about, has clearly read his Gospels and thought about them. His book, which covers the same ground as a classic Passion, is fresh and intelligent. He gives Judas, who is brought further into the foreground than usual, a valid motive for his betrayal of Christ; he sincerely believed that the mission had gone too far and should be checked before it caused trouble. He hits on some singularly appropriate ways of rephrasing familiar lines. 'For all you care,' says Jesus at the Last Supper, 'this wine could be my blood.' At the start of the evening I was noting down the horrible vulgarisms – 'Messiah' rhyming with 'fire', 'Sour' as a grinding dissyllable. Later I found better things to write about.

The score by Andrew Lloyd Webber goes a long way beyond conventional rock music. Familiar rock rhythms lie behind many of the numbers, but there are constant ingenious changes of pace. Five in a bar and seven in a bar keep us on our toes. I found interesting touches in the orchestration; a six-piece rock group sits on stage, complete with electric piano and synthesiser, and a more conventional band in the pit. Amplification is of course excessive, but some happy sounds emerge. The melodies are fairly closely confined to conventional rock clichés of thought, and this has the disadvantage that they cannot offer much characterisation in the various parts; but at least they are tunes that dig themselves into the memory and raise the spirits.

The problem of staging what is virtually no more than an oratorio in adeptly expanded popular style must have been hard, and it cannot be said that Jim Sharman has altogether solved it. He has rightly avoided much in the way of acting; apart from anything else, everyone is handicapped by the need to cling to a hand microphone. (Is there *no* way of overcoming this? Can't efficient throat mikes be developed?) So what we have is not much more than a very lively concert performance of this lively score. There is a permanent set; most of the movement – I hesitate to call it action – takes place on a small raked floor between two wings that house the group and provide perches for the chorus, who also use a gallery across the back of the central area.

On this set the principals come and go with no more than an occasional effort to suggest more than an old fashioned Bible picture. The chorus routines I found uninspired; the chorus is more effective when employed purely vocally, as in the horrifying screams of 'Crucify him!' Mr Rice has used the chorus well, emphasising the instant change of mob behaviour as Shakespeare did in *Julius Caesar*. There are some moving moments to see; the chorus of angels, for example. There are some rather brash ones, and the costumes by Gabriella Falk are undistinguished. There is one astonishing move into music-hall comedy where Herod, a degenerate playboy, sings an amusing point number :

> Prove to me that you're divine,
> Change my water into wine.

It may not be canonical, but it's remarkably effective, and Paul Jabara does it splendidly.

Paul Nicholas presents a dignified figure as Jesus, though the interpretation is unusual – frequently short-tempered, more at home chasing the capitalists out of the temple (an episode that won a cheer from the gods) than blessing Mary for her gift-wrapped jar of ointment of spikenard. His music has a tessitura of two octaves or so, and he sounds a little hoarse. Judas gets a performance of serpentine menace from Stephen Tate, very good indeed; he not only overcomes the handicap of the microphone but sometimes turns it to positive advantage with his handling of it. There are nice appearances by Dana Gillespie as Mary, Richard Barnes as Peter, George Harris, richly baritone, as Caiaphas.

There are faults I haven't mentioned, and won't. To my mind they are amply outweighed by the undeniable devotion and excitement that glow from this remarkable opera.

Billy

Drury Lane   *2 May 1974*

In Billy Fisher, the by now almost legendary Yorkshire boy who re-treats from every personal crisis into fantasy and lics, Michael Craw-ford has found a part that not only suits him down to the ground but enables him to display the full range of a talent never before more than partly unveiled to London audiences. I've been hoping for this to happen for about a decade, since (to be specific) he appeared in a good but unsuccessful comedy called *Travelling Light*. He lately illuminated a wretched part in a farce with acting of depth and sympathy; in an uninspired television comedy series he gave weekly displays of truly rounded characterisation.

In *Billy*, the newest version of Waterhouse and Hall's *Billy Liar*, he not only plumbs the depths of the fascinating undertaker's clerk with understanding, but he whisks at the drop of a circumstance into a series of invented personalities – president of a nation, scion of a rich family, successful pop singer, whatever comes to mind – that all retain a touch of the basic quality of the simple Yorkshire boy. Mr Crawford acts with every inch of his frame, with his face, with his arms (even when one of them is in plaster, as unhappily now), his wrists, his legs. Moreover, though his voice is small, he can put feeling into John Barry and Don Black's songs; and he can dance any kind of routine from small-town dance-hall to Warner Brothers musical.

I have complained before that British musicals tend too often to be founded on stories that are already too well known and well loved in another form, and it cannot be denied that Dick Clement and Ian La Frenais have added little to the *Billy Liar* that we know. Nor, for that matter, have the song writers; there is a rinky-tink quality about Mr Barry's tunes that is unusual for him. I suspect it is a deliberate attempt to give them a simple small-town quality to match the world of the simple small-town Fisher family. One of them at any rate – 'I missed the last rainbow' – is pretty enough to remember, and the others are cheerful and energetic, but I need something of Rogers-and-Hart quality to reconcile me to the interruption of a familiar story.

As a matter of fact there isn't much story. There is a thread of plot about Billy's engagements with three rival girls, virginal Barbara (Gay Soper of the charming voice), anti-virginal Rita (Elaine Page of the vigorous attack) and Liz (Diana Quick) who is his soul-mate and almost persuades him actually to live one of his fantasies in reality. But most of the evening consists of the realisation of these fantasies; and this is where Patrick Garland, the director, and Ralph Koltai, the designer, have added a quality that keeps the pulse beating solidly, or better than solidly, all evening.

Fundamentally this is an anti-glamorous production. It doesn't rely on elaborate colourful sets or tremendous routines. In fact for part of the evening there's little to be seen but dark grey walls and mock-concrete balconies and staircases. But Mr Koltai has a store of electrical apparatus concealed in the sets, and the stark basics can blossom into a suburban house or a dance hall or a football ground at the touch of a switch with silently creeping scenery.

In the house we encounter Avis Bunnage and Bryan Pringle and Betty Turner as Billy's family. Truth to tell, they have little to do but adumbrate his background, though they do it very nicely. But in the football ground or the town centre or the dance-hall we have Onna White's fascinating and unusual dance routines, which rely less on the mechanical accuracy of old-fashioned chorus-line than on the evocation of social surroundings. That they can do this without ever seeming serious, remaining constantly vigorous and amusing, is Miss White's special merit.

Through it all goes Mr Crawford, the frail, skinny, foolish hub of this enchanting joy wheel. I keep moaning that managements won't promote new candidates to star office. Well, Mr Crawford's ability has now been justly recognised; he has been cast as a star and treated as a star, and all we must fear now is the risk of his being permanently type-cast as a sub-man. Touchstone would be nice in a couple of years, when he can leave *Billy*; but Hamlet might be interesting, too.

162

A Little Night Music

Adelphi   *16 April 1975*

A Little Night Music is exactly the kind of musical I like, and a superb example of it. It is about love, the only proper subject for musicals, but it takes an adult view of love, which consists largely of infidelity and delusion. The songs by Stephen Sondheim are outstanding; the musical score is the most cultivated since *West Side Story*, and the lyrics are witty and tender and full of delicious internal rhymes. The story, by Hugh Wheeler, out of Ingmar Bergman's *Smiles of a Summer Night*, has a genuinely dramatic quality and provides opportunities for solid characterisation as well as romantic singing. And in this production the singing is so discreetly amplified that it really sounds like singing.

The story, which for once deserves attention, encompasses three generations. At the centre point is Desirée Armfeldt, an actress as famous for her amours as for her acting; Jean Simmons's return to the London stage in this part after (can it be true?) thirty years is welcome indeed, for she has it most perfectly in her grasp, blending the experience of middle age with the lasting beauty of youth. Her mother, a successful retired cocotte, lives with her memories of elegant liaisons with Barons, Counts and Kings, regretting the decay of elegance among the younger people but entertaining with style in her Swedish castle. She is played by Hermione Gingold, who knows all there is to be known about the projection of style, and plays with matchless expertise, every word of her songs as clear as a bell and rich with meaning.

Desirée has a pretty daughter Fredrika, a girl on the verge of life, played with likeable gaminerie by Christine McKenna. Fredrika and her grandmother watch the events of a weekend from opposite ends of the scale. The weekend occupies the second half of the evening; the first half is concerned with assembling the materials for this hospitable time-bomb. Desirée renews acquaintance (and something more) with her old lover Fredrik Egerman. Fredrik has a young second wife, Anne, and a son, Henrik, about Anne's age, by his first wife. Henrik is a theological student overdue to erupt into life. Desirée also has another lover, a fiery Dragoon officer with a reluctantly complaisant wife. As ammunition for a house-party on an endless Scandinavian summer night such a combination is certain to be unstable, and instability occurs in every probable combination until the dawn and a more sensible sorting-out of generations brings the play to a close.

Harold Prince's production moves the business along swiftly (after the first ten minutes, when we have to work hard at sorting out the company) and smoothly, and the company could hardly be better. Fredrik is played by Joss Ackland offering a depth of characterisation not common in musicals, and singing delightfully; his rendering with Miss Simmons of 'Send in the clowns' was deservedly given an up-roarious reception. David Kernan makes a splendid dragoon, and Maria Aitken is very funny as his long-suffering wife. Young Henrik is played by Terry Mitchell, who not only sings well but goes through the motions of being a tolerable 'cellist. In smaller parts, there are Diane Langton, with a rousing song, 'The miller's son', that earned her a tremendous cheer, and five guests who serve as a chorus both in the musical and the Greek sense.

The score demands attention. It is not immediately tuneful in the popular way, and the harmonies are often subtle. Themes are re-peated to make points in the manner of Richard Wagner. It is worth close listening, and I am sure that the more one goes the better one will enjoy it. It is ably directed from the pit by Ray Cook.

The sets by Boris Aronson are entrancingly lovely, a forest scene in which little fragments of landscape can be made to slide here or there to vary the picture.

It is possible that *A Little Night Music* has its faults; but I am not in the mood to mention them now. Evenings as enjoyable as this do not come very often.

My Fair Lady

Adelphi   *26 October 1979*

There is little doubt in my mind that *My Fair Lady* is the best musical there has been since I began going to the theatre. The story comes with only one important change from Shaw's most romantic play, and much of Shaw's dialogue is retained. To this splendid script are added the clever lyrics of Alan Jay Lerner, full of cunning word-play and of idea-play that can look Shaw in the face, and the fine musical score of Frederick Loewe, which descends more apparently from his youth in Germany (where he studied with Busoni among others) than from his adopted America. The result has everything to be desired – drama, romance, intelligence.

I am one of the rare people in my generation who never saw *My Fair Lady* before, either on the stage or the screen, and I am not handicapped by recollection of any former magic. I know the performances only from the records. And I cannot believe that Rex Harrison can have been a better Higgins than Tony Britton. Mr Britton gives a beautifully acid performance of that arrogant artificer, his awareness of others totally lost beneath his devotion to his professional pursuits. Using the accepted blend of speech with song, Mr Britton is able to act vividly as he sings, and even more vividly of course when he does not.

Liz Robertson, his Eliza Doolittle, emerges unquestionably as a star with her performance. As guttersnipe or as society lady, she is ravishing to look at; she sings the songs beautifully, both the point numbers ('Just you wait, 'Enry 'Iggins') and the romantic melodies ('I could have danced all night'); and she acts with the skill needed for this important acting part. I wasn't altogether convinced by her cockney vowels, but in any case Shaw made such a phonetic jumble of writing them down that anyone may be forgiven for essaying a personal rendering.

I was not overwhelmed, though it's only fair to say that the house was, by Peter Bayliss's Doolittle. There is too much artificiality about it, too much music-hall cockney, to fit in with the naturalistic playing of the others. It's true that his two big numbers, 'With a little bit of luck' and 'Get me to the church on time', are only done in the company of the chorus of costermongers and flower-girls, but even so I felt we had made too abrupt a change of gear.

Richard Caldicot makes a good Pickering, sneaking an occasional comic moment into what is fundamentally a pompous character; and Peter Land gives his all to Freddy Eynsford Hill – an unrewarding part, for though he has one of the best songs ('On the street where you live') and is the only character for whom Eliza shows any emotion ('Show me'), he is not accorded the more-or-less happy union that Shaw gives him in his afterword to the play. Aficionados will spot Anna Neagle looking as lovely as ever in what is now the minute part of Higgins's mother.

The director is Robin Midgley, and he is to be congratulated on the able way he has spent the Arts Council's grant on this happy production. The designs by Adrian Vaux depend mostly on the ingenious use of flats; the only three-dimensional scene is Higgins's sitting-room.

Guys and Dolls

Olivier   *10 March 1982*

Let no one think I am going to write a calm and analytical notice. This has been my favourite musical, whether or not I think it the *best*, since I saw it at the Coliseum in 1953, and Richard Eyre's fine production at the National has only reinforced my feeling for it.

To begin with, the book by Jo Swerling and Abe Burrows, using material from stories by Damon Runyon, is a good romantic comedy even apart from the songs. Nathan Detroit, who runs the oldest-established permanent floating crap-game in New York is a truly interesting three-dimensional character, and squat, balding Bob Hoskins brings him to what must at least be very like life. He has been engaged for fourteen years to Miss Adelaide, a chanteuse at the Hotbox who longs for a quiet home with wallpaper and bookends, and Julia McKenzie, both as singer and player, gives the best performance I have seen from her, funny and sentimental and oddly honest – see the difference between her cabaret song, 'Take back your mink' and her real feeling in the duets 'Sue me' and 'Marry the man today'.

The second plot uses less caricatured figures. Ian Charleson has no need to make Sky Masterson funny; he is just a big-time gambler who is involved in funny situations. One situation at least, the arrival of the gamblers at the Save-a-Soul Mission, seemed funny enough to last night's audience to rate a round of applause, a tribute seldom given to a wordless situation. Mr Charleson is perhaps a little too restrained, but he sings beautifully in a pretty tenor voice, and that is his main function. Julie Covington as the Mission sergeant Sarah, whom he takes to Cuba for a bet, also keeps on the right side of comedy, and she too sings delightfully, especially her just-less-than-sober song on the beach in Cuba.

The great thing about the songs, apart from Frank Loesser's ably varied tunes, is that they arise naturally from the story, and the lyrics are couched in a language that not only makes high-quality light verse on the page, but is written in the same Runyonesque style as the dialogue. Besides the lyrical showpieces for the principals like 'I'll know when my love comes along' and 'My time of day', there are great numbers like 'Fugue for tinhorns', which is indeed a fugue, and 'Sit down, you're rocking the boat', so well sung, and acted, by David Healy as Nicely-Nicely Johnson that the audience wouldn't let him go.

The choreography by David Toguri is both picturesque and comic on its own account; the crap-rolling routine that begins the game in the sewer is cleverly imagined. The play looks and sounds exciting all the evening on John Gunter's ingenious sets that never leave a gap between events; and the band under Tony Britten, set to one side on the open stage, makes just the right sound, never overcoming the voices. You can hear all the words, even in the chorus numbers, perhaps because the chorus is small; and the words are always worth hearing.

The acting in even the smallest parts is really acting, never merely going through the moves that lead up to the next song. There is nice work by James Carter as Big Jule, Harry Towb as Lieutenant Brannigan, John Normington as Abernathy. When the sailors fill the Hotbox before Adelaide comes on to shed her wraps in 'Take back your mink', each person on the stage has something specific to do; there is literally never a dull moment. To quote from Sarah's song of freshly-released affection, if I were a bell, I'd be ringing.

CHAPTER EIGHT

Exotics

From 1964, the Royal Shakespeare Company and Sir Peter Daubeny presented a decade of springtime seasons under the name of World Theatre Season. Sir Peter had always been a pioneer in importing foreign companies when he was in private management. The World Theatre Season, which began as a celebration of the centenary of Shakespeare's birth, gave him a golden opportunity to comb the theatrical world for our benefit. In the first season we saw leading companies from France, Germany, Italy, Poland, Soviet Russia, Ireland and Greece. Some of them came back for second visits; to them were added companies from Israel, Czechoslovakia, Japan, Sweden and the US.

I have only picked out a few of my favourites; but the seasons were of immense interest and even of value to the English theatre, for foreign directors were invited to work here. Karolos Koun of the Greek Arts Theatre directed *Romeo and Juliet* for the Royal Shakespeare Company, and Ingmar Bergmann directed *Hedda Gabler* for the National.

Perhaps when the recession is over we may have seasons like this again.

*

Dead Souls

Aldwych   *27 May 1964*

The Moscow Art Theatre Company has done wisely in opening at the Aldwych with Mikhail Bulgakov's adaptation of Gogol's story. It's something that most people know, at any rate in outline, and the story is very easy to follow. The book is dramatised in twelve short scenes, organised – purely for the convenience of the stage-hands, I imagine, since each scene requires a new set – into four acts. This really involves rather too many breaks, and there were moments when I felt the evening was passing with less than ideal celerity; but there are so many compensating virtues to be grateful for that it would be curmudgeonly of me to hold this against the production as a serious fault.

In the first scene we see Chichikov, played by V. V. Belokourov, with just enough resemblance to Napoleon to make us say 'Oh yes, of *course*!' when the rumour begins to spread that that is who he is, bribing his way into the Governor's presence. The Governor, in the next scene, is enchanted by Chichikov's oily charm; and in the next, Chichikov is at the Governor's reception meeting landowners. We then see him at work trying to buy from these landowners, and a few more, the serfs from their estates who have died since the last census but are still officially alive until the next census. Although each of these encounters is quite different, this is where I began to feel that the script was becoming a bit repetitious; the landowner might give away his serfs as a token of affection, or haggle over their price, or play draughts for them but the point of each incident was that Chichikov wanted the 'dead souls' and got them, and this phase occupied five consecutive scenes.

However, we then proceed to the Governor's ball, which is mounted with such beauty and liveliness that nascent impatience evaporates at once; and from there to dinner, with a score or more guests at a long table looking really gorgeous in their bright uniforms and evening gowns. But here Chichikov meets his Waterloo, for the drunken Nozdryov, the one landowner who resisted the sale of his deceased retainers, comes on and spills the truth : Chichikov's apparent affluence is based on fraud. Chichikov passes the last scene in prison – but only, of course, for long enough to bribe the Colonel of the Gendarmerie to arrange for his acquittal.

Gogol's high comedy has been transmuted into farce in this production, but it is farce of a very superior quality. The characters come to life like animated figures from drawings by Caran d'Ache or Daumier, and their personalities are drawn in minute detail. There are some exquisitely funny moments – the statuesque pose of the Governor (played with outstanding subtlety by Y. V. Stanitsin) as he prepares to receive Chichikov at his desk; the sentimental exchanges between the over-cultured Manilov and his wife (Y. L. Leonidov and G. I. Kalinovskaya); Nozdryov (B. N. Livanov) cheating at draughts; the marvellous scene between Chichikov and the boorish Sobakevitch – a wonderfully funny performance by A. N. Gribov – in which Chichikov beats his prospect down from 100 roubles per serf to two.

There are also, it must be admitted, some passages of rather familiar farcical procedures, such as the after-you-Cecil-after-you-Claude encounter between Chichikov and Manilov, and the repeated reluctance of Chichikov to give up his money until he has his hands on a receipt; but these are done with such elegance and freshness that they don't seem stale for a moment.

The current production is said to be identical with that of Stanislavsky, who first produced the play in 1934. The two producers now in charge, V. G. Sakhnovsky and E. G. Telesheva, can certainly be gratified by the freshness and sparkle that persists under their direction after 30 years constantly in the repertory. The brilliant costumes and the admirable sets are the work of V. A. Simov.

L'Amante anglaise

Royal Court   *26 September 1969*

In 1966 there was a strange affair in France when pieces of a body were found in goods trains on the railway all over the country. The pieces put together made a woman, and the routes of the trains put together converged at a bridge in Viorne, in the district of Corbeil.

This crime has so fascinated Marguerite Duras that she has now made out of it two plays and a novel. The first play, *The Viaduct*, was presented recently at Guildford with Dame Sybil Thorndike as the woman to whom the crime was traced. This was a conventional piece, rather suggesting Simenon in style; but while it was actually in rehearsal, Mlle Duras was busy on a totally new version, and I understand was somewhat put out when Dame Sybil declined to scrap what she had done and start again.

This new version is *L'Amante anglaise* (and I should say here that there is no English lover in it; the name is a McLuhanish pun on *la menthe anglaise,* an edible garden plant). It is a far simpler, yet a more powerful play. It consists only of two long interrogations, the first of Pierre Lannes, the husband of the accused woman, the second of Clair Lannes, the woman herself.

In the course of these two investigations, conducted by an anonymous functionary who seems part policeman, part psychiatrist, part *juge d'instruction*, the bizarre life of the Lannes household takes shape in our minds. The dead person was Claire Lannes's cousin, a deaf-and-dumb woman who had been brought into their home twenty years before to run the household. Their three lives remained rigidly independent. Claire left all the work to her cousin while she consorted with Alfonso, a woodcutter from the little Portuguese colony in Viorne, or else dreamed of her former lover of long before, a policeman in Cahors. (The words 'Alfonso' and 'Cahors' were found scrawled on the cellar wall with a piece of coal.) Pierre's only social contacts were with local prostitutes; and fat, deaf-and-dumb Marie-Thérèse was able to find herself friends among the Portuguese, the Portuguese, as Pierre observes to the interrogator, not being particular.

Pierre's interrogation sets the scene in detail but does little to help us see why his wife should have committed such a gruesome crime – apart from the fact that she was mad, a fact that he throws off with as much emotion as if he were saying she was colour-blind. Jean Servais shows us exactly what kind of a man this was – all passion spent, life a mechanical accession to the basic demands of nature.

Claire, brilliantly played by Madeleine Renaud, is a much more fascinating character, yet she is presented to us only by the same economical formula of question and answer as she sits spotlit in her chair. Mad she undoubtedly is; though all we see is a simple, rather jolly, middle-aged woman, her explanations to the interrogator (simple and rather jolly as she makes them sound) are macabre in the extreme. She has always dreamed about killing people she lived with, she says, so sooner or later she was bound to do it really. This is the best excuse she can offer. She had to cut the body up, to make it disappear. What she has done with the head, which was never found, she resolutely refuses to tell.

This is where the play ends. And indeed how could it go on? Claire's mind is as impenetrable as the institution where she will spend the rest of her days.

The simple but cogent direction is by Claude Régy, and the part of the interrogator, spoken at first from the darkness of the stalls, later from the gloomier reaches of the stage, is well taken by Michael Lonsdale.

1789

Cartoucherie de Vincennes   *27 February 1971*

1789, which is bringing enthusiastic crowds from Paris to a disused armoury in the park at Vincennes, is produced by Ariane Mnouchkine; but it is a joint creation, in text and *mise en scène,* by the whole company of the Théâtre du Soleil. This is the first of their productions I have seen, and it certainly indicates something special. The subject of the French Revolution was chosen for a collective creation as something every member of the company would be likely to know about and have ideas about. It shows in a series of tableaux what the Revolution must have seemed like to the ordinary man of the time, and how quickly its gains were lost as the Government slipped back into old patterns under new names.

The unlettered French poor knew that they were hungry and ill-housed; but they can hardly have known much about the real activities of the king and nobility under whom they suffered. These were as unreal – and as real – to them as people in fairy-stories; this is how Mlle Mnouchkine first presents them. *'Il était une fois un roi'* – and there he is, like an illustration from a story-book, and there are the nobles, practising thoughtless cruelties as inevitably as the giant in *Jack and the Beanstalk.*

The development of the Revolution is shown in various genres that mark a gradual increase in popular understanding of the situation. Fairytale gives way to puppet-show, to actual political appeal, to agitation directed personally toward the man in the street, until the production bursts suddenly into an episode of unparalleled splendour. In an almost silent house, men have been moving among the crowds – us – reporting the fall of the Bastille, at first softly, to individuals and small groups, then more loudly and openly to bigger and bigger crowds until the sound of their voices, reinforced by a turbulent thunder of drums, becomes a shout. A man jumps up on to a platform to broadcast the news, ending with a great cry of triumph, *'Le peuple est vainqueur!'*

At these words all the lights blaze up on the hitherto gloomy scene, the music bursts out with 'The Entry of the Gladiators', and on every side the symbols of the people's victory are presented in the manner of sideshows at a fair. In the general rejoicing, members of the audience join hands and dance euphorically around the arena. The people have got their Revolution – the biggest circus in the world.

The manner of presenting *1789* is as original as its conception. In the great, bleak spaces of the armoury, a big acting space is surrounded by five raised stages connected by catwalks. There is a tier of seats along one side; but the audience may wander where it likes, and all the acting area is full of people, including a lot of boys who give the feeling of the terraces of a football ground. People even climb up on the stages, leaving obediently when they are needed by the actors. In this way the sensation of being part of the people of *1789* is marvellously transferred to the spectators of 1971.

After that great burst of revolutionary joy, the rest of the play is bound to be anti-climactic. A rocket's descent, needful as it may be under the existing laws of gravity, can hardly be expected to match its rising. There are still some fine things, such as the impact of the Rights of Man on the blacks of Santo Domingo (*'on a parlé des hommes, mes doudous, pas de nègres'*), and the vast, subtly controlled puppet King and Queen brought from Versailles by the women of Paris on 6 October. But it's not so exciting to be reminded that 'liberty only exists through obedience to the laws'; and though on paper the actual quotations from the Parliamentary debates have a cold grip like handcuffs, they make less impression in a huge room like the Cartoucherie theatre, however much art is put into their projection.

We still have Marat, though, to call for *les émeutes populaires;* and as an *émeute populaire* had only the previous day got the schoolboy Gilles Guiot out of prison, and the dreadful C.R.S. were still in the streets, it was clear how the audience felt. The clear lesson in *1789* is that a revolution was needed again as soon as the first one was over; and, by extrapolation, that a revolution is *always* necessary. A civilised society is an unstable equilibrium, like the inside of a locomotive's boiler. It's the pressure of the steam on the piston that keeps the machine on its way towards that *perfection du bonheur* that Saint-Just saw as the terminus of the Revolution of 1789.

La Ville dont le Prince est un Enfant

Aldwych   *25 March 1971*

'Romantic friendships' between big boys and small boys at school seem to be pretty universal, and if you ask me the horror with which

they are regarded by staffs is absurdly exaggerated. Henry de Montherlant in *La Ville*, has probably touched the truth when he suggests
that this horror is a reaction by the master against their ever having
a tender feeling towards a small boy themselves. He allows his Abbé
de Pradts, vice-principal of a boarding-school at Auteuil, to give way
to a weakness for 14-year-old Serge Souplier; as Souplier is already
having an *amitié particulière* with 16-year-old André Sevrais, disaster
is inevitable, and disaster comes on the small boy, the big boy and the
priest alike.

It should be made clear that there is absolutely nothing prurient in
the play. Sex is never even hinted at. Affection is the emotion that
drives the characters towards their fate, affection and its by-product,
jealousy; and discipline is the barrier against which it has to fight.
The argument is conducted on philosophical and religious grounds.
The actual story is comparatively slight; de Pradts warns Sevrais to
keep away from Souplier, but relents to the extent of allowing their
association if Sevrais will promise to use it for good. (Souplier is
a bad boy.) Later he finds them in apparently compromising circumstances in the sports store, and precipitately has Servais expelled. The
headmaster, however, sees what de Pradts is up to, and has Souplier
expelled too; and the play ends with a long moral confrontation between the two masters.

I wasn't deeply involved emotionally in the story; but I did feel
involved in the argument, which is presented by Montherlant with
power and with grace. The play reproduces events that happened to
himself at school and led to his expulsion, and naturally enough the
sympathy is channelled towards Sevrais, the character filling his own
role. (You might spell his name *c'est vrai*.)

This leads to a weakness, as I consider it, common in this kind of
story. Sevrais's feelings are deeply explored; he is a very articulate
boy, and when he is not presenting his own case he's as often as not
being discussed by someone else. De Pradts's case is presented even
more fully. But Souplier's case is never made at all.

These juvenile affairs are the first initiation children have into
what they will later recognise as love, and can occupy their minds to
an extent no subsequent affair ever will. Yet Souplier (played with
beautifully natural relaxation by Dominique Pennors) is treated as if
he were a stage prop. He's there for people to argue about. And
indeed, though they argue with a frankness and a fluency unfamiliar
in English schools, no one ever asks how *he* will feel about it all. 'Woe
to thee, O land, when thy King is a child' (the quotation is from

Ecclesiastes); but woe, too, to the child that becomes a king before his time.

Jean Meyer and the Théâtre Michel have the sole acting rights of the play; the author will not allow it to be played by anyone else or in any other language, though the BBC has given two performances in English on what was then the Third Programme. Monsieur Meyer certainly earns his accolade; his production is sensitive and convincing and his company admirable. Paul Guers is de Pradts, a mixture of sternness and sentiment; Sevrais is played by Gil de Lesparda with a hint of intellectual superiority that keeps him from ever giving way to his emotion, even in the scene where he and Souplier pledge eternal blood-brotherhood. In the last scene, there is an imposing performance by Yves Brainville as the Supérieur; the scene between him and de Pradts is cunningly inflected with a reminiscence of the first scene between de Pradts and Souplier.

La Ville which runs until 10 April, marks the start of the 1971 World Theatre Season. It has been running in Paris since 1967 (when the author revised his text, originally published in 1951). Montherlant isn't easy, as a rule, for English audiences, but this is a play to be seen.

The Possessed

Aldwych   *30 May 1972*

Andrzej Wajda is best known to us as a film director (*A Generation, Ashes and Diamonds, Kanal*), and his direction of *The Possessed* for the Cracow Stary Theatre is basically cinematic. Small rudimentary sets are pitched for scenes that may be as short as a minute or less; sound is used independently of the action on the stage; direct address to the audience suggest close-ups. The swift scene-changes, effected by a corps of 'invisible' hooded stage-hands in the Japanese style, prevent any diminution in the tension; sometimes, when a fade to black is indicated between scenes, tension is maintained by using taped sounds of penetrating emotional power, of which more in a moment.

Wajda's version began as a production of Camus's adaptation of Dostoevsky, but it soon broke clear of Camus's comparatively conventional play, taking in more of the Russian social background that is

so important an element in the conspiracies of Stavrogin, Verkhovensky and the rest, and presenting them in a dreamlike – nightmarelike
– scenario that truly suggests Dostoevsky's idea of an underground
society possessed by the legion of Gadarene devils emerging from a
sick Russia.

Two main plots appear – Verkhovensky's murder of Stavrogin's
mad wife Maria, freeing him to marry his current mistress Lisa Droz-
dov, which is his price for Stavrogin's services as leader of the conspiracy; and the killing of the student Shatov as an earnest of loyalty
by the inner five the day after his wife has returned to him and had a
baby. But there is a great deal of subsidiary detail included, and I
sometimes felt that the principal lines might seem stronger if some of it
were omitted.

The first minute sets the mood of the evening. As soon as the house-
lights go down, our ears are assaulted with a terrible stereophonic
cacophony of belches, groans, cries and murmurs such as you might
imagine inside the head of a maniac. Projected on the back curtain,
a horse-drawn chariot races straight out at the house. Picture and
sound fade, and the lights reveal that the stage is covered with a rough
layer of mud; the mud encrusts the shoes, trouser-legs and skirts of
the players. We may think, from time to time, that we are in Barbara
Petrovna's elegant salon, or Shatov's miserable cabin, or the room
where Alexey Kirilov toys with thoughts of suicide before an icon;
but in fact we are always at the top of that steep Gadarene hill where
the possessed will run violently down into the sea and be drowned.

The sounds recur at every moment of emotional peak – when
Stavrogin has his epileptic seizure, when Shatov is murdered by his
fellow-conspirators, when, in a truly appalling climax, Dasha goes out
to join Stavrogin and finds him hanging at the end of a suicide's rope.
I have never known anything that tore in such a raw fashion at my
nerves. It is a short cut to hysteria, but it is a mighty effective one.

The acting is strongly externalised, each character's qualities em-
phasised as far as possible short of caricature. Wojciech Pszoniak's
Verkhovensky becomes increasingly excitable as his anarchistic plans
become wilder, until at the end he windmills about the stage like
someone from Lewis Carroll. At the other end of the scale is Aleks-
ander Fabisiak's quiet, contained Shatov; and squarely between them
is the aristocratic superiority of Jan Nowicki's Stavrogin, a man commanding devotion through his own certainty of superiority. There is
some fine work in smaller parts, too – Izabela Olszewska as mad
Maria, Wiktor Sadecki as Stepan Trofimovitch, Andrzej Kozak keep-

ing fit for suicide, Jerzy Binczychi's pathetically *déclassé* Lebyatkin, and more.

No one interested in the capacity of the stage to embrace the widest of canvases should miss this production, which brings to an end a World Theatre Season well up to the usual standard.

Kabuki

Sadler's Wells Theatre   *6 June 1972*

I suspect that European audiences react to the Kabuki theatre quite differently from Japanese. What the Japanese are seeing is an exciting, or a sentimental, or a pathetic story, stylised to the degree, say, that Shakespeare is. The excitement and the pathos are apt to pass us by, unless we happen to understand Japanese. What we admire is the spectacle, the grace of movement, the wonderful use of colour in the sets and the costumes, the subtleties of the lighting.

The Kabuki company now at Sadler's Wells Theatre presents two plays, or strictly speaking one play and three acts of another. The three acts of the very long *Kanadehon Chushingura* come first, and together they provide an outline of the whole plot, which I don't mean to retail here. In the first act the Governor of Kamakura makes approaches to Lady Kaoyo, who is identifying the helmet of a lately killed enemy so that it can be laid on a shrine, and tells her that her husband Hangan's future depends on her pliability. In the second scene he taunts her husband until in desperation he draws his sword – a capital offence, for which he is condemned to commit *seppuku* (formerly known to us as *hara-kiri*), a fate he meets in the next scene. The final extract shows Hangan's now masterless retainers, the forty-seven *ronin* who give the play its title, before the city gate, crying out for justice, but dissuaded until a more suitable time. (They do kill Moronao in later acts, then all forty-seven of them commit *seppuku*).

Each scene has its own particular excitement. The first, before a sacred shrine, is a big, colourful production; the development of the story depends a good deal on the dialogue and on the commentary provided by an off-stage *joruri* singer, who keeps the story going to the accompaniment of musical instruments, but it is fine to look at, and the stillness of the players when they are in repose is stunning.

The most impressive scene is the one where Hangan commits his ritual disembowelling. There is almost total silence as servants bring in the proper mats, the knife, the four shrubs that stand at each corner of the mats. Hangan (Nakamura Shikan, showing a wonderful blend of stoicism and dismay on his white-painted face) slowly removes his outer clothes until he wears only vestments of pure white. The sense of gathering terror in the act is marvellously gripping.

The scenes outside the gate are different again, the accent being on movement and action; it is a truly exciting moment when the revenging *ronin* come thundering up the *hanamichi*, the gangway that leads from the stage to the back of the stalls.

The second play, *Sumidagawa*, is a complete contrast. It has a simple story about a madwoman who hears from a boatman on the Sumida River a story of a child, abandoned by slave-traders, who died and was buried on the river bank. The woman recognises the child as her long-lost son, whose loss it was that drove her out of her mind. It is the story of Britten's *Curlew River*.

The performance is mostly danced, a small band of *samisen* being placed on the stage near the head of the *hanamichi*. While the band tells the story, the woman and the man dance their interpretation of the tale, only occasionally exchanging a few words of dialogue. The play was borrowed by the Kabuki from the classical Noh theatre and I understand the performance is little changed, only moved from the traditional Noh stage to a more naturalistic setting – a setting incidentally of the most entrancing beauty.

The two parts are played by the two senior members of the company, Nakamura Utaemon and Nakamura Genjiro. Utaemon plays the woman; there are no women in Kabuki companies, but actors who specialise from their youth up in women's parts, and Utaemon, who has been playing them for fifty years, is utterly feminine without the least suggesting of the effeminate male. It is hard to imagine anything more graceful than the performance of these two artists. Indeed the whole company give us something splendid that should on no account be missed.

Umewaka Noh Troupe

Aldwych   *5 June 1973*

All Noh plays are basically two-handers. Both those in the Umewaka company's first programme are by Zeami, born in 1363. The stories are not likely to matter much to Western audiences (nor, I suspect to Eastern; there's a passage in one of them so corrupt that even the players don't understand it). In outline they go like this :

Sagi, The Heron. A heron starts to fly away when startled by the Emperor's party; but when told that the Emperor wishes it to return, it comes back and performs a dance in his honour.

Kiyotsune. The ghost of Kiyotsune, a general who drowned himself when assured of defeat, returns after eight years to appear to his wife and persuade her to accept the lock of his hair offered her as a keep-sake by his former retainer, refused by her out of mingled shame and sorrow.

What does matter is the matchless beauty of the performance. This is now the fourth Noh programme I have seen in the last five or six years, and I find more in it each time. The costumes, to begin with, are rich with embroidered silks, never representational but delicately suggestive. The heron costume is all white, with a flying bird incorporated in the headpiece; the ghost of drowned Kiyotsune wears a surcoat of watery blue over his tunic. There are wide sleeves and immensely broad trousers with flat panels at the back, and the actors manipulate them into subtle patterns with gestures that look simple and conventional but on examination reveal cunning potentialities.

Noh combines speech, song, mime and dance, but naturally it is the dance that speaks most immediately to a foreign audience. Both these plays – indeed all Noh plays except, according to Arthur Waley, Zeami's *Hachi no Ki* – end with a dance for the *shite*, or protagonist. Here again, though nothing is representational, there is suggestion so nice that apparently identical motions may carry quite different feelings. In the dance with which Manzaburo Umewaka concludes *Sagi* (a dance so highly reputed that no actor dances it until he is sixty years old, and which won for Umewaka the coveted Emperor's medal), he makes the traditional Noh stamps with a birdlike neatness. Yasuyuki Umewaka as Kiyotsune stamps like a general recounting his memories of battle. Yet the basic movement is just a raising of the knee in a 'mark time' action.

Conventional dramatic tension comes out strongly at times. Before the entry of Kiyotsune, the chorus has a passage recounting Kiyotsune's wife's sleepless longing for her man that ends in a prolonged bass cadence. There is a silence. Then the flute player plays a slow melody. Kiyotsune's subsequent entry is wonderfully effective. Here, though, I must interpose a word of criticism, though I know there is nothing to be done about it : the stage of the Aldwych is not big enough to accommodate a full-size twenty-foot square stage and a full-length *hashigakari* walk-way for the entries and exits, and the *hashigakari* has been severely shortened. (It has only one pine along its length instead of the proper three). So some of the entries, especially the first entries of the *shite* players, seem to me to have lost some of their proper power.

However, it is not an evening for complaints. So a round of credits : Makio Umewaka for the *waki* performance – the straight man, as it were – in *Sagi,* and Masaji Fujitani for the pathos she puts so economically into her playing of Kiyotsune's wife. To Sengoro Shigeyama, Masayoshi Shigeyama and Juro Zenchiku for their comic antics in the *kyogen* interlude, *Futari-Daimyo.* And to James Leith, who gives a small introductory talk and recounts brief summaries of the plays with enough clarity and wit never to seem intrusive.

The Bacchae

Burgtheater, Vienna 16 *June 1973*

Euripides's *The Bacchae* is everybody's favourite play nowadays for bringing up to date and relating to the current world. At Newcastle you can see it under the title *The Orgy.* John Bowen's version was set in a modern megalopolis. Maureen Duffy set it in a ladies' lavatory.

Luca Ronconi, in his Vienna Festival production for the Burgtheater, takes the view that it is most clearly shown to belong to our age if it is shown to belong to every age : '*eine diachronische Aufführung einer griechischen Tragödie*', he calls it. He bases it at the time of the Renaissance – the city of Thebes is modelled on the wonderful permanent set of the Olympic Theatre at Vicenza, the offstage music of the Bacchae calls with the Christian sound of Monteverdi – but shifts in period when it suits him. The hideous details of Pentheus's death are told by a character in modern dress to a group of factory-workers (the only point, as a matter of fact, at which I felt the impulse to be running slow).

The playing, isolated from the productional excitement with which Ronconi has gilded it, is in the traditional heroic style of the Burg-theater, a style difficult to avoid in this vast house when there are great speeches to deliver. What lifts the whole thing into the realms of magic is the director's visual imagination.

When the curtain rises, Dionysus is seated down-stage looking away from us at a great wooden arch. As he begins his prologue, this arch rumbles towards us as if to demonstrate the power of the god; as it reaches him, it turns slowly on the revolve and Dionysus walks through it descending as it were from one world to another.

The arch is in fact a false proscenium. A curtain falls, or rises, in its opening, and behind it there appear or disappear scenes that range between the richness of the Olympic Theatre set (of which, incident-ally, the front slides away later to show the details of the perspectives behind the entrances) to the simple but astonishing Biedermeier arm-chair that furnishes the stage when Pentheus is being arrayed in his drag for the reconnaissance of the Bacchantes' retreat. The complexi-ties of Pier Luigi Pizzi's scenery are handled with enviable smoothness.

The chorus is treated as an integral part of the drama; there is no halting of movement to allow rows of ladies to recite in unison, or imposed but irrelevant dancing to keep the eyes filled while the words go on. Ronconi's Bacchae are always engaged in a dramatically meaningful activity. Perhaps the most exciting moment of the evening is the scene where they come among the women of Thebes to infect them with their new ideas.

The acting of Wolfgang Schadewaldt's German text seems to me admirable. Sebastian Fischer's Pentheus is puzzled but still a leader to the last moment; and appropriately he, who has to put on women's clothes, is the most emphatically masculine of the male characters, who tend to wear long gowns while Pentheus is allowed breeches. Norbert Kappan has a touch of the faun in his face that suits Dionysus well, and his cool command of every situation, even where he is required only to sit and observe the behaviour of other people, is notable.

Judith Hoelzmeister's distracted Agave is given extra depth by the knot of Bacchantes who sit on kitchen chairs upstage observing her as she tells the tale of how she had killed her son believing him to be a lion.

The production is an exciting taste of the way in which Gerhard Klingenberg is hauling the Burgtheater from the eighteenth century into the 1970s. In his determination to bring a new individuality into the Austrian theatre he is inoculating the Burgtheater, too long hobbled by the edicts of Emperor Josef II, with new elements from many directions in the process of building up a truly Austrian tradition.

That this tradition will be both stimulating and cosmopolitan may be seen in his programme for 1973–74. Directors will include Felsenstein, Jean-Paul Roussillon, Peter Wood; plays will include Aristophanes's *The Birds* (another Ronconi production), Tom Stoppard's *Jumpers*, Goldoni's *Mirandolina*, Joyce's *Exiles*, Schiller's *Maria Stuart*, Albee's *Seascape*. Klingenberg hopes to get Paula Wessely to play Edward Bond's *The Sea*. This is the kind of schedule that sets national theatres a worthwhile example.

Bunraku

Lyceum, Edinburgh   *2 September 1976*

Bunraku is the art of the National Puppet Theatre of Japan, based in Osaka, the traditional home of Japanese puppetry.

The puppets are about one-half life-size, beautiful little figures dressed with all the splendour of the Japanese theatre. Male puppets are operated by three men; the leader works the head, the eyebrows and the right arm, his assistant works the left arm and the body, and a third operator controls the legs. Female puppets have no legs, and may therefore be worked by two men. There are also some less elaborate puppets for bit parts which can be worked by one.

The stage presents only the actual movement in the plays. The story is read from a book by a *joruri* reciter at the side of the stage, and he is accompanied by a player of the shamisen, a banjo-like instrument with three strings. On the stage the puppets are taken through their parts with the operators in full view. In the Japanese theatre, however, anyone dressed in black is invisible, so although there may be as many as fifteen puppet workers and stagehands on the stage, to a devotee no one is to be seen but the characters in the story.

And in my experience it is true that, after a bit of practice, this is true. At the Lyceum I was sitting in the circle, which is not an ideal place to watch *bunraku* theatre from, since too much of the works is showing; none the less, by the time we had reached the story of the

Double Suicide in the Tenjin Woods in the second half of the programme, my attention was confined to the dolls, and how they were
manipulated was no longer of immediate concern to me.

The two tales in the company's first programme are both by the
master, Chikamatsu Monzaemon (1653–1725). The first is the tale of
an exiled priest who gives up his chance of rescue in favour of a
woman; the second with an ill-starred love affair that ends in suicide.
Even if I could, I wouldn't tell the stories in detail; for British viewers
the pleasure is in the beauty of the dolls and the scenery, and the
subtle skill of the puppeteers.

Though there are moments of big dramatic impact, such as the
arrival of the ship in the first play, and the moment at which the
priest Shunkan snatches the sword from the scabbard of his adversary
in the second, some of the quieter moments are equally impressive,
the little movements of a weeping woman's head, for instance.

In the final scene of the suicide play, there are two *joruri* reciters,
speaking and singing, sometimes in turn and sometimes together, and
three shamisen players; also the principal operator of each doll is
allowed to show his head, instead of cloaking it in a mask.

Bunraku got its name from the family of Bunrakuken in the early
seventeenth century, and the company that is now the National
Puppet Company stayed in the hands of its descendants until 1909.
The theatrical company that then took them over found public interest
so much on the decline that nationalisation was the only way to keep
the art going – a sadly familiar tale to Western ears.

Peking Opera

Coliseum   *4 July 1979*

Forget the formalities of the Japanese theatre. Forget the classic origins
of the Peking Opera in 1790 (pretty recent compared with ours, anyway). Forget the elaborate code of meanings attached to the colour of
costumes, the makeup of faces and so on. Forget the word 'opera'.
Peking Opera is not an intellectual entertainment; it is a glittering
synthesis of speech, song, mime, dancing, acrobatics and fencing, and
it is meant for the amusement of the ordinary man.

'Peking Opera' is a general term; this particular company comes

from Shanghai. The four pieces they gave last night illustrate different aspects of their talent.

At the Cross-roads Inn was the first. Its story should be familiar to
us, for it is the origin of Peter Shaffer's *Black Mischief*. Ren Tanghui,
guarding the rear of an exiled general's retreat, stays the night with
the good innkeeper Liu Lihua. (You know he's good, if you've read
the rules, because he carries a duster; this is one of those symbols I
just recommended forgetting.) Liu believes that Ren is the general's
enemy, so as soon as the candle is out, though it never was lit and the
stage remains brightly lit, he attacks him. They then have a long fight
in what we must imagine to be the dark. It's not only very funny, but
immensely clever. Qin Weicheng, who played Liu last night, is an
acrobat of great skill – exceptional skill, I would say if it were not so
general among the company.

The Phoenix of Fire is a dance representing a battle between egrets
and vultures for an island prettily represented on a backcloth. The
band, which sits visibly in the wings, gives us a rest from the endless
clashing of cymbals and lets us hear some music on strings and wind
instruments. At the climax, the Giant White Egret (Qi Shufang)
turns into a phoenix and so defeats the vultures, and in doing so she
shows extraordinary swiftness. There are eight vultures throwing light
spears at her, and she returns them, with her arms, her own spear or
her legs, infallibly to the vultures that threw them. She even manages
two at once, using both legs – not once, but three times in a row. This
dancer also has a beautiful routine with long flame-coloured streamers
that she waves in sinuous patterns.

The Jade Bracelet is a simple love-comedy that depends a good
deal on the dialogue. The Chinese around me in the audience laughed
like anything at this; but there is also some attractive visual fun from
Zhang Qiuwei as the mother of a girl who divides her time between
feeding her chickens, with endless cries of 'Oush!', and flirting with
her young man.

The Yandang Mountains has a plot about a battle between two
generals (who appear with four flags flying from their shoulders, thus
symbolising an army, I understand). But it is really just an astonishing
display of fighting and acrobatics, so quick and so accurate that they
hardly seem possible under Newton's laws of motion.

I have not even mentioned the beautiful costumes or the simple but
effective décor, with nothing on the stage that is not immediately required. I need only say that they are at the same level of excellence as
the performances.

CHAPTER NINE

Hamlet, Prince of Wales

'And what's he like?' Guildenstern asks Ophelia – not in Shakespeare's play, it is true, but in W. S. Gilbert's *Rosencrantz and Guildenstern*, a later version. Ophelia does not respond with any gush about 'the expectancy and rose of the fair state'. She says:

> Alike for no two seasons at a time.
> Sometimes he's tall, sometimes he's very short,
> Now with black hair, now with a flaxen wig,
> Sometimes an English accent, then a French,
> Then English with a strong provincial burr,
> Once an American, and once a Jew,
> But Danish never, take him how you will!
> And strange to say, whate'er his tongue may be,
> Though we're in Denmark, AD ten-six-two,
> He always dresses as King James the First!

'Hamlet,' wrote Peter Hall in his programme notes for the 1965 Stratford production, 'turns a different face to every decade.' The sixties were the decade of the beatnik, the hippy, the flower-power drop-out. The Polish critic Jan Kott – and yes, the sixties were the decade of Jan Kott, too – saw Hamlet in black sweater and blue jeans, reading Sartre and Camus and Kafka: an existentialist Hamlet, possibly even a Marxist Hamlet. This was not unlike the Hamlet of David Warner. The Court was reeking with politics. Reynaldo was a secret agent. Polonius was the *éminence grise* of King Claudius, the strong man of eleventh-century Danish affairs. David Warner as Hamlet was an ineffectual student, out of his depth among the intrigues of the Court. He certainly belonged in his decade. The trouble is, he doesn't belong in the play. For if there is one quality that Hamlet displays more than any other, it is pride. When the time was out of joint, he had been sent to set it right.

He was clearly disappointed when, after his father's death from snakebite (as he thought) he failed to succeed to the Throne. As we know from the information carefully planted in the Gravediggers' scene, he was thirty years old. To be passed over at that age in favour of his father's younger brother, a man in the prime of life, meant that if he were ever to be king at all (and Claudius was good enough to say that he would support his ultimate succession) it would not be until he had reached middle-age at least. He was condemned to the existence of Prince Charles when what he wanted was the life of Henry V.

Naturally, from the first soliloquy onwards, he is against Claudius. Claudius wasn't a bad king, as kings went at the time. The Court accepted him in spite of his incestuous marriage. His first act of policy was to send ambassadors to Norway to conclude an honourable treaty in settlement of the unhappy situation resulting from his brother's having killed the King of Norway in single combat. This action may have saved Denmark from invasion by Fortinbras and his storm-troops.

Hamlet disliked him from the word go, so much so that when he heard the Ghost accuse him of murder, he almost took it for granted – 'O my prophetic soul!' he says, *prophetic*, he knew it all along. And as if murder were not enough, he goes on and on about Claudius's marriage to Gertrude, his mother, which was indeed incestuous by the day's standards.

In his book *Hamlet and Oedipus*, Ernest Jones proposes that this feeling was due to Hamlet's own incestuous affection for his mother. All his life he has felt deprived of a fair share of her life, and when for a moment he has a glimpse of a world where it might come to him, the vision is brutally blotted out by Gertrude's instant remarriage.

A more convincing explanation is offered by Grigori Kozintsev, who directed the Russian film of the play. In an essay in his book *Shakespeare: Time and Conscience* he stresses the Ghost's lines:

> Let not the royal bed of Denmark be
> A couch for luxury and damn'd incest.

The royal bed, he suggests, here stands as a symbol of the continuance of the royal line. Hamlet's preoccupation is less with his mother's misbehaviour than with his having been cheated of the Crown.

This twin obsession with incest and usurpation persists all through the play. When Hamlet returns from the abortive trip to England, and is apparently as sane as can be, he sums up the King to Horatio like this:

He that hath killed my King and whored my mother,
Popped in between the election and my hopes,
Thrown out his angle for my proper life.

These are not the words of any introspective melancholic. They're not the words of a loyal son determined to avenge his father. They are the words of an active and ambitious Heir Presumptive.

We do not know much about the elder Hamlet, 'so excellent a King', as his son called him, beyond the fact that he had killed the Norwegian King, that he was devoted to his wife, and that presumably he had no objection to the boozing that his son found 'a custom more honoured in the breach than in the observance'. I see him as a hard-fighting, hard-drinking, hard-swearing swashbuckler (and certainly in Saxo Grammaticus's *Historiae Danicae* he is called 'the most renowned pirate that in those days scoured the seas and havens in northern parts'). I can't understand either the melancholy Hamlet of the old tradition or the political Hamlet of the new voicing for such a monarch the ample admiration so often on his lips.

Who else did Hamlet admire? Horatio, to start with; but Horatio, in spite of his good part in the play, isn't much of a chap – 'spinelessly sycophantic', one of my colleagues has called him. He is Hamlet's shadow.

A more significant object of Hamlet's admiration is Fortinbras, and it seems to have been mutual. It's fashionable nowadays to make Fortinbras into a kind of SS *Oberstürmbannführer*. But Hamlet calls him 'a delicate and tender prince', even when he was leading his band of irregulars against a worthless patch of Poland. Indeed it was Fortinbras's example at that moment which recalled Hamlet to his neglected duty of regicide. With his dying breath, he named Fortinbras as his successor : hardly the choice of our irresolute intellectual. And Fortinbras in return observed over Hamlet's body that 'he was likely, had he been put on, to have proved most royal'.

Moreover, we have confirmation from a very different source. The most detailed description of the Prince comes from Ophelia – not as we know her a girl likely to have had heterodox social views, not until later anyway. This is what she says after the 'nunnery' scene :

Oh what a noble mind is here o'erthrown!
The courtier's, soldier's, scholars', eye, tongue, sword,
The expectancy and rose of the fair state,
The glass of fashion and the mould of form,
The observed of all observers.

This is a key speech in the delineation of Hamlet's character. It tells us so much we are not told elsewhere. She would not have said 'soldier' if Hamlet had never been a soldier; and of course it is unlikely that Hamlet could have lived thirty years in the shadow of his piratical father without some kind of experience in the field. 'Scholar' may mean no more than that he had been to the university. But 'the expectancy and rose of the fair state' must indicate that the common people were looking forward to his ascending the Throne (and Claudius also admits that 'he's loved of the distracted multitude'). The warlike Danes would hardly have felt that way about some vacillating philosopher.

There has been some argument whether Hamlet was in fact thirty years old, as the Gravedigger says. The passage serves no other purpose; it appears only in late editions, and may perhaps have been connected with the looks of the actor playing the part. (And later, 'He's fat and scant of breath.') Even if we accept that he was thirty, there is also a possibility, put forward by A. C. Bradley, that he had not begun his education until he was fifteen or so, in which case he might only lately have come down from Wittenberg.

Yet his first words to Horatio were 'Horatio, or I do forget myself,' as if they have not met for some time, and Horatio, we know, was actually up at Wittenberg until the time of the King's funeral and the Queen's remarriage.

When Hamlet told Claudius that he wanted to go back to Wittenberg after the wedding, it seems to me that he was not, as at first appears, simply trying to get away from a Court that had become distasteful to him. Once over the border, he could begin to think about taking over the Throne so unjustly denied him. Without attracting too much attention, he could have assembled a little junta of Old Wittenbergians and, under cover of their studies, have planned a coup d'état.

The intelligent Claudius realised this possibility and forbade him to go. He knew how insecure was his tenure of the Crown, and he needed to have the strongest claimant under his eye.

If we assume, though, that Hamlet came down from the university at the normal age, what had he been doing in the five or six years until he was thirty? Hanging about the Court? This wouldn't make him 'the expectancy and rose of the fair state'. More probably he had been seeking opportunities of emulating his piratical father's reputation. We need not rely only on Ophelia's word that he was a soldierly young man. He was a better fencer than Laertes, of whom it was said that ' 'Twould be a sight indeed if one could match him.' When the ship taking him to England was intercepted by pirates, Hamlet was the first man to board the pirate vessel, and he quickly won over the pirate crew with the force of his personality. Then there was his ruthless treatment of Rosencrantz and Guildenstern, whom he cold-bloodedly sent to their deaths by way of a joke – a proceeding that even shocked Horatio.

Is it any wonder that he resented the loss of the succession which he regarded as his right? Hamlet often drops important thoughts into what seems to be trivial conversation. 'What is the cause of your distemper?' 'Sir, I lack advancement.' Rosencrantz takes him up, 'How can that be when you have the voice of the King himself for your succession in Denmark?' 'Ay, sir, but "while the grass grows" – the proverb is something musty.' The proverb was 'While the grass grows, the horse starves.' Hamlet had no intention of spending his youth as the next man in while his uncle enjoyed himself at the wicket.

'Denmark's a prison,' Hamlet says, and the sympathetic Rosencrantz understands at once. 'Why then, 'tis your ambition makes it one.' Hamlet's ambition was no secret from his friends. Even in the soliloquies, pride is often a main ingredient. 'This is hire and salary, not revenge' – not the revenge of a prince. 'Oh what a rogue and peasant slave am I' – when actually I am a prince. This list of his sins 'such that it were better my mother had not borne me' amounts to pride, ambition and revenge.

It is easy to argue that the soliloquies are more melancholy than proud, but the conflict of pride with melancholy is one of the most interesting qualities of the character. One of the proudest men in recent times was Winston Churchill, and he was so afflicted with recurrent fits of despair that he had his private name for the condition. He called it the Black Dog. 'To be or not to be,' 'Oh what a rogue and peasant slave' are Hamlet's fits of Black Dog, no more.

One is bound to ask how it is that this proud, ambitious, revengeful young man-at-arms lets two month go by without making any attempt to carry out his dead father's charge. The answer must be that simply killing Claudius might have satisfied the Ghost, but would not have satisfied Hamlet. Hamlet required Claudius's death to be followed by his own succession. Even in a primitive Court like this, you could not publicly kill the King one moment and sit on his Throne the next. I wonder how long Claudius mulled over his intention to kill his brother? How many plans did he dream up and discard before hitting on that scheme of poisoning him during his siesta? Claudius had the advantage, moreover, that his brother was not expecting to be murdered, whereas he knew very well that Hamlet was after him. Two months does not seem such a very long time.

You can understand the Ghost's impatience when Hamlet fails to run his sword through the praying King. The Court was already alerted to the possibility of some such attack. Hamlet would have been arrested and got out of the way at once. So with a soliloquy whose argument is generally felt to be exceptional in Elizabethan tragedy, Hamlet moves on to continue his search for a scheme that will get rid of the King without getting rid of the Throne.

Hamlet was an expert schemer. It must have been a setback when he was sent off to England with his schemes uncompleted; but as soon as he found out what awaited him there, he schemed his way home and would no doubt have resumed plotting at once, having without delay got in touch with Horatio, already in the know, if he had not been distracted by the unexpected sight of Ophelia's funeral. It was not until he was certain of his own death from Laertes's poisoned rapier, and so knew that he could never be King of Denmark, that he finally allowed himself to kill Claudius.

The character of Hamlet that I see keeps reminding me of the Duke of Windsor when he was Prince of Wales. Here was this fascinatingly handsome young Prince. He had been at Oxford; he served with the Guards during the war; he was certainly 'loved of the distracted multitude'. He too, though the circumstances were not the same, was disappointed of the succession. In fact if one wants to pursue the parallel still further, his father King George V had married his elder brother's fiancée, though it was tuberculosis and not the juice of cursed hebenon that carried off the Duke of Clarence in 1892.

It would be silly to take the comparison too far. But when one is offered an existentialist Prince, or a bourgeois Prince, or a beatnik Prince, there's no harm in looking at a real life parallel to check whether the many and confusing clues have come up with an acceptable answer.

*

Amleto

For all the inadequacy of my Italian, Franco Zeffirelli's *Amleto* played by the Proclemer-Albertazzi company gave me one of the most exciting evenings I have ever had in the theatre.

It is a profoundly original creation. Signor Zeffirelli, rejecting all previous interpretations, has re-thought the play from the beginning, and has come up with something utterly new and vitally stimulating.

The production is non-realistic in style, unlike the Zeffirelli productions we are accustomed to. There is a steeply raked stage that softens the break between stage and cyclorama and gives an illusion of extra depth. The back half of the stage can be masked in different ways by various runs of curtains made from the same smoke-grey material as the cyclorama. The lighting is kept low almost throughout.

The front of the stage is built in concentric arcs that frame a kind of well-head almost at the front of the apron stage. These lines are more than ornamental; they have a special significance with respect to Hamlet. When he begins his first soliloquy, 'O that this too too solid flesh,' he takes two or three deliberate paces inwards across the arcs, inward, that is, toward the centre of his personal problem. Later, when the idea of self-slaughter has burgeoned in his mind until it has reached the point at which he toys with the actual prospect, he first circles this well, like a man with an unwelcome appointment, and then descends a few steps into it, into the nadir of his existence, for the great 'To be, or not to be,' soliloquy.

Incidentally, Gerardo Guerrieri, the translator, seems to have had second thoughts about the beginning of this speech. As first rendered, it ran *'Essere o non essere, e tutto qui'* – to be or not to be, that's all about it. What Giorgio Albertazzi said last night was *'Essere o non essere, questa e la problema,'* which is much less of a departure. Signor Zeffirelli confessed as late as lunch-time on Monday that he was not sure which version would be used. I think he and Signor Albertazzi between them have made the right decision.

'E tutto qui,' all the same, would be characteristic of Albertazzi's Hamlet. Zeffirelli claims that he is an existential Hamlet, and he is certainly not concerned with the spiritual aspect of anything he does. On the other hand he is deeply concerned with his relationships with his fellows; and being an Italian Hamlet, for all his blonde rinse, his emotions blaze where we are accustomed to have them smoulder.

Why should not an Italian Hamlet weep when he says 'But break my heart,' and why should he not wipe the tears away openly with his hand when Horatio and the officers of the guard come to him?

When Hamlet has his first close encounter with the Ghost he almost chokes with fright. There is in fact at that point no ghost to be seen. When the watch first see it, they follow its movements over the front of the stage; it is only to Hamlet that it ever shows itself, and then only in the form of a little flickering light that moves slowly along the dark battlements (how much darker than usual, and how rightly so). A whispering Pinfold-voice tells the dead King's tale; in the scene in the Queen's chamber the ghost's lines are omitted altogether while Hamlet bends his eye on vacancy. The intention no doubt is to show the subjective nature of the ghost in Hamlet's mind. but I must confess to having found something lacking.

While Albertazzi's Hamlet naturally stands out head and shoulders above everything else, there are other fine performances that I shall remember with gratitude, most particularly those of Annamaria Guarnieri as Ophelia and Anna Proclemer as Gertrude. This Ophelia, a little teenage upper-middle class girl thrilled to bits at having attracted the Prince so soon after her coming out, and distracted literally to madness when his affection is withdrawn, is quite lovely. I hope it will be possible for us some time to see her as Juliet, a part which she has played also with Albertazzi.

Anna Proclemer is a most beautiful Queen to look at, but the beauty seems in some way to be held on mortgage; no one old enough to be Hamlet's mother could hold on to it in a crisis. Her second husband Claudius (Massimo Girotti) is a trifle too handsome for his part, which is explicitly unattractive ('the bloat king'); but he gives a performance of some subtlety, and it is fascinating to watch the suspicion growing in his face as the players, terrible hams that they are, enact his crime before him.

The familiar Zeffirelli is seen in all the scenes where there are many characters on stage together; everyone has a detailed, finished part to play, sometimes in apparent conflict with the players actually speaking. His profuse resource in inventing things for people to do imparts a very special finish to his production. The music which he uses generously to underline emotional situations – some of it electronic, some purely instrumental – is always effective and never intrusive.

The play runs for well over four hours. It is worth missing any number of trains for, whether you speak Italian or not.

Amleto Again

Old Vic   25 September 1964

A second visit to Zeffirelli's *Amleto* – and not to have made a second visit while the chance was there would have been mad – gives me a chance to write more about some of the parts which it was impossible to describe in my first notice.

One of the interesting things about this production is that these parts develop much more during the evening than they're generally allowed to. Hamlet himself can go through as many metamorphoses as Diabelli's waltz, but the rest tend to have personalities, complex and subtle no doubt, but constant as the northern star under the impact of the terrible events of the play. Not so here. Anna Proclemer's Queen is an outstanding example. We see her first as a woman still flaunting the classic beauty of her youth, though when she speaks to Hamlet we can at once detect the maturity in her voice. To be beautiful is one of her functions as a queen, and she is punctilious about her public image. Even when her son is in mortal danger from Laertes's envenomed foil she is able to provide a simulacrum of decorous enthusiasm.

But by this point she has already suffered a terrible change. That awful day in her bedchamber when Hamlet stabbed Polonius and communed with the invisible spirit of her first husband left its mark on her. Her hair has turned completely grey, and the still lovely features are taut and lined. The Queen has lost her hold on life. I never saw a Queen who dies so unresistingly when she found out about the poison in the cup.

Laertes (Alessandro Ninchi) is another character who grows up before our eyes. When he leaves for Paris, he and Ophelia are still almost children. The golf-bag full of rapiers slung over his shoulder might have been the guitar of a student setting out to hitch-hike down to Cannes for the summer. But when he comes back, he is a man – decisive, stern, controlled. Even his face is different. In spite of his grudging concessions, he never forgives Hamlet at the end for all that has happened.

Ophelia, of course, develops in another way. Hers is the tragedy of inadequacy. Zeffirelli sees Polonius more as a civil servant than a courtier, and Ophelia (despite her brother's candidature for the throne) is a little *bourgeoise*. To have come near to marrying the Crown Prince while only a young girl, and then to have it snatched away from her in such a brutal way, is too much for her, and her brain snaps. All the business that Zeffirelli gives her to do is about maternity, rocking the child, making its bed, and so on, and this renders the sudden swift descents into coarse sexuality ten times as searing. This is a wonderful performance by Annamaria Guarnieri, marvellously devised and marvellously executed.

Polonious, oddly enough, seems to me to develop less than he ought to. He is a divided character, this devoted father who is prepared to use his daughter as a pawn in the court intrigues. Both Mario Scaccia and Gianni Galavotti, who played the part in the second performance I saw, make him a scheming villain from the beginning; the scene with Reynaldo, which indicates no more than an excess of paternal concern, is played as if it were the prelude to a sinister plot. As soon as Polonius, over-persuaded of his duty to the crown, begins to sacrifice his honour to his position and really becomes a villain, all is well.

I am told that business at the Old Vic for this production has been less than brisk. It has only two more days to run, so it is a bit late to do anything about that except to say that those who might have seen it and didn't will regret it for the rest of their lives. In spite of the alien language – or possibly because of it – I came out of the theatre feeling that I knew quite a lot more about *Hamlet* than when I went in; and I am certain that Giorgio Albertazzi's Hamlet is one of the very greatest performances of our day. It would be folly to miss it. Sleep on the Embankment afterwards if necessary (though now the play has settled down it ends soon after eleven); go without lunch for a day or two; do *anything* to fill up those empty seats for the last two days. It is something to remember for a lifetime.

Hamlet

Royal Shakespeare Theatre   *20 August 1965*

Hamlets come in a variety of shapes and sizes, but they should always remember that whatever individuality they bring to their readings they must be Princes. Before his madness Hamlet is described 'the glass of fashion and the mould of form' and at the end Fortinbras insists that 'he was likely, had he been put on, to have proved most royal.'

The trouble with David Warner's Hamlet is that he is not royal at all. 'Hamlet,' says Peter Hall in his programme notes, 'turns a new face to every decade.' David Warner's face belongs to the 1960s all right, for he has made Hamlet a beatnik, not only in his dress and appearance, but in his behaviour as well. Within its limits the character is consistent; but it is not a character that could do the things Hamlet does. Much of Hamlet's concern is with pride, pride in his birth, pride in his family, pride in the fortunes of Denmark and dismay at their decay.

This Hamlet has no pride. He is a snuffy little post-graduate student from Wittenberg who is pitchforked into a situation he cannot even begin to cope with.

The trouble, I think, is that Mr Warner isn't ready, by five years or so, to tackle this part. He gets almost nothing out of the big speeches, and his delivery is full of mannerisms – the flat monotone speech, with upward inflections at sentence-ends, that remind me of Michael Foot in full spate before the House of Commons, and the long, meaningless pauses in the middle of sentences that slow him down beyond bearing.

What is more, he doesn't act very much. When he says 'the air bites shrewdly, it is very cold,' it is clearly not cold at all. When the ghost appears (a 10-foot robot containing Patrick Magee), he exclaims: 'Angels and Ministers of Grace defend us!' before he even looks at it.

It is a fault in this company that they tend to bring people on too fast. Glenda Jackson is another victim as Ophelia. Before her madness she is a tough, confident deb with one of those voices that sound as if she were trying to make herself heard on a bad telephone line. From such a start, pathos is impossible to achieve in her insanity; and her decision to accompany her mad songs on the lute alienate our sympathies still more since she seems to be perfectly well in command of everything she is doing.

Peter Hall's production on the whole is very slow. It uses a very full text, fuller I dare say than Shakespeare ever used, and it runs for close on four hours. There are occasional effective moments – Ophelia's funeral in the rain, for instance, with Laertes jumping out of the grave to tackle Hamlet round the legs, and all the duelling in the last scene, where the tension rises to a high pitch.

There is a novel Polonius, a tough Court official quite different from the one Shakespeare described, who could *never* have been mocked by the players; this is nicely done by Tony Church. Brewster Mason is smoothly hateful as the King, and David Waller is funnier than most grave-diggers are.

There is a characteristically lowering set by John Bury.

Hamlet

Birmingham Rep   *16 February 1970*

This is basically the same production that Peter Dews gave us last spring, with the central platform radiating *art nouveau* staircases down to the stage and up to the flies – a pretty but sometimes over-obtrusive design by Finlay James.

Since I saw it last, however, the production has changed notably. Hamlet was played then by Richard Chamberlain in a high romantic vein, and the production was kept on that level. The costumes, suggesting the court of Tsar Nicholas II, matched the gold scrollwork on the stairs to generate an air of Ruritanian fantasy, and the company's passionate performances kept pace. But now we have Alec McCowen giving us a Hamlet that I can best describe with the surprising word 'realistic', and the passion has been taken out of the production to be replaced, quite effectively, by practical common sense. Even the costumes, if my memory doesn't deceive me, have become less Balkan and more general-purpose, or perhaps they only look that way in context.

I don't mean anything disparaging by saying that Mr McCowen's performance is realistic. Indeed it is possibly as intelligent a Hamlet as I ever saw; princely too, and fastidious, though it is marred here and there by an evident self-consciousness in the delivery of the lines. 'And so he goes ... to Heaven,' he says in that terrible speech where the Prince declines to murder his praying father in case he might find salvation beyond the grave. Since the chance of Claudius's going to Heaven is the whole drift of Hamlet's thought there, a pause is meaningless. (It is an Army pistol, not a sword, that Hamlet fingers as he sees his chance here, so the line 'Up, sword, and know thou a more horrid hent' has to be left out.)

Throughout the evening, you feel that Mr McCowen and Mr Dews have asked themselves anew why every line, every word, should come just where it does. Instead of launching into a long speech of advice to the Players, for example, Hamlet is actually rehearsing the Player who will speak the part of the Third Player, which fits in nicely with his interpolation during the play, 'Leave thy damnable faces and begin.' The soliloquies come out least effectively. They are spoken in a flat tone, as if the Prince were giving himself a private rehearsal of a subsequent public speech. If there's one thing you can't do with a soliloquy, it's to make it realistic – though I must say the opening of 'To be or not to be,' a bored comment on a book he has been reading, is a jolly good try.

Anna Massey gives Ophelia the hard, loud voice of a deb on the telephone. This suits her well enough until she loses her reason; but there's no pathos to be obtained from firing 'How shall I my true love know?' at her mother like Mireille Mathieu; and when she drops from song to speech, she speaks the nursery-rhyme lines as if they held a wealth of meaning.

Brian Oulton repeats his magnificent Polonius from last year; this silly, dignified, touchy old man is wonderfully evoked. There's a good King from Hugh Sullivan, an unscrupulous Ruritanian monarch who could easily seem as charming to Gertrude (Mary Wimbush) as he seems revolting to her son. As usual, Voltemand and Cornelius are omitted, so we never learn that Claudius's first action as King was to conclude an honourable treaty with the Norwegians.

John Baddeley gives us a nice Gravedigger, but (no doubt in the laudable pursuit of realism) the younger generation of courtiers, Horatio, Marcellus, Rosencrantz, Guildenstern, even Osric, seem more or less interchangeable, if not indistinguishable.

Hamlet

University Theatre, Newcastle

The opening of the Tyneside Theatre's *Hamlet* has just the right feeling of unease and suspicion. The guards never quite know who they are challenging or being challenged by, and the Ghost, huge, silent and dominant, brings a real whiff of the supernatural.

This insistence on vivid, active narrative is the virtue that Gareth Morgan pursues throughout the evening. When Hamlet goes mad, he

goes really zany, mad not only north-north-west but in every direction
from south-south-west to south-south-east. John Fraser's design has
a matt black stage and costumes as formal as chessman, though on
state occasions the Court wear ruffs to indicate the play's date.
('Though we're in Denmark AD ten-six-two,' wrote W. S. Gilbert
of the Prince, with an exceptional knowledge of the date of a mythical
story, 'He always dresses as King James the First.')

But this production belongs neither in 1062 nor 1602; it is an
exercise in pure intrigue, a staff college demonstration of relationships
under strain. Done in mime, it would be impressive. Unfortunately,
most of the acting is fatally inadequate.

It is, I imagine, Gareth Morgan's positive intention that the verse
should be treated as a communication medium and not as poetry, but
this leads to trouble. Jack Shepherd as Hamlet offers no identifiable
emotions at all. He speaks either very fast or slow; when fast, he only
pronounces about three syllables in five, and when slow he offers
eccentric accents – 'Throw away the worser part of *it*, and live the
purer with the other *half*.' Paul Bacchus as Claudius might be reading
the minutes of an annual general meeting, but minutes that have for
some reason been framed in iambic pentameters. Horatio, Laertes,
Fortinbras join the zombies' chorus; it is as if the director, having
drilled the company into their exciting patterns against the black,
relied entirely on their motions to show what was going on. Michael
Barrington's Polonius and Gravedigger are shining exceptions to this
generality, and Lu Jeffery's Ophelia and Celia Gregory's Gertrude
aren't bad either. Miss Gregory's Queen, obviously a loose woman,
wears a red Elizabeth I wig, echoed in the ginger wig of the Player
Queen.

Do the motions express what they should express? Well, Hamlet,
following the Ghost offstage with a defiant 'I do not set my life at a
pin's fee,' grovels on the ground for the whole of his confrontation
with his father. Having announced 'I will speak daggers to her but
use none,' he knocks his mother about unmercifully.

The text used is shortened mainly by cutting out the chatty bits.
(We even have Voltemand and Cornelius, though not Reynaldo; they
crowd behind Polonius and read Hamlet's letter to Ophelia over his
shoulder). The cuts are not always wise; 'So Rosencrantz and Guildenstern go to't,' says Horatio, though Hamlet has not told his plan for
their death. The company make a fair number of cuts of their own,
too, Mr Shepherd in particular; I never thought we could get so
close to 'more honoured in the breach than in the observance' without

actually hearing it.

Something has, in fact, gone wrong. I know a bit about the merits of both company and director, and this is characteristic of neither. Perhaps they should start all over again from the beginning, for there is certainly the seed of an interesting *Hamlet* in this disaster.

Hamlet

Phoenix, Leicester   *13 February 1975*

The play is staged on a double-deck set (designer, Paul Bannister) composed of rough timber and iron scaffolding, and the players wear the clothes of our own day. Not of the equivalent characters of our day, though, not of kings and queens and princes, but of the young people who formed the majority of Monday night's admirable audience, whose average age must have been about twenty. The dialogue is spoken as if it had been written last week by Alan Ayckbourn. It's quite often gabbled so fast that words are lost; there are some wrong words and an occasional mispronunciation. The clowns' lines have been rewritten in modern language and some extra jokes inserted. The production is one of the most exciting *Hamlets* I have ever seen.

Its success is due to the total faith the company, under Michael Bogdanov's direction, put in Shakespeare's lines. They sound as if they came naturally and spontaneously to the players' minds, and the result is that the sense is always presented in utterly natural intonations, and the music, instead of being imposed by conscious artifice, emerges from the words that Shakespeare wrote.

Shakespeare's mastery is specially revealed when it is disputed. The Gravediggers are very funny; but each time you hear a Shakespearian line rephrased you realise how much more witty and economical Shakespeare was. Mr Bogdanov has demonstrated that something was rotten in the state of Denmark by reorganising the start of the play so that it begins with Marcellus and Horatio chatting about the daily cast of brazen cannon and the shipwrights' seven-day working week, while Hamlet on the lower level wonders in silence about his father's death (presented in dumbshow upstage). Only after this does he come to the real start of the play, and we see at once how brilliantly Shakespeare had suggested the 'strange eruption' of the state with his nervous, trigger-happy sentries on the battlements.

Once back on the main line, we get an uncommonly full text, which by brisk playing and imaginative use of the multiple stage is encompassed in about three and a quarter hours. My other complaints are comparatively slight. Rosencrantz and Guildenstern shouldn't be rewarded with a pound note each; they may look like Hell's Angels, but they are courtiers. The King's on the wrong side of the audience at *The Murder of Gonzago*; Horatio can't watch his face. It must be wrong to have a bully-boy kicking Hamlet in the crotch to extract from him where Polonius's body is; the King is present, full of 'thine especial safety' and 'thy loving father', and Hamlet is swopping quips with him.

The Prince is splendidly played by Hugh Thomas, who took the part over at forty-eight hours' notice from a sick David Gretton. It is a performance of great skill, even though his black-sweatered, bespectacled, Kottesque Hamlet doesn't happen to match my own idea of the character. Of the rest of the team (eleven of them play twenty-eight parts, including no fewer than nine Players), John Darrell's Polonius stood out for me, a grey Civil Servant in a three-piece suit who reads his farewell advice to Laertes clause by clause from a notebook. Small happy details abound, and never cause any unease by their conflict with the Shakespearian idiom of the talk.

The Phoenix is now Leicester's junior house and gives special attention to young people's theatre. If this *Hamlet* is characteristic of what Michael Bogdanov gives them, they are a very lucky generation. *Hamlet* is on until 1 March, and is worth crossing half of England to see.

Hamlet

Old Vic   *11 December 1975*

Peter Hall has given us a pretty straightforward *Hamlet*. It is played on a bare stage, decorated oddly with a circular motive, before a plain grey wall pierced at the centre by an imposing gateway. The cast is as full of stars as an American film : starring Albert Finney, Philip Locke and Denis Quilley; also starring Robert Eddison, Susan Fleetwood and Gawn Grainger; guest stars, Angela Lansbury, Simon Ward and Roland Culver. Mr Hall drives them through the fullest possible text as fast as they can possibly go. With one interval, at Act 4, Scene 4, where Hamlet resolves that his thought be bloody or be nothing worth, the play lasts just on four hours. As in Mr Hall's last production of the play, there are two and a half hours to go before the break.

We start off splendidly; those uneasy calls on the battlements create an atmosphere of real trepidation. It comes as a surprise, however, when Horatio enters to take his place on watch, for he is a grey-bearded, bespectacled old don in academic dress, by no means the man you would expect Hamlet to address as his fellow-student, worn in his heart of hearts. Philip Locke's performance is consistent with his appearance rather than Horatio's usual reputation; he is slow and reflective in all he does, even when, somewhat unexpectedly, he sits and dangles his legs in what is to be Ophelia's grave.

Hamlet is equally unusual. Seated on the left of the royal couple, already out of mourning and resplendent, there sits a mature man with a bushy beard and a head of untidy hair. Apart from his inky Jacobean raiment, you might take him for a ghillie. As Mr Hall told us when presenting David Warner in the part dressed as a post-graduate student of Essex University, Hamlet turns a new face to every decade. Albert Finney, once he has got out of his black, still has something of the current student pattern about him, but it is quite new. His breeches stop halfway down his calves, revealing socks rolled down over his shoes. He is perpetually untidy. When he returns from his sea voyage he is wearing something borrowed from the crew, I imagine, and he is not abashed at keeping it on for his fatal fencing match.

A mature Hamlet of this kind makes good sense. As the Grave-digger tells us, he is thirty years old; as Ophelia says, he is a soldier and a scholar, the mould of form. But Mr Finney, though he acts the part well enough, does not speak it well at all. His verse-speaking is very level and monotonous, so that the meaning of the words is often concealed. There were one or two lapses of memory; and some of the action Mr Hall has given him won't do. For instance, when he says 'Look, where my abridgement comes', he is looking at solid door panels through which he can see nothing; he even has to open the door to let the players in. When Claudius kneels in his vain prayers, Hamlet comes rushing in as if he had planned the moment, only to remind himself that he is on the wrong tack.

Claudius, who is Denis Quilley, utters his prayers remarkably well.

Mr Quilley gives us a civilised monarch, an elegant King whose first act of policy is to make peace with the Norwegians antagonised by his roughneck elder brother, after whom I suppose we are to believe the younger Hamlet took. At the lines 'When sorrows come, they come not single spies,' he goes to his Queen to console her, folding her tenderly and not at all lecherously in his arms.

What there was about Queen Gertrude, as Angela Lansbury gives her, to tempt him to such extremes is difficult to see. She is clearly no more than a politically-contracted consort whose object in life is simply to sit on the throne; only once does she display any of the softer emotions, and this is in the closet scene. She has been on the verge of hysteria; but when she sees her son talking to the empty air (or rather the ghost of her late husband, raised through a trap, but invisible to her) she melts into a likeable motherliness. She is not able to show a similar attitude towards poor Ophelia, but this is because the verse seems to defeat her around here, especially in the 'There is a willow' speech.

Ophelia (Susan Fleetwood) is a tough girl when she is sane, rather bigger than her brother Laertes (Simon Ward in a neat beard). But after she loses her wits, Peter Hall has her dressed as if she were straight out of the funny-farm, her hair cut short and untidy, her clothing confined to a single filthy chemise wearing ragged at the hem. In such a guise she could not persuade me that she was a court lady who had gone mad. Moreover the new songs Harrison Birtwistle has composed for her make things worse, for they are complex enough to demand attention to the music, which in the circumstances is a mistake.

Roland Culver makes a splendid Polonius, wise and dignified, a suitable chancellor to such a king as Claudius, and he speaks the verse as well as anyone in the company bar Robert Eddison as the first Player. (First Player should put Hamlet to shame when he does his Pyrrhus bit with such restraint after the Prince has been breaking all the rules he deems it his duty to give the actors.) But although this Polonius was a bit absent-minded, he hardly seemed to merit Hamlet's description of 'great baby'. The description is consistent, though, in a way; it matches such a phrase as 'the bloat king'; it is simply an example of Hamlet's distorted view of the members of the court, most of whom, incidentally, are old, bald and grey.

There are some lesser delights in the production that gave me some pleasure. I loved the Irish gravediggers of J. G. Devlin and Stephen Rea. Gawn Grainger gives a good, conventional Osric (and Horatio

ought really to look at him when he says 'This lapwing runs away
with the shell on his head,' or we shall think he doesn't know what
the line means). Mr Ward and Mr Finney play a very spirited bout
in the last scene; but I thought it odd that the 'unction' killed Mr
Ward almost at once, but left Mr Finney standing up in no apparent
pain until he decided to lie down and pass over. David Yelland speaks
Fortinbras's final words above the Prince like a blaze of trumpets.

Hamlet

Royal Court						*2 April 1980*

There's not much music in this *Hamlet*, but there's a freshness that
brings to many of the lines a feeling that we are hearing them for the
first time. Sometimes indeed we are : with unforgivable impertinence,
the First Player's speech about Priam has been replaced by some
awful lines by Christopher Logue, who speaks them admirably.

The production is not treated as a star vehicle for Jonathan Pryce,
nor does he in any way try to make it one. He is inclined to flatten
out some of the more poetic verse by putting a full close at the end
of every phrase, and he is a bit niggardly in his allowance of humour,
one of Hamlet's better qualities. But he never works against the text.
That is to say, what is left of the text, which has been ruthlessly and
rather insensitively cropped. depriving us of all the vital first scene,
one of the gravediggers, and several vital lines, such as 'And shall I
couple hell?' and (in the closet scene) 'Is it the King?' Then we have
to do without the Ghost.

This is a liberty hard to justify. Hamlet is given some of the Ghost's
lines, though not enough to tell all the omitted information. He breaks
off his own dialogue with a choking sound that suggests imminent
sickness and speaks the Ghost's lines in a new voice, as if possessed.
Thus both the battlement scenes are virtually lost.

The King, in Michael Elphick's hands, always sounds like a good
con-man, that is to say, he speaks with apparent belief in what he
says but never persuades one that he is more honest with his fellows
than he is with God, whom he approaches with a minimum of respect.
Gertrude, on the other hand, is a decent sentimental woman, and
Jill Bennett spreads her sympathy so universally that she might almost

have married Claudius just to take his mind off the murder.

I very much liked Geoffrey Chater as Polonius, who is never too silly, but I liked only one of his children, the boyish Laertes of Simon Chandler, whose excesses are due only to his having been suddenly carried away by juvenile temper. Harriet Walter's Ophelia is a big, butch girl who in her mad scenes seems to be musical without being insane. So her burial on a spare shelf in the royal mausoleum with its cupboards full of skulls was no more than she deserved.

On the whole William Dudley's sets are very good, making use of lines of arches movable into different positions to change the venue. Glimpses through trompe l'oeil shutters show sinister details, a skull here, an hour-glass there, a cloaked figure half-way through a door. It was wrong, though, to give Hamlet that great arras in his mother's closet, under which he has to crawl to stab Polonius point-blank, and then to use it as the background for Fortinbras's arrival on his way to Poland.

CHAPTER TEN

The Private Collection

There are some evenings that one recalls with an affection independent of their merits. I don't mean that they have no merits; I like to think that I shouldn't have enjoyed them unless they had some. And when I write 'affection' or 'enjoy', let no one think that the emotions I mean are necessarily at all like the emotions one has on the day of one's engagement or when drinking a glass of 1928 La Tache. No right-minded person could hear the last scene of *King Lear* and not be overcome with horror. One of the plays I have isolated in this section is truly beastly. But pleasurable or not, my private collection consists of a little bunch of productions of which I specially like to be reminded.

Alan Ayckbourn's *Mr Whatnot*, for instance. What I thought of it, you can read below, and you can be sure that an evening involving Ronnie Barker, Judy Campbell, Ronnie Stevens and Marie Löhr could never be a total loss. But as we left the theatre, I, still a comparative newcomer to the business of wrapping up my thoughts in instant prose, found myself with Philip Hope-Wallace.

'They'll all go and say how trivial it is,' he said, indicating a bunch of fellow-critics, 'as if there were nothing in it worth noticing at all.' It was characteristic of that lovable man that he should look for the merits in a piece that clearly had little chance of popular success before he conceded its shortcomings. What he wrote in *The Guardian* that night I don't know; but at any rate Mr Ayckbourn was not discouraged enough by the short run of *Mr Whatnot* to give up.

I have always said that when I win a major prize in the football pools I shall take a small theatre, something like the Fortune, and put on a season of plays designed only to please myself. Half a dozen of these plays from my private collection would be considered for inclusion. Whether one could form a company capable of playing, say, the yobbo students of *Little Malcolm*, the advertising executives of *The Happy Apple*, the American petty gangsters of *The American Buffalo* and the Liverpool bus-crews of *Fat Harold and the Last 26*, I don't know; not as well as I would want them all played, I'm sure; but at any rate with three-quarters of a million at my disposal I ought to be able to hire a tolerable bunch of players to perform my repertory.

And who knows, my judgment might be so completely justified that I should finish the season on the credit side.

*

The Formation Dancers

New Arts   *19 March 1964*

Frank Marcus's new play is a very funny comedy about adultery.

The participants are two asymmetrical couples. On the one hand we have Gerald, a pompous, self-satisfied literary critic with an endemic need for an affair to resolve his tensions, and his wife Maggie, who is sufficiently engulfed in married life not to mind when he has one as long as it keeps the household stable in the long run. On the other hand there is Paul, an even more pompous and selfish art-dealer, but in place of his wife (who is away on holiday for the duration of the play) we have Perdita, his mistress, an intellectual beatnik from a Chelsea bed-sitter.

The interplay between these four characters has a kind of idiot formality. Paul is invited to dine with Gerald and Maggie, and takes Perdita. Gerald's tensions are due for relief, so behind Paul's back he arranges for Perdita to join him on a trip to Manchester, where he is to lecture. When Paul suspects what is going on, Maggie decides that she will wean her husband away from Perdita by pretending to have a lover, and Paul is cast for the part. The ensuing complications are neither very ingenious nor very novel, but the play is kept bounding along by Mr Marcus's talent for buoyant dialogue and his acute delineation of character.

The dialogue, like the plot, has a formal tinge within its apparently naturalistic ripple. Most of the laughs – and they are numerous – arise not from any conventionally comic exchanges but from our recognition that *this* is exactly what this character or that would say in exactly these circumstances. For this method to be effective the characters must be very precisely observed, and Mr Marcus's specimens could hardly be better displayed. Gerald, played with ineffable conceit by Robin Bailey, writes articles on Bingo for *Encounter* and profiles of pop-singers for the *New Statesman* : he has a weakness for making lists of things, and in his last meeting with Perdita, when he is trying to prolong their association beyond the end that clearly threatens it, he tells her with no sense at all of its untimeliness that she is his one hundred and forty-eighth girl.

Maxine Audley has a less interesting time as Maggie, who is, after all, the play's one tenuous link with normal adult behaviour; but the detail the author has written into the part is again so utterly right and Miss Audley sinks herself into it effectively. Paul is a man who cannot imagine any of his actions or opinions being challenged : Gerald Flood has imbued him with just the proper brand of bovine romanticism.

Perdita is the most rewarding character of the four. Beatniks of her calibre, and they can be found with reasonable frequency in the cellar coffee-bars of Chelsea, present a problem in that they must be able to converse intelligently without losing their beatnik quality, and Mr Marcus has succeeded most ably with this one. It is the first time I have heard this brand of way-out intellectual talk so convincingly reproduced on the stage. Joanna Dunham, looking very pretty and a bit too clean, has got almost completely into the skin of the character, and will I suspect get more so in time.

Clive Donner, a graduate from the film world, directs with wit and imagination. There are imaginative little felicities to warm the heart from time to time, such as the gout of flame that jets from Gerald's cigarette lighter as he is about to demonstrate to Perdita some particularly romantic ploy with it. Sally Jacob's sets are changed in blackouts against which the actor speaking each curtain-line is shown in a dramatic pose under a green spot, while music by Ron Grainger for harpsichord, drums and bass distracts our attention.

Lightweight it may be, but *The Formation Dancers* is a genuinely witty little piece, and very attractively played. I laughed a great deal.

Mr Whatnot

New Arts   *7 August 1964*

It has been Alan Ayckbourn's curious whim to write his play half in dialogue and half in mime. As if this weren't hard enough, he has deprived his hero of a voice altogether. There are no rigid rules about the way he applies his formula; some props are real, some are imaginary; some conversations are spoken, some mimed, some carried on in a mixture of the two media.

Lest there should be any risk of reality breaking in, the director, Warren Jenkins, has dispensed with a set, and uses instead three screens on which appropriate slides are projected – very pretty slides, incidentally, by Peter Rice. Moreover, all the sound effects come from an electrical reproducer and the cast do wonders of synchronisation as they play the piano or tennis, drive cars or ride bicycles, in time with the tape.

The idea is quite a gay one, but its success depends not on its intrinsic qualities but on what it is applied to. Frankly, I doubt if it ought to be employed in anything longer than a half-hour cabaret turn. Having taken the decision to use it for a whole evening, Mr Ayckbourn should have found something a good deal stronger to harness it to.

His story is a very simple one of a handsome young piano-tuner – Peter King, voiceless, agile and likeable – who is called to a Stately Home to tune the new piano and falls in love with the daughter of the house. His pursuit of her is simplified by the fact that everyone mistakes him for a guest, though nobody knows his name. It's a story, in fact, out of the same packet as *Salad Days* but even less sophisticated.

The cast is a strong one. The resident peer and peeress are Ronnie Barker and Judy Campbell; Ronnie Stevens, in a boater and blazer from the twenties and a wig that makes him look like Lord Peter Wimsey, is their daughter's fiancé; Marie Löhr puts in an appearance as a ferocious hunting lady. Although they all squeeze every drop of flavour out of their parts, aided by prodigies of direction, the author has only given them stereotypes to work with. Given some good lines they might have sustained our interest; regrettably, I'm afraid mine flagged a good deal in spite of my determination that it should not. The kindest judgement I can pass is that *Mr Whatnot* provides us with a good idea gone wrong.

I don't think it's a total loss, there are moments in it that made me smile, but they're too far apart. What it really needs is a good going-over with the scissors, wielded by someone rather more in touch with current West End standards than Mr Ayckbourn appears to be; then, with half an hour cut out of it, there will be room to insert half-a-dozen songs. Vivian Ellis has already contributed a couple of tunes that mutter almost unheard in the background; a few more as good as they are might be just the tonic this odd little show requires.

The Play of William Cooper

Northcott, Exeter   *5 February 1968*

– *and Edmund Dew-Nevett*, to complete the curious title of this curious play by David Selbourne. William Cooper is a half-wit and Edmund Dew-Nevett is the spirit of sophistication who comes (driving on to the stage in a white Sunbeam Alpine) to corrupt him with ideas above his station.

Other influences on the unhappy but talkative William are Richard Puckeridge and his wife, or mistress, Joan, who grow rich by exhibiting a man dressed as an ape but continue to touch him for loans, and Tiger Bright, representing sex. Their mutual relationships are chronicled in a kind of loose verse based on everyday speech patterns but occasionally taking off into more rarefied spheres. There is a strong feeling of Beckett about, but Mr Selbourne is less cogent and more verbose than his master.

I found the play, in fact, singularly short of intellectual or emotional content. But this doesn't mean that the evening was without interest. On the contrary, it was riveting; for Robin Phillips's production is brimful of poetry and invention, and he has secured such performances from his cast as do not come one's way all that often.

The Sunbeam Alpine is one of Mr Phillips's touches; all William's visitors arrive in some unexpected way. Richard and Joan share a tricycle. Tiger enters on a swing, trailing a 50-foot train of muslin. The author has also asked for three ragged children and a black-faced man; but Mr Phillips has replaced them with moving, chattering patches of light and a black balloon that slides threateningly across the stage as if of its own volition.

The evening is full of such magical touches; and Daphine Dare's designs and John Baker's lighting have an equally engaging quality. Because the play concerns ideas and qualities rather than events, it is given a non-representational setting. A single circular panel punctuates the black drapes across the back of the stage; on it are projected simple designs indicative of the mood of the current scene.

In front of this, William stands on a white, comma-shaped patch on a black stage, and most of his visitors approach along a white curved pathway orbiting his little reserve. Above his head, hardly noticeable at first, hangs a half-circle of vertical bars; at one end, as William's separation from the real world dominates his mind, this falls slowly to engulf him in a cage.

I don't remember being so interested in a young producer's work since I saw Peter Brook's *Dark of the Moon.*

Michael Byrne is the excellent William, Jonathan Elsom is Dew-Nevett, Valerie Minifie is Tiger, Davyd Harries Richard and Christine Ozanne Joan. They, and Mr Phillips, give Mr Selbourne's hollow verse a quality that suggests real poetry. But it's a quality, alas, that soon withers away in recollection.

Claw

Open Space   *31 January 1975*

Howard Barker's *Claw* is very much the kind of play I like; the economical production by Chris Parr suits it admirably; and the playing is excellent from top to bottom.

It presents a contrast between real power and imaginary power. Noel Biledew was born illegitimate while his father was in a prisoner of war camp during the war. He grew up with such bad eyes that he had to wear pebble-lens spectacles, a circumstance that gave him a sense of being unwanted, since his school-friends naturally weren't keen on having him in their teams and thought his appearance comic.

Soon after leaving school he began a career in search of power as a pimp, with the help of a girl he met at the Young Communists, and he soon built up such a clientele that his clients included a Cabinet Minister. An affair with the Minister's wife inevitably led to trouble; and after a violent confrontation, Noel (who adopted the nickname

'Claw' as a teenager to symbolise the sway he intended to have) threatened to reveal to the newspapers the extent of the Minister's immoral behaviour. No way: a word in the right quarter, and he disappeared from public life.

The whole of Claw's life up to his disappearance is shown in a series of short, cogent scenes purged of irrelevant detail, as simple and strong as Phil May's drawings. Bitterly funny, some of them are; the picture of Claw's sad old father (beautifully played by Roger Sloman) bashing his son over the head with a framed portrait of Karl Marx as he spends his ill-gotten gains in Fortnum's tea-room is enchanting. The austere concentration of the writing produces some good effects; a vision of a world in which 'Boys with bad eyesight will be loved even by their cuckolded stepfathers,' though it encapsulates the whole tragedy of Claw's life, is also a very funny thought.

The play ends with a long scene in what looks like a condemned cell. Claw in grey denim eats breakfast on one side of the stage; on the other, two white-jacketed attendants recall their past. One was an Ulster gunman, one was a hangman, both have been saved from their respective fates by the offer of Government work in this secret station. Claw's desperate distress conjures up a vision of his father in a wheelchair, dying in a home for incurables. His father tells him, before he learns what his end is to be, of his error in failing to distinguish the cheap power of the thug and the crook from the real, embattled power of privilege.

Nothing is perfect, and I think *Claw* is too long; there are incidents and speeches that could be cut without harm. But I found it spellbinding, whatever its faults. Claw is played with deep understanding by Billy Hamon, and there are able performances by William Russell and Isobel Dean as the politician and his wife, June Brown as Mrs Biledew, and indeed by the whole company.

Fat Harold and the Last 26

Theatre at New End   *19 December 1975*

Fat Harold is the inspector in charge of a Liverpool bus-depot one foggy night. Two things afflict him. First, a driver, after using his bus as a taxi for all benighted passengers on and off his route, has now set off after a car in which he thinks he saw his wife with another man. Second, he has threatened to report a bad-tempered, unreliable driver – a 'cowboy' in bus-depot jargon – for trying to sell a ticket twice, and the cowboy, Kavanagh, is determined to start a fight.

The action takes place in the depot, an emotional cul-de-sac where things can only get worse until they reach a climax. Alan Bleasdale, the author, charts the progress of the quarrel with much skill and a sure grasp of the men's language and behaviour.

On either side of the central fight are two other busmen, Uncle, the slow-witted shunter, and Bignall, the sensible, peace-loving shop-steward. Bignall starts on Kavanagh's side; but when the endless needling leads to violence he sees that Kavanagh can no longer be supported and switches to the inspector's side against him.

There is hardly any more to the story than this, but the representation of the men's relationships is unfailingly interesting from start to finish. Moreover, all four parts are played with above-average skill – Don McKillop as the failed Fascist, Harold, Paul Angelis as Kavanagh the rebel, Robert Hamilton as Bignall, and Anthony Haygarth as Uncle, whose mind never rises above the dirty books that he can barely understand. Robert Walker directs, and the bus-station has been designed by Jane Ripley.

Valediction

ADRIAN : I take it that you will not be in for dinner.

BERTRAM : You know very well that I am never in for dinner. If you are feeling sufficiently obliging, you may leave me out a scrap of bread and cheese.

ADRIAN : There is still a little of the game pie in the refrigerator that you might have with a half-bottle of the Krug. But tell me, don't you find it excessively tiresome not to dine properly at night? It must be more than ten years now since you took up this practice of passing your evenings at the play.

BERTRAM : That is a very courteous estimate. In fact it is at the moment a matter of two decades.

ADRIAN : I have been studying courtesy all my life. It is an interesting historical phenomenon. I expect you encounter it constantly on the stage.

BERTRAM : On the contrary, manners on the stage would be considered excessively forthright at a truck-drivers' pull-in. Not only do the characters comment unkindly on one another's behaviour when they are not actually driving a knife between their shoulder-blades, but they frequently do so in language coarse enough to raise eyebrows at a football stadium.

ADRIAN : You are speaking of what is called the fringe.

BERTRAM : I am speaking of the theatre in general. I have heard actors who have been given the highest honours by the Sovereign use words that Her Majesty can never have heard of.

ADRIAN : And has this always been the case? Come, join me in a glass of this delicious Beaumes de Venise and tell me how the theatre has changed during the twenty years you have given it your attention.

BERTRAM : The theatre of today labours under handicaps not felt twenty years ago. For example, it no longer enjoys the protection of the Lord Chamberlain.

ADRIAN : You cannot be serious.

BERTRAM : I am always serious, even when I make jokes. I was talking lately to an elderly actor. He said to me, 'I don't think the critics today are any good. They never make any jokes.' I explained to him that the kind of jokes we make are sometimes too rarefied for universal consumption. I am not making a joke about the Lord Chamberlain, however, who I am sure is a perfect dear. When he licensed a play, it was safe from the depredations of Mrs Whitehouse. What is more, once it was licensed, I knew that I could take my mother or my aunt, even my Aunt Edna, without subjecting her to abject vulgarity.

ADRIAN : My aunt only goes to the play if she can be sure of hearing some abject vulgarity. She likes such plays as *Measure for Measure* and *The Country Wife*.

BERTRAM : Does she like hearing obscene language?

ADRIAN : It makes her feel at home.

BERTRAM : Now it is you who are not being serious. If it were not that I am sure you are about to offer me another glass of Beaumes de Venise, I should stop talking about the theatre altogether and turn to some more interesting topic, such as politics or steam railways.

ADRIAN (*two hours later*): But you cannot deny that the Bulleid Pacifics on the Southern needed massive rebuilding quite soon after going into service.

BERTRAM : Even then, they were inferior to Maunsell's 'Lord Nelson' class, which had the highest tractive effort of any locomotive in the country. I think it is time that I changed for the theatre.

ADRIAN : You are going to see something vulgar and obscene, no doubt.

BERTRAM : I expect so. The actors will use common vowel-sounds, because no one checks them for doing so. If there are any foreign names, one half of the company will mispronounce them one way, and one another way. The text will be decorated with four-letter words, as if they were appoggiaturas in a Handel aria. The plot will be concerned with some liberal call for reform such as you read about in the *Guardian* newspaper. No scene will last longer than two minutes because the author has learnt to write by watching television. Most of them will last even less.

ADRIAN : Then I take it you will spend an unhappy evening.

BERTRAM : On the contrary, I expect to enjoy myself deliriously. Going to the theatre is always enjoyable. It is even more enjoyable than the opera, because you can hear the words. If you see a good play, well acted, in a comfortable seat, you have the highest pleasure in life. If you see a bad play, ill acted, from an uncomfortable seat with a bad sight line, you can stimulate your mind with the problems of what must be done to make it better.

ADRIAN : Such as asking for a better seat.

BERTRAM : Managements are excessively obliging in such matters when they are dealing with the newspapers. No, Adrian, you must not disparage bad theatre. Apart from anything else, I have to confess something that I have not mentioned to any one for twenty years, that it is easier to write a good adverse notice than a good favourable notice.

ADRIAN : I am sorry that you should have mentioned it now.

BERTRAM : So am I, now I come to think of it. My intrinsic honesty sometimes gets the better of me.

ADRIAN : You will have to keep it well concealed if you intend to write about the theatre for another twenty years.

BERTRAM : I don't think I shall be allowed to write about the theatre for another twenty years. As a matter of fact, I am not sure there will be a theatre after another twenty years. I am thinking indeed of asking my editor if I may start a weekly column about steam railways, which seem to me to be inadequately covered at the moment. I shall be exchanging one historical subject for another. However, this is something that only time can solve. A plain woollen tie, I think, don't you? I am going to the Barbican.

Index